Adirondack Characters
And Campfire Yarns

Early Settlers And Their Traditions

With articles and stories collected,
organized, and written by William J. O'Hern

Adirondack Characters And Campfire Yarns
Early Settlers And Their Traditions

First edition printing 2005

Publisher's Cataloging-in-Publication Data

O'Hern, William J.
  Adirondack Characters And Campfire Yarns: Early Settlers And Their Traditions
    p.   cm.
  ISBN – 0-9743943-0-0 (Cloth)
  ISBN – 0-9743943-1-9 (Paper)
  Includes index
  1. Pioneers–New York (State)—Adirondack Mountains. 2. Trappers—New York (State)—Adirondack Mountains—Biography—Anecdotes. 3. Hermits—New York (State)—Adirondack Mountains—Biography—Anecdotes. 4. New York (State)—Adirondack Mountains—Social life and customs. 5. Adirondack Mountains—New York (State). I. O'Hern, William J., 1944-   . II. Title
F127.A2O35 2005
974.7'53—dc22

Previously unpublished material edited by Neal Burdick and Mary L. Thomas.
Book and cover design by Roy Reehil.
Printed and bound in the United States by Thomson-Shore, Inc., Michigan.
Printed on 50% post-consumer recycled paper.
Published by The Forager Press, LLC, 23 Bridge Street, Cleveland, NY 13042.
The Forager Press, LLC is online at: www.theforagerpress.com.

Cover and title page photograph caption:
Burt Conklin's Lumber camp near West Canada Creek would have been abuzz with activity around the time that this picture was taken in 1897 by traveling photographer Grotus Reising. Most of the people in the picture are members of the Conklin family and the rest are friends and hired hands. From left to right: Pascal Conklin, Dee Courtney, Johnny McCullen-Teamster, Astrander Buck, Roy Potter, Golusha (in doorway), Burt Conklin, John Pardee, Phil Perry, Roy Conklin (the boy in front of Phil), "Red" Jack Conklin, John E. Conklin (with dog), unidentified man, Lyman Conklin, another unidentified man, Jessie Conklin (John E. Conklin's wife), Maude Conklin, Mrs. Burt Conklin (Alice Cummins) and Bessie Conklin, sitting down.
FRONT COVER, BACK COVER AND TITLE PAGE PHOTOGRAPHS COURTESY
EDWARD BLANKMAN (THE LLOYD BLANKMAN COLLECTION)

Dedication

The majority of the stories contained in *Adirondack Characters and Campfire Yarns* are the result of Lloyd Blankman's efforts to honor Adirondack pioneers and woodsmen. This book would never have crystallized without Lloyd's initial research and his son Edward's passion for all things Adirondack. For that, I thankfully dedicate this book to Lloyd and Edward Blankman.

Contents

II – ADIRONDACK TRADITIONS

Preface

THE SUMMER HIKING and camping crowds leave by Labor Day. The hunting public ends their season. The beautiful forests of the southern Adirondacks become virtually empty, returning to their natural state of quiet simplicity. This is excellent news for people who like solitude.

I favor unconfined recreation. The majority of marked foot trails in the West Canada Creek and Black River headwaters lead to ponds, lakes, rivers, or low mountains. Trails do not lead to the far-removed places I enjoy seeking out. The contest on many of my excursions is to find the locations of former "green-timber" traplines, hunting and fishing shanties built from forest resources, and to identify strategically-placed logging camp sites. Having knowledge of an area's history gives my adventures greater meaning.

Several years ago I reproduced a copy of W. E. Wolcott's *Map of the North Woods* by Shady P. Groves, drawn in 1891. It's one of the many Adirondack artifacts that I have collected over the years. On the reproduction I highlighted the trapline trails that "French" Louie Seymour (1831–1915), the colorful West Canada Lakes character, slogged over. His trails covered territory few modern bushwhackers have ever seen.

I carried that old map on outings into the West Canada Lakes country, not for the scanty navigational information it provided—topographic maps served that purpose—but for the nostalgic feeling of walking in the footsteps of an Adirondack legend. It served that purpose well.

I am a dyed-in-the-wool Adirondack history buff and I've spent time most winters traveling, researching, listening to stories and reading about the historic Adirondack destinations that fascinated me the most.

I also collected artifacts. Some are faded, others tinted yellow and brown-toned, dog-eared and fly-specked. Glimpses of bygone days in the Adirondack Mountains stored as they came in a Fanny Farmer chocolate box, a red and white cardboard Royal Medjool pitted dates container, a Peter Schuyler-Victor cigar box, and a vintage Utica Club beer case—no bottles included! Other snapshots were given to me in little stacks tied with old Christmas ribbon, in metal recipe tins and in family scrapbooks. Others came singly. My most prized pictures showed up in a worn manila envelope. It contained just negatives—the old square, thick film variety. They belonged to Lloyd Blankman. His son, Edward, had them stored on an upstairs closet shelf.

Most are snapshots, casual family photographs taken with a hand-held camera without regard to technique. I have no idea who some of the men and women are. Lloyd's notes identify others.

Twelve are very old professional photographs: thin photographic paper fixed to a thick cardboard backing. One shows French Louie and Truman (Trume) Haskell standing in front of Louie's camp at Big West. Lloyd wrote on the back: "Taken about 1900. Given to me by Trume Haskell. One of my best and rarest pictures." Another shows a buckboard bound for Barber's on Jocks Lake road. One of my favorites is of guide Giles Becraft standing with a party of two "sports" on the shore of Jocks Lake. Dut Barber, owner/operator of Barber's Lodge, stands next to his woodsman guide.

Another favorite shows "Red" Jack Conklin and buddies in 1926 at Red's camp on Gulf Brook back in the woods north of the Haskell Hotel. Hunting success is evident in many of the photos of his camp. That area today is a bushwhacker's longing.

Those dingy pictures and yellowed journals of bygone days guided me to places where trappers trapped and loggers ran river drives, to one-room school houses and stone fences around the fields of hardscrabble farmers. Many trips to the headwaters of the Black River and West Canada Creek were inspired by stories about the first wealthy sportsmen traveling there by horse and jumper and the guides who led them to the bounty of that pristine wilderness.

Year after year, I collected. Eventually I found that I was depending more and more on materials directly connected to a handful of amateur Adirondack historians: Lloyd Blankman, Rev. A.L. Byron-Curtiss, Harvey L. Dunham, Mortimer Norton, and Thomas C. O'Donnell. They too had spent much of their lives collecting pictures and stories about the backwoods folks of the highland interior. Now I was collecting them.

They were all sportsmen. They loved the Adirondack Mountains, and they all found the region's history to be as captivating as its varied landscape, as captivating as I find it now.

People who knew them describe men haunted by the chase. They amassed a wealth of woods lore over their lifetimes. Perhaps because the men instinctively knew technological progress would replace the pioneers' readiness, they made voluminous and amazingly detailed notes to record the skills of survival afield and the ability to live in a harsh climate.

All the men lived during a time when gathering scores of amusing anecdotes and information was painstaking. Many of their subjects were old or had died. The personal histories of natives they sought were already being obscured by the gathering mists of legend and hearsay.

The most important thing to me is that they gathered a supply of sidelights on the nature and texture of mountain life that is factual. Their recordings bring to life the distinctive voices of hermits, moonshiners, gum pickers and anglers with stories of families, feuds and sporting in the North Woods when Adirondack waters were a trout haven.

They wanted people to remember the names of the men they researched, respected and revered. Men like French Louie and Johnny Leaf, the St. Regis Indian who would kill a deer for a pint of whiskey. The bear-teasing Frank Baker, guide for the famed Dut Barber at Jocks Lake, now Honnedaga. Burt Conklin, a local frontier legend. Ferris Lobb, hermit of Piseco Lake. Johnny Jones, Bill Pardy, Roc Conklin, Will Light and other unadulterated "wildcrafters." These men became some of the best-known characters in the lively headwaters country, because of the numerous newspaper and magazine articles the collectors produced.

Their notes, writings and photos are extremely helpful to me as I plan what I call historical bushwhacks—trips where I make use of the extensive personal papers, diaries, unpublished manuscripts, published articles, and photographs that generous relatives and friends of the men have offered me.

I admired these men for spending a lifetime searching and recording historical information. My adventures were thoroughly enriched because of their interest and research. I realized I should do something with their notes, pictures and out-of-print stories, to continue their work; I just didn't know *what*—until an accident brought my thoughts together.

One winter night, as I twirled my swivel chair away from the computer to dart out to the kitchen for a handful of pretzel rods, I tripped over my cat, Rascal, who had curled up underfoot. I fell on the rug, "a double s over tea kettle," as my grandmother used to say. As I went down, my arms went out to soften the fall, but my aim was misplaced. As I grabbed for the desktop I accidentally knocked over a pile of photographs that included photos from Rev. Byron-Curtiss' albums and those Edward Blankman had loaned me. Mixed in with scattered vintage images was some correspondence from a 90-year-old occasional pen pal, Walt Hastings.

I cursed as I lay sprawled on the floor. Papers and photos were everywhere. The hours I had taken to organize the pictures seemed like a huge loss. As I berated myself for not putting rubber bands around the various stacks, my eyes fixed on a letter from Walt. It was the last letter he ever sent me. I picked it up and began to read.

In reminiscing about the history and happenings of the area in question . . . I dug into some old deeds and as far as I can determine, my Granddad arrived on the North Wilmurt scene in 1900, give or take a couple of years, some 30 years after the Reeds . . . arrived to settle at the mill. . . . I have no idea how long Granddad was at North Wilmurt before he met Addie [Hull]. . . . Addie was a good friend of Granddad's. [As a result of his infantile paralysis] Addie's method for getting from here to there was by crawling. He wore a pair of hip boots cut off at the feet (so the toes would not catch on roots and rock) and a pair of heavy rubber gloves similar to those worn by power company linemen. With his double barrel shotgun slung beneath his chest he would crawl on all fours, like an animal, to a favorite deer run to watch and wait. Because of his infirmity, balance was a problem and to prevent being toppled over from the "kick" of the gun, he would sit with his back against a tree. After bagging his deer, he would crawl back home to get help to retrieve the carcass. On a visit to his home in 1932, he told me many stories of his life and showed me 28 notches cut on the inside groove of the forepiece of his shotgun, each one representing a deer he had killed.

Walt's letter went on, but Rascal interrupted my reading as he returned to the room. He now wanted the warm spot under the light. I watched him jump up and settle down. "Lucky cat," I muttered.

As I fumbled over the photos, now totally out of any sequence or context, I began to look at them in a way I had never seen them before. Walt was still alive and kicking, but Byron-Curtiss and the others were all gone now. The pictures appeared ghostly on the floor, like faces in clouds, a mosaic of vanishing history blowing in the wind.

Instead of reorganizing I found myself randomly reviewing individual items. I focused on details I originally had overlooked. A new order was revealing itself. Pictures were no longer grouped according to whom I had received them from, but by what story they told. Pioneering natives, loggers, stage drivers, guides, well-to-do early camp owners could be categories. So, too, could moms and dads. Barefoot children, posing with rifles, standing by elders. Girls adorned in bows and ruffles with long curly locks, clutching bouquets of ferns. Boys dressed in bib overalls with a single pant strap buttoned at the waistband. Children rowing, carrying packbaskets or riding in them. Proud exhibits of fish hanging from stringers or singly from the ends of makeshift fishing poles. Gangs of loggers posed at their lumber camps. Clothes revealed whether it was warm summer, cool autumn, cold winter or buggy springtime.

For each, I had questions: What became of you, whatever your circumstances? Are any of you still alive? What families still live in the mountains? Do the settings in the pictures still look about the same, or has the landscape so changed that all that remains of those days are the ghosts of those who once roamed the land and the now-silent voices of the people frozen in a moment of time, calling out, "Hurry up and take the picture!"

I handled, sorted and filed one picture. I didn't have a clue who the little boy in the blue-tinted photo was. I came across his picture in a copy of a 1912 edition of *The Life and Adventures of Nat Foster: Trapper and Hunter of the Adirondacks*. It had been placed inside the front cover. I believe it is Joseph Byron-Curtiss because his father, Rev. A.L. Byron-Curtiss, wrote the book. Tom Kilborne said it was one of twenty-seven books he inherited when he purchased the Reverend's camp. A rubber stamp was used to identify where the book was stored. On several pages, a red and blue ink sign reads, "Nat Foster Lodge, North Lake. Adirondacks. P.O. Atwell, N.Y."

I know the names of the two sporting writers standing on a beaver dam across Fall Stream in Piseco because someone penned the celebrities on the picture postcard. I estimate the picture to be close to a hundred years old, but from personal experience I can attest that paddling that stream is just as challenging now as it would have been when the photo was taken.

Two photos showed interesting portraits of a young Byron-Curtiss and a fishing buddy. Someone scrawled with an old-fashioned pen—the type that required periodic dipping of the steel stylus into a jar of permanent ink—"Row, Row, Row." Nothing there gives a clue to the person's identity, but I showed it to one old-timer in Forestport who thinks it might be Ira Watkins, a turn-of-the-century guide who lived in Atwell. I figure there is a good chance he is right. There is also a good chance that every natural setting shown in the photographs could be rediscovered today: The landscape of the headwaters has changed very little in the last one hundred years.

Mortimer Norton once said that outdoorsmen tend to overlook significant features of the North Woods—"its mountain meadows and wild flowers." Lloyd Blankman would have added, "and the lore of the mountains as well as the Adirondack characters."

Lloyd's essays colorfully recreate life in the Adirondack Mountains in firsthand accounts. They contain little formal history, because unlike the works of scholars who sift and arrange facts into understandable sums and patterns, Lloyd's stories are the stuff of history before it is worked by the hands of historians.

I knew Lloyd had dreamed of organizing his newspaper and magazine articles, along with the published and unpublished works of Harvey Dunham and Mortimer Norton, into a book. It was to be titled "Adirondack Characters," after the banner of his column in *The Courier*, Clinton, New York's hometown newspaper.

A similar book of campfire yarns and Adirondack characters, which would include those authors themselves, was taking shape in my mind. It wasn't long before I was making further inquiries to find relatives, additional materials, and permission to use them.

In the summer of 2002 I visited Lloyd Blankman's son Edward and talked with him about the project. I quietly suggested to Ed that I would like to finish his father's dream, by way of incorporating material I had collected that bore a likeness to stories told by Lloyd. I wanted to produce a book that told the stories of early settlers—stories that originated from the West Canada and Black River headwaters.

Almost immediately Ed replied, "You have my permission to use all the material my father gathered and was given permission to use." He disappeared into another room, coming back shortly with two boxes containing additional treasures of antiquity.

"You're tapped into an interest of mine," he said. "My father enjoyed gathering fresh and authentic material for his lectures. Yes, go ahead. As a matter of fact I would love to write an introduction."

Funny how things go. If Rascal had not been underfoot, the idea to assemble these early Adirondack folklorists' anecdotes and photographs into a book might never have crystallized. I'll say thanks now, Rascal, because I certainly didn't then.

My other colleagues in the preparation of this book are Lloyd Blankman, Rev. A.L. Byron-Curtiss, Harvey L. Dunham, Thomas C. O'Donnell, and Mortimer Norton. They were all woodsmen at heart, their haunt the southwestern Adirondacks. There they fished and hunted, and were "regulars" sharing their lives with the natives of the region. The writers are long deceased, but their stories, articles and memories about a variety of Adirondack characters, their vocations and their uniquely Adirondack way of life live on. This book weaves their works together with mine to present a glimpse of Adirondack pioneer life, an artifact that can provide future readers with an appreciation for a plain-spoken way of writing and some good old campfire yarns.

William J. O'Hern, March 2004

Introduction

By Edward Blankman

I WANT TO EXPRESS my great appreciation to "Jay" O'Hern for his superb effort in compiling my father's writings. My father was very enthusiastic in his love for the history of the North Country. He visited every place that he ever wrote about, and he enjoyed talking with as many people as he could find who could recall the "Golden Age of the Adirondacks." His interest was especially sparked by the publication of Harvey Dunham's *Adirondack French Louie* in 1952. Dunham and my father spent many days and nights at Segoolie, the author's camp, reminiscing with the old characters such as Bill Potter about the days gone by.

My father and I visited with many people on our own forays into the woods in the 1950s and 1960s. He would never

Lloyd Blankman as he prepared to give a lecture, carrying and wearing artifacts from the people he wrote about and admired.
COURTESY EDWARD BLANKMAN
(THE LLOYD BLANKMAN COLLECTION)

fail to come home with some special memento that he had bought or that someone had given him. It might be part of the roof from one of Louie's camps or a campstool that the hermit had made. Dad had one of the finest collections of early Adirondack material, including Louie's hunting knife. He had collected hundreds of vintage photographs, three Rushton canoes, Newhouse bear traps, early sleds, Giles Becraft's Adirondack League Club guide pin, Tim Crowley's spruce gum spud, Mortimer Norton's trout spoons, and much more. Many of these items were given to the Adirondack Museum in Blue Mountain Lake after my father's death.

He gave talks to schools and service organizations about the Adirondacks and prepared a number of different programs from which the groups could choose. He also wrote stories that were published by *The Courier*, Clinton, N.Y. and *North Country Life*, later *York State Tradition*.

It is a great pleasure to see so many of these stories in print again as it would have fulfilled a long-held dream of my father.

I
Adirondack Characters

WHEN I WAS A BOY I would listen in awe to the stories of exploration told by avid fishermen, hunters, and mountain climbers who stopped by as they passed from Seventh to Eighth Lake on their return from some deep woods haunt, to share their experience at my parents' tent site at Eighth Lake campground.

Grandpa managed the Potter Boat Company, a sales and repair shop that sold Evinrude outboard motors, boats, and accessories. In those days business was relaxed. Customers stopped by the shop to talk before and after trips to the lower lake country. Sportsmen and recreationalists, whether campground passersby or customers, were easygoing, friendly folks who offered tidbits of their adventures afoot in the Adirondacks. Some were natives who worked the land with horse teams. Others had ancestors who had cut down trees and built log cabins. One man had been given a contract to cut the timber on hundreds of acres of land; he was to have as half-payment a portion of the acreage after the timber was cut. Others worked on crews that cut out improved roads and built bridges. Those who talked about trapping in the mountains, hunting black bear, boating and fishing the big waters, and bushwhacking to reach the summits of trail-less peaks were intriguing storytellers. The men who rode rolling logs and broke up jams seemed to tell the most exciting and danger-ous tales. How could I not want to join the river drivers who broke log jams to send rolling, tumbling, masses of logs rushing down river with several men riding along? They had to jump from log to log until they could reach the riverbank or a boat. Sometimes a man would slip, be carried under and lost forever.

As a result of my exposure to mountain life, I couldn't wait to grow up: I wanted to see the wilderness. I wanted to go beyond the beaten path with only the supplies I could carry in a packbasket.

A large portion of my summers was spent living at Camp Oasis, my maternal grandparents' riverfront camp. They knew how to make do on their own. They raised most of their own vegetables, fruits, and meat. Gardening was second nature. I remember gathering eggs in the A-frame hen house and learning the lessons of life and death at the chopping block. Root cellars were as ordinary as the coal bin and the stacks of cordwood. Blocks of ice were bought to keep perishable foods cool. Few grandparents today would give their young grandson a hatchet, even with proper instruction. I enjoyed the grown-up feeling gained from being trusted to take billets of wood and split them into the proper size for the wood-fired kitchen range. Responsibility came early in a child's life.

One of the most important qualities Grandma and Grandpa had was self-sufficiency. Their conviction was passed on to me.

When I was about twelve years of age I began picking baskets of raspberries. Heritage red raspberries are everbearing; they provide a good yield over a long period of time. I marketed them at a roadside stand, along with angle worms raised in our camp's garbage pit. I earned twenty-five cents a quart for red raspberries. One well-heeled gentleman asked me to keep his family supplied with berries. At the end of several weeks I handed him twenty one-quart baskets of berries at twenty-five cents a quart.

"Great Scott!" he exclaimed, "I made my money by hard work, and as a boy, I would have been glad to get five cents a basket for berries. It seems to me the price has gone up."

"Yes," I replied, fully aware of my toil. I had helped string and tighten the wire between the poles, trained bramble canes over wire supports, kept the berry patch weeded, and mowed between the rows with a heavy iron-wheeled push mower. "The price has gone up," I explained, "but the berries are cultivated and require more work."

There was little disposable income for what folks might refer to as fun today. Rural children of my generation knew how to entertain themselves the way modern children can't, or won't. The simplest things were big deals. Being outside was important: investigating the riverbank, building huts in the woods, roaming cow pastures, and playing made-up games. I can remember being near the big box Zenith radio listening to "Gunsmoke" and "The Lone Ranger." I would lie on the camp's sheepskin rug on the floor in front of the cobblestone fireplace. I would be perfectly silent one minute and shouting the next as the broadcast sound effect of a galloping horse or squeaking saloon door came over the airwaves. I took it seriously, becoming so wrapped up in the story that I thought it was true. Then I would go to bed, afraid to close my eyes because a villain might find his way to our camp.

I was no less absorbed when a hunter dragged the carcass of an enormous black bear or whitetail buck from a pickup through the front door of the meat market.

"Where did you get the big brute?" I might have inquired.

"We shot him in the wilds around Hoffmeister up in the West Canada Crick country," might have been the reply. "We've got ourselves a huntin' camp up that way. Built it from an old barracks we bought from the government after the air base closed."

"Be jagers!" I thought. A hunting camp! Wilderness! Wild animals! Names of far-away places in the Adirondack Mountains. I was intrigued.

My youthful imagination was a rich source of entertainment. As a result of my interest in listening to the stories of men and women who visited and lived in the mountains, I developed an insatiable thirst to experience the pleasures of exploring the Adirondacks. I've logged almost sixty years of pleasure in "God's country" now, and I'm still counting.

Today the North Woods provide a totally different experience from the Adirondacks of my youth. The aged folks I knew in those days knew an even more profoundly different North Country. Those who went deep into the woodlands found land to range and privacy far back from the newly constructed highways that brought rushing crowds of motorists.

Enter Lloyd Blankman. He was a senior gentleman in my youth. Like my parents and grandparents, he knew from firsthand experience that family and community were the most important things to rural folks during and after the Great Depression. Nothing was closer than blood, followed by community spirit. And nothing brought people closer together than going through hard times.

As a boy, Lloyd Blankman knew the dread of entering the "little house out back" in winter, the blisters earned working a buck-saw or a hand hoe. He knew the smell from a village drug store where the pharmacist ground his ingredients, and the care needed by a tired boy following the evening milking as he carried pails of milk from the barn to the cool farm cellar. He seldom slipped into store-brought clothes. Patched-up hand-me-downs made up the bulk of a child's wardrobe.

Lloyd Blankman also loved the same region around the Adirondack headwaters in which I have spent so many years knocking around. His avocation in old age was to ferret out the history of the natives who lived in the southwestern Adirondacks. Whatever sporting he enjoyed in his life always led him back to the native Adirondackers in the lower mountains. Nestled in those headwaters, he found the rich folklore that he decided to record.

Over a span of twelve years Lloyd Blankman talked with dozens of family members of mountain residents. He personally interviewed notable old-timers who held that they had many advantages in the "old days" that their kin are deprived of now—abundant wild meat, economic opportunities, and freedom from government overregulation. Most folks had plenty to eat and wear but, whipped by the Depression, had no money. They learned to get by the hard way—not because they viewed experience as being the best teacher, but because they couldn't find or afford any other way. Blankman, as an interviewer, understood how the older generation felt. It was his wish to record for future generations what rested within the memory of men and women living in his beloved Adirondacks. He gathered their stories and began presenting them in his weekly newspaper column, "Adirondack Characters."

The setting is Herkimer County, in the southwestern corner of the "blue line" that outlines the Adirondack Park, in the middle of the twentieth century. These are the stories of those Adirondack characters.

Collection 1
Great Adirondack Guides

THE ADIRONDACK WOODSMAN and guide stories of Lloyd Blankman's time were inexhaustible. Old-time independent guides helped mold the folklore of the region they lived and made their livelihood in.

The old men would stare eagerly down the tracks from a railroad station, awaiting the arrival of their city sportsmen. At first their eyes could grasp no more than telegraph poles, wooden ties and parallel steel rails that seemed to join in the far distance, broken only by the shadows of trees and boulders and the angular outlines of an Adirondack Mountain depot, houses, hotels, stores, cafe, saloons, and houses positioned trackside like Northern orioles that build hanging nests over buildings. Then suddenly, with all the strength of a hawk's eyesight, they would see in the far distance dark puffs from a train's smoke stack. Sports arriving.

Because they were often looked on as local heroes, due to their woodsman's labor—trapping, lumbering, and guiding—popular tales of their doings got about. These popularized men-of-the-woods were most often the offspring of farmers who arrived in the North Woods expecting to make a living off the precarious topsoil-thin land. Pioneers found the long winters and poor soil of the mountains unsuitable for large-scale farming. The most resourceful settlers remained, turning to the woods and water for their livelihood.

Burt Conklin, George Wendover, Giles Becraft, Alvah Dunning, and Jim Dalton were representative sons of pioneers-turned-woodsmen who turned to guiding. All were hardworking and skillful in woodscraft. All were popular with sportsmen they guided, except for Dunning. Dunning was a primitive man. Neither nature nor civilization ever tamed the streak of savagery in him. His hostility to some of the men he guided—the fools who thought the earth round—made it easy to believe that he had beaten his wife and had had a nasty quarrel with Ned Buntline, the dime novelist, on Eagle Lake. As more and more fools invaded the forest and closed in on his successive retreats, Alvah acquired a legend of his own. He was the wild frontiersman ever protesting, "Don't fence me in!"

In the early 1950s, the release of *Adirondack French Louie,* written by Harvey L. Dunham, fired Lloyd Blankman's imagination. Himself an avid outdoorsman, Blankman found the anecdotal, informal history of old-time trappers, loggers and guides extraordinary. Blankman loved the North Woods.

He was especially knowledgeable about the headwaters of the Black and West Canada Rivers. Wishing also to contribute to local history, he became deeply involved in seeking out old-time woodsmen and their families who still lived in the backwoods—those who had their own ideas and ways of living—lifestyles that were so different from those of people in the towns and cities.

Perhaps too, Blankman found Dunham's book revived similar memories of his own boyhood. Lloyd began going with his father on fishing excursions to West Canada Creek when he was ten years old in 1913. The Adirondack Mountains have changed so completely that it is difficult to revive a comprehension of what "French" Louie was really like. The book had given Lloyd a huge dose of nostalgia.

Lloyd Blankman drew material from his interviewing efforts to craft rural images of the closing scenes of old-time men of the mountains. His columns were clearly aimed at an Adirondack lore audience.

With his Clinton newspaper column successes, Blankman realized his own potential as an interviewer.

The work included in this collection represent a single man's effort to record earlier-era mountain personalities. Few others were collecting these old-timers' histories during a time in American history when the war between North Korea and the United States was at its peak. Blankman, through his personal effort, became a recognized regional collector of Adirondack memorabilia.

 NAT SHEPARD
Lloyd Blankman

Nathaniel "Nat" Shepard (1865–1922)

Nathaniel Ward Shepard, one of the best known and most popular guides and woodsmen in the Southern Adirondacks, died at the home of his daughter, Mrs. James Harvey, Town of Ohio, August 21, 1922, age 57 years.

Most of his mature life was spent in the great forest he loved so much. Nat was a friendly and generous man, who made friends easily, and they held him in high regard. He was a true lover of nature and was happy when in the woods primeval.

From the age of 21 for the remainder of his life he was employed as a lumberman and guide in the Town of Wilmurt. He married Ruth Conklin and they raised a large family of five children.

Soon after Nat's death his son Henry wrote a poem called "My Dad," in memory of his father.

This poem was conceived in the mind of a man with a talent for expressing himself in verse, and was inspired by the love of a young man for his father.

MY DAD
By Henry P. Shepard, 1923

Old timer, you've taken the long, long trail
That goes winding over the Great Divide
And I reckon tonight your campfire light
Will shine from the other side.
'Twas a long hard climb to the top, ole man
But you've reached the summit at last
And they say that the trail is wide and smooth
From there to the Golden Pass.
I'm kinder lonesome tonight ole man
And I'm hankering to hear yer voice
And I reckon the grip o' your ole right hand
Would make my heart rejoice.
We've hunted and fished together ole pal,
Where the trails were far apart
And each lake and valley and mountain and stream
Seem to be a part of my heart.
As I think tonight of the camp on the hill
Memories manifold throng;
And in fancy I hear the voice that's now still
Mingled with the White-Throat's song.
The fire's gone out in the little old stove
I reckon a cobweb hangs o'er the door;
And the Rose-breasted Grosbeak sings from the tree
Where he sang for you oft' before.
Somehow I can't feel that yer gone ole Pal
For as the seasons come and the seasons go
And I camp each year in the little ole shack
You'll be with me there in the fire-light's glow.
Yes, I'm kinder lonely tonight ole man
Perhaps 'taint right ter feel bad;
But you were the best OLE PAL I ever knew
I reckon that's 'cause you were Dad.

🌲 I ONCE KNEW AN ADIRONDACK GUIDE
Henry P. Shepard

During a spring 1950 interview in the mountain hamlet of Cold Brook, Lloyd Blankman encouraged Henry Shepard to write his recollections of his well-known father, Nat Shepard. The following is Henry's remembrance.

Yes, I once knew an Adirondack guide. I like to think that I knew him perhaps better than any one of his many friends and acquaintances. I spent many happy, unforgettable hours in his company in far-away places. In our years of association and companionship I came to love and respect this soft-spoken, mild mannered, unassuming man of the Great Outdoors with his vast knowledge of the deep forests and the wild creatures that dwell therein.

I should like to record an incident in our lives that happened on one of our many forays into the wilds on one of those Yesterdays back there on the trail a piece.

I was in high school at the time and had a two week's vacation over the Christmas holidays. The Old Timer was running a trapline out from a camp on Little Black Creek Lake and had asked me if I would like to spend my vacation back in camp with him on the trapline.

I don't need to describe the reaction of a sixteen-year-old boy to such an invitation nor go into a detailed description of the anticipation of, and the preparation for, the trip.

The morning after Christmas Day we left for the camp and reached it shortly after midday. I remember the camp was cold as only a camp can get when left unoccupied for a few days in wintertime. A roaring fire in the old kitchen range that served both for cooking and heating soon made it comfortable, and food was the next item on the agenda.

That afternoon was spent replenishing our supply of fuel. We sawed, split, and carried into camp a huge wood supply and stacked it up around the stove. The mercury dropped that night to 30 below zero and the next morning our lake was frozen over. I shall never forget the picture it made when the morning sun shone upon it. Here was a lake, over a mile long and nearly a mile in width, frozen over while the water was calm. It looked like a huge sheet of glass and was at least six inches in thickness. The entire lake was a mirror reflecting the shore line perfectly. We crossed on the ice that morning to work the trapline that started at the inlet and led northward over the mountain range towards South Lake, and I remember wishing that I had included my ice skates in my duffel.

The weather stayed clear and cold for the next two days, and then, in the afternoon of the second day, snow began falling. The skies had cleared by morning and when the sun had climbed the range of mountains to the southeast, it shone down upon our lake, covered now by its blanket of pure white, transforming it into a sparkling sea of glistening diamonds. We were starting out again and, pausing for awhile, we stood spellbound by the beauty of it all. Not a word was spoken by either of us.

As we were about to start on, the Old Timer remarked that this would be a good time to show him how straight a trail I could make across the ice from camp to the inlet. Let me explain that on our winter trips whenever we came to an open field or lake to cross, he showed me how to make a straight trail just by focusing my eyes upon some object in the distance and traveling straight to it. We had always made a sort of game of it and would vie with each other to see who could leave the straightest trail behind. Now here was my chance to put a straight trail across the lake. Selecting a large tamarack tree on the farther shore, where our trail left the lake, I fixed my gaze up on it and struck out with the Old Timer following close behind.

We had reached a point about half way across the lake when a flock of blue jays on the shore at our right let loose with a chorus of screams and squawks that could be heard all around the lake. I stopped in my tracks and turned around to face the Old Timer with a question on my lips.

He just grinned and said, "Nothing but blue jays, Lad." Then he went on. "The blue jay is the scatterbrain of the forest. Yes, he is beautiful, I'll admit, in his gaudy dress and jaunty top-knot, but he is an alarmist, a meddler, and the world's worse gossip. Whenever he sees something unusual, he has to scream it to the world from the top of the highest tree. He just can't keep a secret. Could be they have ganged up on an owl, or they see a Porky asleep in that tall hemlock, or that there is a buck bedded down on the ridge and they see us coming up the lake and are telling him to get out of there. His warning scream has saved the lives of more than one sleeping buck. I know he has put an end to many a stalk for me."

As we moved on, I glanced shoreward several times, hoping to see the cause of the commotion. I could see nothing, of course, and gradually the din became fainter in the distance.

When we reached the shore, we stopped for a few minutes to put on our snowshoes and rearrange our packs before starting out on the trapline. I had finished putting on my snowshoes when the Old Timer called to me, "Step over here a minute, Lad. Here is something I want you to see."

I was standing beside him in an instant. Placing his left hand on my shoulder and with his briar pipe in his right hand, he pointed the stem out across the lake. "Do you see the trail you made, Lad?"

Yes, I could see it—I can still see it very vividly more than forty years later. The picture all comes back to me again—the lake, the two of us standing together on the shore and looking out over the snow-covered ice. There was our trail, a deep furrow through the snow, with the rays of the sun casting a bluish shadow on one edge of it. I could see nearly all of it from start to finish, and over it all, the sparkle and glitter of sunlight on snow.

I was not proud of that trail, though, for it definitely was not straight as I had planned it to be. The Old Timer had noticed it and just couldn't let it pass. "You see, Lad, when you started, you planned to go straight and you did a perfect job of it as long as you kept your eyes upon your objective. Notice that your trail is straight and perfect up to the point where you became interested in the jays. From there you made a long, sweeping arc but finally got back on the line again and came through straight enough at the finish. Here is an object lesson, Lad, that can be applied to our daily lives.

"When we start out up Life's Long Trail, if we wish to blaze it straight and true, we must first of all have an objective to guide us. That objective should be the Cross, Lad. Keep your eyes focused upon it every step of the way, never once losing sight of it, and you will find that the Trail you blaze through life will be a straight one.

"Of course, there will be jays all along the trail to attract your attention and steer you off your course, but if you will keep your eyes upon the Cross, your trail will be a straight one. You will get a heap of satisfaction in being able to look back from that farther shore upon the straight trail you have blazed down through the years. Keep your eyes on the Cross, Lad."

I shall never forget the incident nor the lesson taught. I have listened to many learned and scholarly clergymen, speaking from beautiful pulpits, and never have I heard a more eloquent or convincing sermon than was delivered there in God's Great Cathedral, yesterday, December 30, 1909, by this old guide of the Northern wilds who had felt the touch of God's hand in the solitude of the forest.

His name? Oh, yes—he was Nat Shepard, an old Adirondack guide who lived in the town of Wilmurt in northern Herkimer County and who spent many years as a guide for the Adirondack League Club at Honnedaga Lake.

Many of you who read this may have known him, but I like to feel that I know him just a little better than any one of his many friends. You see, he was my Dad.

Mr. and Mrs. Henry P. Shepard at Richards Falls, their favorite trout fishing hole on West Canada Creek. The falls are also known as Wilmurt Falls today. The photograph was taken in 1939.
COURTESY EDWARD BLANKMAN (THE LLOYD BLANKMAN COLLECTION)

Giles Becraft, (second from left) a good companion, and an excellent guide.
COURTESY EDWARD BLANKMAN (THE LLOYD BLANKMAN COLLECTION)

🌲 ENJOYMENT – GILES BECRAFT
Lloyd Blankman

Giles Becraft (1850–1893)

Giles Becraft was one of the greatest of the Adirondack guides. His father ran Becraft's place, later to become Matteson's Mountain Home, in a clearing on the edge of a beautiful stillwater, on the East Branch of the West Canada Creek. Back of the house a mountain rose two thousand feet in two miles and here was beautiful Wilmurt Lake, surrounded by spruce trees and loaded with trout.

Here Giles grew up from a boy. The wilderness was everywhere. He learned the country intimately and became an expert with a rifle and the fly. Lucky was the party who had Giles for their guide, as he was a good companion and he knew the woods thoroughly.

The Adirondack League Club at Honnedaga kept a roster of fifteen or twenty guides on call and Giles was one of the best of them. This quiet and unassuming man died suddenly of a heart attack on the Piseco Lake road, in 1893 at the age of forty-three.

His children were not yet grown up. One of the sons became well known in the paper industry and he died in Utica in recent years. His daughter, living in Dolgeville, gave the writer her father's Adirondack League guide pin.

🌲 SLIM MURDOCK AND THE GUIDING TRADITION

William J. O'Hern

One of my fondest memories is of sitting with eighty-six year old Slim Murdock and listening to the stories that he told. He would open up his old photo albums and point to the woodsmen he used to know and say, "Jay, this here is the old hewed log cabin where Gerald Kenwell lived while his father, Wellington, and other guides were building the Sportsman's Hostelry along the south branch of the Moose River far back in the Moose River Plains wilderness. And see here, this forest patriarch is old 'Pop' Baker. Pop used to guide for the Adirondack League Club when he was young. He hooked up with the Chapins about 1899. Henry Chapin was a millionaire from Rochester, New York. He contracted Wellington to build a grand, rustic lodge in the heart of his 300-acre preserve at Beaver Lake

Slim Murdock 1921.
AUTHOR'S COLLECTION

back in the Plains. It was virgin land then. And oh, what a beautiful setting Camp Nit was, set under the immense whispering pines. And look here; you have just got to hear about Billy Buckshot. This might be the only picture in existence of this bony-framed fellow. When he got too old to guide, he too took to being a caretaker at some wealthy folks' camps near the blue waters of the Fulton Chain of Lakes he loved so well."

"Now see this mustached, large-framed fellow. Who do you suppose that might be?"

Our conversations would go on and on. Slim would recall: "Bob West, now there was a guide of great physical strength. He was also well versed in woodcraft and how to survive the hardships of the wilderness."

"Laura and Gerald Kenwell grew up back there along the south branch. Gerald represented that type of pioneer childhood no longer in existence today. When he was only nine years old he'd walk the perilous miles clear over to the Big West in the West Canadas to bring French Louie a pack basket full of snakes for Louie's potato patch." And so the conversation would go. "Phil Christry was an excellent shot. Len Harwood could swing an axe with the strength and dexterity of Paul Bunyan, and . . ."

I'd barrage Slim with all sorts of questions. My queries would bring a smile to his aged face when he talked about the olden days and how everybody who went into the Adirondack backcountry relied on the services of a guide.

Over the years, my old friend Slim's memory flowed as he reminisced about the personalities of the Fulton Chain guides he knew in the southern Adirondacks—most guides had their favorite localities where they were especially well-acquainted with the lay of the land.

"Slim" was not his birth-given name. Old photographs bear witness that in his younger days he was tall and slim. Slim was one of many of the old-time mountaineers and woodsmen, descendants of that earlier generation of original settlers who made the wilds of the Adirondack Mountains their home.

My venerable friend earned his reputation as an proficient hunter, trapper, fisherman, and expert with dynamite. Slim was also a guide and packer for his uncle, Gerald Kenwell, one of the best-known guides in the Fulton Chain. He operated a hunting and fishing camp nineteen miles back in the Moose River Plains along Otter Brook. Otter Brook Camp was much different from most of the typical guides' camps of the day, and yet there were many similarities.

Slim grew up in Inlet, New York, among numerous grizzled surviving patriarchs of the Adirondack forest, woodsmen who were famed as some of the "most honest, hard working and loyal" guides a sport could hire.

He was a younger counterpart of the original Adirondack guides who came to the mountains, learned well the territory where they lived and worked, and hired out to tourists, businessmen and sportsmen who began arriving in the Adirondacks for extended vacations about 1850.

Tourists needed guides. Guides hefted all the gear, as well as carrying light and slender guideboats between bodies of water along an unmarked forest trail.

The late Long Lake historian Frances Seaman reported that most native guides "worked hard. In those days, a guide was expected to furnish his [own] boat and oars, carry a rifle for securing game for food, assist in selection and obtaining of supplies and food staples, and be able to cook for the party he was guiding. Rowing his party all day was a test of strength, with one or two passengers and their gear. If a guide was well liked and pleased his client, he usually received a good tip in addition to his wages. For two weeks' work, a good guide might receive a tip of $100 or more, along with an advance reservation for his services the next year."

In addition to taking care of his clients, Seaman emphasized, a guide had a family and household to tend to. The men "had to plant a garden, care for livestock and mend fences, cut wood for year-round cooking and heating and procure provisions for their families."

In recalling memories of his mountain-living relatives and the old timers he knew well, a gleam of rightful pride invariably lit up Slim's eyes. Our conversations always revived long-held memories that helped him turn the history pages of his memory back still further.

As often happens in any profession, guiding attracted some men whose character and ability were questionable. They were "scoundrels and outlaws," said Slim, who outraged their clients, overcharged for services, talked clients into parting with an expensive piece of gear, and thought nothing of breaking game laws. "They were a black mark on all the good guides who worked for $3.00 a day in the 1890s."

They professed to be guides but did not represent the title of "guide" honestly and knew little about the profession in which they claimed membership.

In response, a group of noteworthy guides formed the Adirondack Guides' Association on June 27, 1891, at the Berkley Hotel in Saranac Lake. Charles Brumley's excellent history, *Guides of the Adirondacks*, states "The Adirondack Guides Association was lucky to have quality leadership from the start." Saranac Lake guide Hiram Benham is recognized as helping to initiate among all the men gathered, a mission statement that clearly defined the purpose for professional organization.

In late September of Slim's eighty-sixth year of life, he asked if I would take him back to the Plains. He wanted to see the forest, the south branch and the former site of Otter Brook Camp. Slim's request was heartfelt. I knew how much he cherished his years working in the backcountry, but his request was not easy for me to follow through on. I was hesitant. In fact, I was downright worried. He had recently been released from the hospital. He said his hospitalization had not been "all that serious"— just his thirteenth "mini-heart attack"—but he assured me he was as healthy as any boss bear.

Winfred "Slim" Murdock on pack horse at Chapin's Crossing, south branch of the Moose River about 1921. AUTHOR'S COLLECTION

"Besides," he reasoned, "if I die there, I'll be right where I want to be when I leave this earth. So don't you go worrying about me."

Slim put forth his best arm-twisting effort. Making the decision was a significant challenge for me, and the choice was not made any easier when he added, "My son won't take me. He won't even let me take my grandson anywhere with me in the car."

I finally decided it seemed sensible to take Slim back "home" one last time. I imagined how I would feel if I were his age. I too would want desperately to revisit a place that held so many fond memories for me. Slim wanted more than mere memories and sweet dreams. He wanted to once again explore the land around Otter Brook Camp.

The weather was perfect on the fall day we visited the Plains. Slim leaned back against a lot of trees and rested frequently along the short trail we hiked to reach the remains of the old guide camp and later a special place he called "The Bears Bathtub."

All day long Slim pointed out locations that were special to him, and recalled memories of his days packing and guiding. I admit that the first time I saw Slim's hand go to his chest as we took a breather, my own heart started beating double time. I think it returned to normal when we reached the partially overgrown clearing where the camp once stood.

"Victory!" proclaimed Slim, his weathered face beaming with elation. I knew then that taking him back to his beloved Plains had been the right decision.

Slim was a special person. He knew the Moose River Plains like the back of his hand—better than any man alive. He pointed to a pile of rotting timbers below a rock cliff. "That there is where the barn used to be. And see here where the hole in the ground is?"

I would take out a photograph that helped me to recreate the setting. "There's a bed spring still in the cellar hole where the main stood. Gerald and I used to sit by the wood stove in the evenings, drinking black coffee and chain-smoking cigarettes. I remember him reeling off tales of the times when he would visit with woodsman 'French' Louie. Old Louie filled his head with tales of living in the mountains that would make the hair on the back of his neck stand up when he was a kid."

Gerald would hang around Louie's camp for days absorbing woods knowledge and enjoying the hermit's adventures—just as I did each time I got together with Slim.

Sports quickly came to realize that they probably owed much of their self-confidence and appreciation of diversity to those guides they encountered in the mountains.

I can say the same thing about what Slim passed to me.

Hats off the old-timers.

Hats off to the Adirondack guides!

🌿 SAM DUNAKIN

Lloyd Blankman

The late Gerald Kenwell of Inlet, remembered seeing Sam Dunakin many times, when Gerald was a boy, six or seven years of age. Sam was then a big, rough, weather-beaten man, nearing the close of a notable career in the woods as a guide.

He was born in New Jersey and came to the Fulton Chain of Lakes about 1844. His first job was chore boy and handy man for the Arnold family, who dwelt in the manor house on the hill opposite the present railroad station named Thendara.

His main interests were hunting deer and bear, running a trapline and guiding parties who came to the Brown's Tract during the summer and autumn months. In camp he played a fiddle and smoked a clay pipe sideways. He wasn't strong on housekeeping, so at mealtime, you were advised to dust off your plate. His dog licked his own dishes clean.

Brown's Tract Guide Sam Dunakin at Fourth Lake.
COURTESY EDWARD BLANKMAN (THE LLOYD BLANKMAN COLLECTION)

On the north shore of Fourth Lake near Burnaps, a rippling stream enters the lake. Here Sam built a camp and named the stream Minnow Brook. A few years later the camp burned down so he built another on the opposite side of the brook.

Sam remained at this location and guided and trapped but mostly drank, until the close of his life many years later. He wasn't what one would call an historic pioneer but was more on the pattern of a lumberjack style.

Honest, Sam Dunakin, whiskey lovin' Sam, became one of the best-known guides on the Brown's Tract during the golden years, when traffic on the chain in both directions was heavy and mostly on the waterways by guideboat and canoe. He was faithful and competent, and took good care of his party and kept it entertained with the darndest stories that were at least half true.

During his later years Sam's full white bearded face appeared on post cards, for sale at hotels, inns, camps and stores, and labeled "typical Adirondack guide." His city customers easily believed this. The hard liquor he consumed aged him and long before would have finished a less rugged woodsman of his age. He was seldom sober during his last years.

Feeble and almost helpless, Sam left the chain in 1906 to live with a sister in New Jersey. Here he died in 1907, aged 79.

After a career of fifty years in the woods, he possessed three pieces of property, a fish rod under his cabin porch, a canoe in the bushes nearby and an axe in the shed, each given to a friend, with the word that when he left the chain he would never have use for them again.

Thus came to a close the life of a man who literally guided thousands of parties by guideboat and canoe from Old Forge to the Saranac Lakes and return.

Jim "Brockie" Dalton (far left) at the Buffalo Head Train Station in Forestport with the Risleys, a family hunting party.
COURTESY EDWARD BLANKMAN (THE LLOYD BLANKMAN COLLECTION)

JIM "BROCKIE" DALTON, GUIDE
Lloyd Blankman

The day of the pioneer Adirondack guide is long past. The guide knew the woods, waters and wildlife of his own territory, but he didn't live long enough to know the whole woods. Few people realize the huge extent of the entire wilderness. The guide naturally learned the countryside where he grew up and acquired a knowledge of the forest by a lifetime of travel in the woods.

Jim "Brockie" Dalton grew up in and around Boonville. As a boy he started working in the lumber camps. Physically he was big, strong and rugged, but soon turned from lumberjacking to guiding and in this field he was to become one of the outstanding guides of that era.

He guided mostly for the Adirondack League Club, first at Jocks (Honnedaga) Lake and then for the remainder of his life at Little Moose Lake.

Just how or why Jim acquired the nickname "Brockie" nobody seems to know. He was also known as the fearless forester of Little Moose Lake. He knew the mountains and lakes of the Moose River territory well, every inch of this country.

When not guiding he made his home in Boonville. When in the woods on the trails he never drank, but when on the outside like many others he frequented the taverns.

No one was more expert with rod, rifle and packbasket than "Jim" Dalton. His packbasket, now in possession of the writer, was the Adirondack style basket invented by the Indians long ago. He knew the packbasket, how to load it, how to fit it to his back, and how to carry it on the trail. He thought nothing of toting a hundred-pound pack on his back, or of slinging a deer over his shoulder and walking out of the woods with it.

Dalton was six feet tall, and weighed over 200 lbs. He was a striking figure to meet on the streets of Boonville, whether in town or forest attire. His hands were so large that a twenty-five cent piece would just slip through a ring that he wore on his little finger.

Jim was an even-tempered man, slow moving, never one to look for trouble, but he knew what to do and could take care of himself under any situation.

The late Thomas R. Proctor of Utica maintained a camp on the south branch of the Moose River and here for over 25 years his personal guide was none other than the fearless forester, "Jim" Dalton. As long as Proctor lived, each year he sent his guide a huge turkey for Christmas.

Many older residents of Boonville today remember this man, who was one of the last of the old-time guides of the Golden Age. He died in Rome in 1945, age 86, and now rests in Boonville Cemetery, where so many early Adirondack characters are buried.

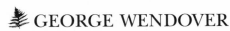

GEORGE WENDOVER

Lloyd Blankman

The North Lake Region, east of Forestport, is a great country—one of the best fur-producing parts of New York State. Fur-bearing animals like the fox, mink, fisher and otter are common here and increasing in numbers.

Just before the turn of the century it was the forest primeval. A century and a quarter ago it was the stamping ground of the pioneer trappers, Foster, Wright and Stoner. Here in Forestport George Wendover[1] was born in 1849.

The region was a sportsmen's para-

George Wendover in his later years.
COURTESY EDWARD BLANKMAN
(THE LLOYD BLANKMAN COLLECTION)

dise. Hunting and fishing parties came by train to Buffalo Head (Forestport) at 2:00 a.m. and then traveled by buckboard to North Wilmurt and thence by trail to camp headquarters. Here in 1900 a party of thirteen on a ten-day hunting trip brought down thirteen deer.

The guide for this hunting party was George Wendover. He became known far and wide and became something of a legendary figure.

He went deep into the woods with the same parties year after year. They found him a gentleman always. He took good care of his parties, and they depended on him as an outstanding woodsman. He was a tall, lean pioneer with leathery face and hands—just a slip of a man who moved fast in the woods—and an expert with a rifle.

He and his son Lon were zealous and skilled workers—skilled in all tasks that camping and living in the woods demanded. They could build a night's shelter of brush or a snug trapper's cabin with an axe or a hatchet.

George lived and raised his family of thirteen children in a small, weatherbeaten house standing to this day in Wheelertown, on the north side of Hinckley Reservoir. He died in 1945 at the age of 96 and was buried in a little plot almost hidden in the woods, a mile or two from his house on the road to Forestport.

---

[1] Grandson Alonzo Wandover reports his family's name has been alternatively spelled as Wandover and Wendover for generations. "The family spells it with an 'a' now. We say the 'a' is in fashion," he joked on December 13, 2003.

George Wendover is second from right in this successful 1904 hunting party.
COURTESY EDWARD BLANKMAN (THE LLOYD BLANKMAN COLLECTION)

GEORGE WENDOVER'S FUN WITH GREENHORNS

William J. O'Hern

They've been icons of the Adirondacks sporting population for over one hundred and fifty years. Thousands of city slickers, also referred to as green-horns, dudes, and sports, trusted a guide to point the way when navigating the mountain wilderness.

The era of the old-time woodsman and resident guide approached its twilight by 1900. Walk into any saloon in the North Country back then, and chances were any number of drinkers would be guides with idle time, all suffering from a debilitating illness of the tongue called storytelling.

The Morrison Inn, across the tracks from the old Forestport train depot, was one such watering hole where "goyds" would congregate. The gathered men of the woods were what any client would call first-class guides—all experienced, congenial, respected, loyal, and crack shots to boot. Add to the list yarn-spinners.

Like all the other guides, George Wendover served his apprenticeship by observing the senior men in action and soaking up all the counsel and wisdom they could hand him. Then too, of course, by carefully examining the habits of the big game animals, he was able to pick up a great deal by himself. He went on to become one of the Black River headwater country's best guides.

George guided fishing and hunting parties deep into the headwaters country. It was said that if George had any decent chance at all he usually got two out of every three running deer he shot at. In aiming his gun he looked down along the side of the barrel and kept pumping the lever and pulling the trigger every time the deer crossed an opening through the trees. The report sounded very much as though he was using an automatic.

Guiding kept George busy during the spring, summer and fall. When waiting for a party to arrive at the train depot, friend Rev. Byron-Curtiss knew George to join the local boys at the Morrison Inn.

Like other trusted woodsmen of the golden age of guides, George was also a storyteller. Gathered together and a bit whisked up, the men enjoyed telling good-natured stories when they got together and recalled the names and exploits of their most unforgettable characters among the sports they shepherded. It was their yarns, Byron-Curtiss said, that gave the saloon a goodly part of its particular notability.

In the 1960s, Lloyd Blankman interviewed George Wendover's relatives. The story that follows is his restatement of one of George's accounts. Such ever-green memories provide convincing proof that George was also a bit of a prankster.

Soon after a party of tired hunters got back to camp, George sneaked out, cut off one of the feet of a hedgehog he had recently caught and sprang the trap on it, pulling the trap out of the hole, until the chain was tight. Next morning, a city boy hustled up to tend the trap. He soon came back with the "bear's foot" that he had found in the trap. He went back to the city with the story in his head of the bear that he had caught and lost, leaving the foot behind.

Of course this was just one of the tricks that George played on any unsuspecting person that he could find.

George liked to have fun at the expense of greenhorns. He invented the Drawboys, who lived in small caves under the roots of large spruce trees. When a greenhorn came into camp the Drawboys were always present just outside among the bushes. They never bothered people when they were awake, but as soon as they went to sleep the little men came in groups and took the city men out the window and—?

Afterword

THE OLD MEN OF THE MOUNTAINS lie in the earth as they have done for so long, surrounded by their private garden of grasses and wildflowers growing from seeds that have blown from the four quarters of the Adirondack range, under old-growth trees and by the familiar maple, beech, spruce, and balsam woods known throughout their lives. Their profiles range from the great to the eccentric. These old woodsmen have endured much at the mountains' hands. They have cut down countless trees and split and stacked immeasurable quantities of cordwood; they have been perilously tossed by swift currents in guideboats and slipped on spring river drives to the mills, sometimes pitching to a watery death. They have been intimately acquainted with both the short-sighted exploiters who saw in the Adirondacks' considerable natural resources only a hasty dollar, the sportsmen with their often feverish eye on the abundant wildlife, and the romantics' imaginations conjuring up quaint and fanciful visions among the old rocks and time-worn slopes. Whether we see the old men in photographs as products of the woods dressed in their summer outfit of long pants and buttoned-up shirt and coat or snugly tucked under their woolen winter get-up, they remain grand and provoking sights well worth thumbing pages of old photographs or thinking of the days when men and women traveled the mountains under their guidance. And they deserve our respectful admiration and gratitude for the part they played in creating a magnetic bond that called city-bred wood lovers' attention to the great natural beauty of the Adirondacks—in their easy, frank way that cemented an intimate relationship between mountaineer and learned man, accepting each other at face value.

Philo Scott, a Cranberry Lake country guide, let on that if he could live an additional life, he was willing to change places with the men he "goyded," such as Irving Bacheller and Booth Tarkington, not because they were distinguished but because the men knew how to live. "Them auther fellers certainly do know how to have a time. It's a great life, en if I could hit the back trail an' live this life over again, I'd be an auther feller fer sure." But "it's ev'ry man to his element, an mine ain't among folks with good clothes en plum grammer."

To Emerson the guides were "uncontaminated with the vicious habits of civilized life." Said William H. H. Murray, ". . . a more honest, cheerful, and patient class of men cannot be found the world over." I like best how Paul Jamieson summarized the Adirondack guides in his June 1966 *New York Folk Quarterly* "Guide and Party" article: "The association of native and outsider is therefore less close and familiar today than in the last century. No composite creation of native's deeds and outsider's nostalgia personifies the region as did the old-time guide. But lore of the woods is still being made by hunters, fishermen, campers, trampers, summer residents, mountain climbers, skiers, boaters and other groups. Outsiders have an increasing share in it as their number and their need grow. 'Out of the woods we came, and to the woods we must return, at frequent intervals,' an Adirondack tourist of 80 years ago spoke for all generations, 'if we would redeem ourselves from the vanities of civilization.' Any return for reasons of the heart is the stuff of folklore."

Collection 2
Old Men of the Mountains

Mortimer Norton believed Adirondack characters should not be forgotten and that accounts of their lives and exciting adventures should be repeated over and over again. He believed the younger generation should learn about the old-time characters like New York State frontiersmen Nat Foster, Jonathan Wright, and Nick Stoner. Canadian "French" Louie who lived on Big West Lake would have been included. The story "Old Lobb of Piseco" is one of Mortimer's stories born of his experience, knowledge and research.

🌿 OLD LOBB OF PISECO LAKE
Mortimer Norton

AMONG THE RUGGED, eccentric woodsmen who wove their unusual, some-times turbulent, lives in the North Woods of New York in an early era, Floyd Ferris Lobb was one of the most unique. The events that occurred during his latter days form an interesting chronicle of the wilderness.

Without any intention on his part, the activities in which Lobb engaged while staying alone on the westerly shore of Piseco Lake, couched in the dense forest of southern Hamilton County, notably influenced numerous sportsmen who invaded the Adirondack Mountains to test their skill at trout fishing.

This impression, rife to some extent even at present, came about because Lobb, goaded either by the impulse to invent or the necessity to appease his recurring hunger, devised a trolling spoon that, in brass, copper, and nickel finishes, was highly appealing to lake trout.

To the fish, its shape, size, and color apparently resembled a golden or silver shiner – two species of minnows prevalent in the lake then and which the trout prized as food—when twitched through the water At any rate, the spoon readily proved to be the most alluring of all those used in the region, and certainly resulted in exceptional catches for the bewhiskered old-timer.

Naturally, visiting anglers became aware of this phenomenal spoon, despite every furtive attempt in the beginning by Lobb to hold it a secret. Their curi-osity was aroused to a sharp pitch; they were anxious to try it out themselves, and to have a few safely stashed in their own tackle boxes for frequent trials. Several fortunate fishermen did manage somehow to obtain samples, and thus inevitably the fame of Lobb's pet trout teaser at length spread far and wide.

In view of this notoriety, more people began to hear of "the hermit of Piseco Lake," and to wonder from whence he had come and why he chose to seclude himself from society.

Being extremely reticent, and almost totally deaf after middle age, Lobb would confide in very few acquaintances and had scarcely any personal friends. He refused to divulge much about the incidents that took place in his boyhood years. As far as the residents and summer vacationers around Piseco were concerned, most of his life was shrouded in an impenetrable mystery. And so it remains!

Nearly everyone who came into contact with the veteran trapper, hunter, and fisherman knew him solely as "Old Lobb." Just where and when he was born, no one could seem to discover beyond that he started life "somewhere in Pennsylvania" at a date probably between 1820 and 1825, and that his parents came from Connecticut.

Stirred by the adventurous tendencies of the pioneer and wanderlust, in his late teens or early twenties young Lobb departed from home, traveled northward, and finally arrived in the cozy village of Poland, a few miles south of the Adirondacks in the scenic and historic West Canada Creek Valley.

Here, it has been told, he opened a small tailor shop to earn a livelihood, and exercised his talents as a musician and writer. On weekends when lumberjacks and other mountaineers drifted into town to drink away their wages, Lobb might be found listening raptly to exciting tales of the North Woods.

These whetted his yearning to partake altogether in an outdoor life, a feeling that was intensified when he heard repeatedly about the wild game— panthers, deer, black bear, foxes, bobcats, beaver, fisher, pine marten, otter, raccoons, snowshoe rabbits, and gray squirrels—that thrived in the region about Piseco. He longed to hunt and trap these animals, to explore seldom-trod tracts of forestland, and to fish in lakes and streams that abounded with trout of huge proportions.

The opportunity to fulfill these desires came to pass sooner than he could have foreseen, and in a way that was hardly expected. A part of his youth, it seems, was enlivened by a wife, but in some manner there arose adverse marital problems that greatly changed the course of his career. It is reported, at least, that "when about twenty-four years of age, disappointed in love, or for some reason best known to himself, Lobb retired to Piseco Lake, where he lived as a hermit until his death in 1891."

In those days it required a long and arduous trek through mainly uninhabited country to cover the thirty-five miles from Poland to the lake. The last seven had to be traversed over an indistinct, windfall-littered blazed trail winding up and down several steep slopes.

*A postcard of Floyd Ferris Lobb, commonly known as "Old Lobb,"
the hermit of Piseco Lake.* COURTESY EDWARD BLANKMAN
(THE LLOYD BLANKMAN COLLECTION)

Penetrating the wilds of Hamilton County around the middle of the nineteenth century was somewhat like pulling a curtain down on civilization. Aside
from a few small, scattered habitations (such as the hamlet of Piseco), logging
operations, and isolated trappers' cabins, a wide and lonely solitude prevailed.

Packing what equipment and provisions he could carry, Lobb clutched his
long-barreled rifle and set out on the dirt road leading to a new life northward.
Emerging from a covered bridge that spanned the storied, trout-teeming West
Canada Creek a short distance beyond Poland, he continued on the dusty way
that eventually brought him to rough-hewn Wilmurt—the place where, in a
more recent year, it is said the post office was abolished by Congress because
of illicit practices.

From here, he followed the thoroughfare that is now highway No. 8 and came to the logging center of Nobleboro at the forks of the West Canada. Nearby, on the western end of Fort Noble Mountain, close inspection then might have revealed the faint remains of the French fortress built during the war with the Iroquois. Then onward he went past Morehouseville until at length he reached the outpost station of Hoffmeister—the end of the stage route.

After passing the night at this spot, Lobb shouldered his heavy pack and started moving along the pathway that led to his final home—the westerly shore of five-mile-long Piseco Lake. On the crest of Hoffmeister Hill he paused to look back upon the scene that stretched southward toward Utica ... an entrancing view of forested ranges rolling to the clear azure horizon, of the verdant valley of the West Canada through which he had journeyed, and of the clearing below where he stood in which reposed the sleepy settlement of Hoffmeister.

Turning to face whatever lay in store for him ahead, the wayfarer plunged into the thick woods and tramped over the broken trail en route to the lake.

Some time later, while trudging on the side of a bluff at the base of Irondequoit Mountain, he got the first glimpse of his destination through a fringe of trees bordering what the natives at the head of the lake called "Gerundegut Bay." This was a long arm extending from the main body and of the lake into which flowed one of the four principal inlet streams that fed Piseco, in addition to the natural springs welling up from its bottom.

As Floyd Ferris Lobb gazed upon the silvery bay, a thrill of exultation must have swept through him. Here at last was the hallowed refuge he had heard about so often—the place that offered the freedom he sought and the chance to fish, hunt, trap, and loaf to his heart's content.

A mile farther along the shore, the weary hiker came to a high, rocky point crowned by stately pine trees. Just beyond he sat down to rest in a sheltered site overlooking the two-mile wide expanse of Piseco, and this struck him as an ideal spot at which to erect a permanent hut. There was no dwelling of any kind at this end of the lake, so he could remain in seclusion and seldom be disturbed by another human being. This was exactly what he preferred.

Lobb set to work without delay at the task of building a crude, open-face, log lean-to type of shelter, with sides shielded by strips of hemlock bark and rough shingles on the roof—the best he could fashion with his axe and such materials as the forest furnished. Under the projecting roof in front, he put together a rock fireplace, so the heat would be reflected inside. Balsam bough tips, carefully laid over the ground, formed his bed, with blankets spread on top. Later, hides from fur-bearing animals he trapped or shot helped to keep him warm and reasonably comfortable on crisp nights.

At the outset, there were few household conveniences. As the years advanced, however, either by dint of overcoming his customary laziness or of

Old Lobb sits in front of his camp beneath the fancy "Lobbville" Sign.
COURTESY EDWARD BLANKMAN (THE LLOYD BLANKMAN COLLECTION)

accepting donations from sympathetic visitors, certain pieces of furniture were added to the hermitage. Notable among these were a table, an Adirondack-originated style of wooden seat, a few extra cooking utensils, cupboards to safeguard food from prowling animals, and a rude bunk.

Essentially, though, the mode of living to which the recluse adhered was primitive, at least until near the end of his career when old age prompted volunteers to construct a small frame camp, in which the accommodations were slightly more modern and he could enjoy some of the comforts of a civilized person. But even then he objected to anything that seemed "fancy" or out of place in the woods.

On the left side of his original open-face shelter, a sign reading "Lobb's" was fastened to a pole holding up one corner of the roof, and by 1860 this sign was a familiar sight to everyone at the lake—native and vacationist alike—and caused this particular portion of the shoreline to be known simply by his name.

In fact, after 1882, when families from distant cities and villages began building summer cottages between Steep Rock Point and Big Sand Point (along Old Lobb's "realm," and much to his displeasure), and the hermit's new camp was made, someone painted an elaborate sign reading "Lobbville" and nailed it above the veteran fisherman's doorway. In this manner the colony of cottages came to be commonly referred to as "Lobbyville," a designation that persists today among the elder settlers at Piseco Lake.

After the self-exiled woodsman completed his bark shelter by the shore, at the base of Wa-Na-Hoo Mountain, he turned his efforts mainly to fishing and hunting to supply himself with food, and to trapping in wintertime to get furs for selling or trading so that he could obtain other necessities.

In those early days, Piseco contained great schools of good-sized native speckled brook trout, as well as numerous big lake trout and common white fish; and the surrounding forest concealed ample quantities of game animals. It was a sportsman's paradise, and exceedingly cherished by Old Lobb.

As might be expected, under the urgency of survival, the lonely mountaineer became adept at catching fish and stalking deer and bear, and was not surpassed by any other inhabitant of the region. He spent endless hours at his favorite occupations, for it meant he could revel in the scenic beauties of nature at leisure, usually without being disquieted by the sight or sound of anyone else.

In connection with his exploits along this line, the writer, who owns a cottage located only a hundred yards or more from where the hermit's bark hut once stood, had the following to say in a story entitled "Old Lobb Proves Faithful," published in the September 10, 1932 issue of *The American Field*:

"Lobb greatly liked to shoot, and was naturally an accurate marksman. He could shoot truer and better than any other woodsman around the lake who chose to compete with him.

"He became deaf, but his other senses were especially sharp. He was what might be termed one of the pioneers of Piseco, and certainly he knew the woods as did one. It has been said that he would disappear from his shelter for many days on long, rough hunting trips, and return with meat enough to last for weeks.

"Lobb would sit motionless on a log or rock by a tree for hours, just for the pleasure of watching and studying the habits of animals. He had opportunity enough to do this, for time meant nothing to him and game was very abundant—often too obliging about making visits to his camp."

Among the traplines Old Lobb ran was one that skirted the western slope of Big Panther Mountain, swung over close to T Lake Mountain, and, after crossing the South Branch of West Canada Creek, ended at Metcalf Lake. Several ponds and streams in this vicinity afforded a lucrative territory for taking various fur-bearing animals, particularly beaver. Since he often came here, Lobb improvised an overnight shelter inasmuch as the distance was too great to inspect his traps, prospect for more fur, and return to Piseco in one day.

The late Charles J. Seavey of Poland, who was one of Lobb's few personal friends, told me that one day the trapper shouldered his Adirondack-type packbasket and headed for the Metcalf Lake grounds. On the way it snowed lightly, just enough so Lobb could not see very far behind. After staying for the night in his open-face camp at the lake, the hermit started back on the homeward trail, laden with pelts.

To his amazement, he soon discovered by the prints in the snow that his own snowshoe—planted tracks of the day before had been closely stalked by a huge panther. This revelation caused a feeling of uneasiness to seize him, in view of what might have happened. He didn't relish being jumped upon suddenly from an ambush and getting severely clawed.

Gripping his rifle a bit tighter, and making certain his keen-edged hunting knife was handy, Lobb kept an alert lookout while en route to Piseco. He was disappointed, though, in not catching sight of the marauder to slay him and possess a fine trophy.

Like other outdoorsmen of his kind, Old Lobb had an inborn, unerring faculty for steering a true course to some desired objective without the aid of anything except his "mental compass" and visible signs. And he could always return to his tiny sanctuary in the shadow of Wa-Na-Hoo Mountain as easily as a well-trained beagle. He hiked fast and far in a day, for his slight, lean figure was toughened by hardships to the exercise undertaken, and to the roughness of the forest floor.

It was during the long evenings spent sitting before his shanty, while watching the flickering flames of the campfire, that Old Lobb mused idly about his inimitable Piseco Lake and ways of capturing the biggest trout that lurked in the depths.

Thoughts would steal across his mind of the times when bands of Iroquois—members of the Mohawk tribe—came up through the wild Sacandaga River Valley from their winter quarters along the Mohawk River and pitched their te-pees on the northern and southern shores during the summer seasons.

Here the Indians would pass the weeks and months in hunting, paddling around the lake and up a five-mile stretch of Fall Stream that entered Piseco at the head, tending to their rawhide fish nets, smoking trout, and making birch bark canoes, showshoes, buckskin clothing, and other equipment.

The Mohawk families luxuriated in the peace and security of the mountains, and in the abundance of fish and game at hand. Some of the neighboring peaks were christened by the Indians, and a few of their aboriginal names remain as ageless mementos of the first tent-dwellers—having escaped the paleface's disconcerting tendency to "modernize" the outdoor world.

The lake itself, so legend relates, derived its title from an apparently ostracized, venerable chief, called Pezeeko, who lived alone for many years near the head not far from a graveyard filled with his kinsmen. Several of the mounds were still in evidence at the time Old Lobb was ensconced in his chosen stamping grounds.

From his rustic retreat, the hermit could look southward to the entrance of the outlet stream and see the point where the Mohawks had made notched stone sinkers with which to weight their fish nets, jars of pottery, and arrowheads of bird-killing and man-killing-sizes from chunks of flint brought from the Great Lakes region.

This place became known to summer cottage owners of a later era as the "Indians' Blacksmith Shop." Each spring, after the lake's frozen surface cracked and ice cakes were shoved high up on the beach to melt, relics of these industries often were discovered along with the sand and stones . . . and this has occurred even within the past few seasons.

Inevitably, whenever Old Lobb reflected upon events pertaining to Piseco, the subject of fishing claimed much of his consideration. He pursued the pastime as a source of food more than from the standpoint of sport, although the act of fishing itself lent him a great amount of pleasure. His ambition was always to connect with a trout larger than he had ever previously caught, for he knew that Piseco harbored lakers weighing thirty pounds and speckled trout going better than six pounds.

"I want to get hold of a trout that's too long to turn around in the lake," he once said to a fisherman.

To fulfill this aspiration as nearly as possible, he conjured up schemes while resting before the glowing fireplace, then fished every day he was in camp and the weather permitted, to put his plans into operation.

Equipped with a linen handline, lead sinker, and spoon, Lobb would troll for hours at a time. Upon occasion, he would row his light Adirondack skiff four miles to the head and make several swings around Pine Island where a channel, rocky bar, and deep depression generally yielded some fine trout. Then he might continue past the curving northern sand beach over to the eastern shoreline, work along the rock ledges into Higgins Bay, move down shore into Benton's Cove, troll over the rocky reefs towards the outlet, cut westward across the sunken sand bar out from the south shore, and wind up at his own landing.

It was a long trip, in distance and time, but it almost always paid off profitably in handsome trout. And yet, Old Lobb was not quite content with the results. There was that giant roaming in the depths somewhere that still evaded his efforts to hook. What manner of lure would inveigle such a wise fish into committing its final mistake?

Stroking his wiry whiskers, the grizzled angler pondered over this problem with much earnestness. He felt that a different size and shape of trolling spoon from what he was accustomed to using might turn the trick, especially if it could be made to resemble the shiners that prospered in Piseco and were devoured so eagerly by the trout.

Securing some brass, Lobb set about experimenting. He cut, trimmed, bent, and molded the pieces of metal until at length he had fashioned a blade that, when assembled with a swivel and treble hook, produced the right performance and appearance in the water while being trolled at moderate speed. The spoon was comparatively short, narrow but oval, and shallow-curved, having a fast twirling movement that was eye-catching to the fish.

When it was perfected to his satisfaction, Lobb tested his creation thoroughly on the lakers lodged along the rocks and channels at the lower end of Piseco, The results, in number and bulk of trout taken, surpassed the fisherman's expectations. It demonstrated that this particular design could hardly be exceeded in effectiveness—at least in local waters.

Delighted with his handiwork, Old Lobb had a mold cast from which he could easily turn out spooning as needed, in brass, copper, and nickel finishes. The brass was the "killer" in the beginning, but gave way later to copper and nickel.

While trolling with this lure, he tried to keep its success from reaching the ears and eyes of inquisitive anglers, but as already mentioned, the news soon got broadcast. Before many seasons had elapsed, both Lobb and his spoon were known in various quarters of the Northeast.

At Piseco Lake, when someone had caught a fine mess of trout and was questioned as to what lure they had been taken on, the laconic reply invariably came back, "An Old Lobb."

Long after his death, the spoons gained such fame, and the demand for them was so great, that the design was appropriated by the Horrocks-Ibbotson Company of Utica, N.Y., and for years hundreds of "Old Lobbs" were manufactured. In addition, the angling sport they afforded was described in numerous articles of mine published in the national outdoor magazines, for I had frequently used the spoons with splendid success and have several (some being originals) to this day.

Lake trout trolling spoons copied from the originals created by Old Lobb and made in a mold owned by Lobb. Photograph by Mortimer Norton.
COURTESY EDWARD BLANKMAN
(THE LLOYD BLANKMAN COLLECTION)

However, times and conditions change through the decades, and today these lures are seldom tried by fishermen, although they will account for sizable lakers in certain habitats. Indeed, the spoons have practically been forgotten, and in their original and best form are no longer to be found on the market. Imitations, under other names, have appeared, but the genuine style created by the lonely hermit has scarcely been equaled.

Old Lobb of Piseco Lake left a marked imprint upon the angling habits of a multitude of earlier sportsmen by the superb catches of trout he made available through his ingenuity even though the motives may have been selfish. By the advent of his contribution to the fishing scene, this abstruse character assumed a remarkable role in the annals of Hamilton County.

While he never brought up a trout "too long to turn around in the lake," he did come into contact with specimens so big and vigorous they either broke his line or straightened out the hooks. Rumor is that his crowning achievement was hanging up a twenty-nine-pound laker. He boated dozens running from five to twenty or more pounds in weight.

In the story which ran in *The American Field*, it is related that "One day Lobb returned from a trout fishing expedition the happiest and proudest man at the lake."

He had started out in front of his camp with his favorite lure, and had at once snagged into a mighty laker. The fish tugged so strongly it was impossible for him to bring it near the boat. Not once did the trout come to the surface, but headed for the depths away from the boat.

It was one time when Lobb worked to land a fish. The angler was so occupied trying to control the movements of his battler that he paid no attention to the oars; consequently, the fish proved to be his propeller and towed the boat a considerable distance.

For three solid hours he tussled with that laker before it would succumb to the gaff. It was the toughest and longest struggle in Lobb's memory.

Upon pulling the trout into the boat, he was amazed to find that he had caught it on the lip hook only of a gang of hooks, and by the trout's tongue. It is a marvel he even had the good fortune to get a glimpse of the fish. It weighed exactly sixteen pounds.

Old Lobb used to still fish about as much as he trolled. By sounding with a lead sinker, he discovered a large pile of rocks in around sixty feet of water directly in front of his hut, about one quarter of a mile out. He set a buoy or "anchor" on these rocks, with a spruce pole protruding four feet above the surface, and baited this area regularly, with pieces of minnows and other fish. In the evening, especially, or in early morning, he would hitch his boat to the buoy, drop over a couple of handlines baited with pieces of suckers, and soon have several of the finest mottled, pink fleshed, native lake trout imaginable flopping on the floor boards.

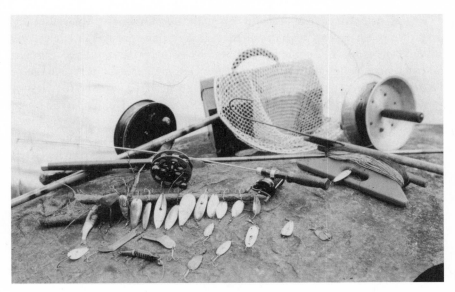

Tools of the trade. Mortimer Norton's fishing outfit. Photo by Lloyd Blankman.
COURTESY EDWARD BLANKMAN (THE LLOYD BLANKMAN COLLECTION)

This location was held to be the most productive by far of any other buoy site in the lake, for years, and the spot is still often referred to by local Waltonians, with a feeling akin to reverence, as "Old Lobb's anchorage."

Being obsessed by a streak of laziness, as well as an insatiable fondness for fishing, this whimsical codger decided that the smart thing would be to accomplish two feats at the same time . . . with no extra labor! His plan was to catch trout and launder his clothing all in one simple process—a neat stunt of which few fishermen seem to take advantage.

On those sporadic occasions when the urge for cleaner apparel stirred him, Old Lobb would tie each piece separately with a cord, attach them behind the rowboat, grab his handline rig, and go trolling. His theory was that after being dragged through the limpid waters of Piseco for an extended period, the clothes should be somewhat purified and contain fewer layers of grime.

Even if his garb wasn't improved in appearance from this method of "wet wash," the doughty angler usually ended up with an enviable string of trout. This, he figured, put him ahead of the game. Why worry about the clothes? After all, wasn't fishing much more important?

Except for prolonged hunting and trapping expeditions in autumn and winter, and reluctant interludes of gathering wood for the fireplace, Lobb passed every hour he could spare pursuing lake and speckled trout with his trolling and still fishing outfits. And the quantity he boated must have been more than most fellows bring to net in their lifetime.

"By the gods!" Old Lobb was heard to exclaim once during his final days. "The fishermen can have all the trout they want. I've had my share."

It was sometime around 1880 when the taciturn hermit was greatly perturbed by an encroachment upon the privacy of his forest haunt. Peace and solitude, unfortunately, could not endure forever in a progressive age, particularly at a lake having the attractive and recreational qualities of Piseco. Dave Palmerton appeared and built a log camp a few hundred yards to the west of Lobb's shelter, right on the slope of Steep Rock Point. He, too, lived alone and took up guiding for fishermen and hunters.

Shortly afterward, a man named Stowe arrived and raised another small log camp with a wooden addition next to Palmerton's; then in 1882 the Potter brothers of Poland, N.Y., erected the first frame cottage on the lake— one and one half stories high, with a front veranda and a storage place for boats underneath. This was situated about two hundred yards to the right of Lobb's hut.

In 1886, the Potter cottage was purchased by Will Tremaine of Rome, N.Y., who, with his wife and five-year-old daughter, Alice, became the initial long-term "permanent" summer settlers on the westerly shore, aside from the eccentric founder of Lobbville. The Tremaines grew to be good friends of the old character, and were among the few people who won his confidence. Even so, he would not converse about his early life, for if it was ever mentioned he would close up like a clam and assume a stubborn, moody attitude.

Young Alice came to know Lobb as well as anyone, save for her father, and used to find pleasure in listening to tales about his hunting and trapping experiences, and watch him troll and still fish in front of her parents' cottage. She was usually on hand to see the catches of trout when he came ashore.

In reminiscing about her early adventures at Piseco and of Old Lobb, Alice, who eventually married Cirrus Cooper, and who spent the summers in "Camp Tremaine" for seventy years until she passed away on June 10, 1956, wrote in part:

> In those days we had to make the trip from Rome with our own horses and wagons, and it took one and one-half days. We would leave home early in the morning with our own team, arriving at Hoffmeister at night, after driving forty five miles over dirt and sand roads that had many hills, which we always walked up to save the horses.
>
> Our democrat wagon was loaded with non-perishable foods e.g. ham, bacon, salt pork, dried beef, and canned goods, and these lasted most of the time in camp. The nearest store was five miles away (Piseco village) and reached only by boat, as there was no road along the side of the lake.
>
> We stayed overnight in the Hoffmeister home with the fine people who ran it—Mrs. Hoffmeister and her four children: Christine, William, Charles, and Gus. The next day one of the boys would take their team, load the buckboard, and take us the seven miles to the foot of Piseco over the rocks, corduroy road, and mud puddles. There were no springs, of any kind, except the 'spring' afforded by the bending boards.

The Hoffmeister Hotel, capacity 15 around 1900. Photograph by Grotus Reising.
COURTESY EDWARD BLANKMAN (THE LLOYD BLANKMAN COLLECTION)

At the foot of the lake, someone had to meet us with a boat and take us to camp, or our own boat was brought in from Hoffmeister and we rowed up in that. Usually a second trip was necessary (after the humans had gone by) to bring the luggage, satchels, and eats.

Our camp consisted of a living room, in a corner of which was a bed, and a bedroom built across one end in which there was a balsam bough bed on the floor, and also a double bed. Then there was a kitchen with wood stove, and a half-story upstairs which needed a ladder to get to and was not used often. The beds had springs of a sort, and for mattresses fresh swale grass was cut and they were stuffed with that.

One of the first things I remember is hearing my father talk about the North Woods, his guides—Dave Palmerton and Gene Abrams—and a great deal about "Old Lobb" and his anchor in the lake.

Never having seen any body of water larger than a small pond, before five years of age, my conception of Piseco Lake was a small pond with a post (Lobb's anchor) in the middle. I think I loved it before I ever saw the lake, and that feeling has grown stronger with the years.

He was always called "Old Lobb" and this is about the only way I ever heard him spoken of in my years of knowing him.

He was a slight little man, and always looked ageless. He was very, very deaf, and the only way to make him understand was to shout in his ear. He had a squealy little voice, and was one of the wonders of my childhood.

If Old Lobb liked you, everything was fine; but if he didn't, he never hesitated to tell you so. Fortunately, my father and he were good friends, and when he would rent his new frame camp to New Yorkers who came up for lake and speckled trout fishing, he always stayed at ours nights.

The trolling spoon he made was used for many years by trout fishermen, and was considered the best of any at the time. My father had the mold and made his own spoons. I always used this myself, and still have some in my possession.

I have seen Lobb sitting at his anchor with his back to the west, when a thunder storm was coming. Being very deaf, he heard no thunder, and sometimes the wind would strike hard, tear him away from the anchor, and send him some distance up the lake before he could get straightened around.

One of his favorite sayings to a young newcomer who he didn't care for was, "You had better go home. Your mother needs you for soap grease."

He once said he would like to be buried on top of Panther Mountain, for that was the highest he would ever get.

At the age of five, the future Mrs. Cooper learned from Old Lobb to row a boat and go trolling and still fishing for lake trout. Occasionally she would also catch brook trout, common whitefish, frostfish or round whitefish which were native to the Adirondacks, and fallfish or "Mohawk" chubs.

Regarding the conditions at Piseco in those days, she says:

Along the shores were gold and silver minnows which were caught, put in a minnow box, and used on gangs of hooks for trout fishing and to bait the anchors, of which my father usually had at least three. I remember going to one of his anchors and catching three nice trout in ten minutes. That was the kind of fishing we had when I was young. I have been in camp when lakers weighing over thirty pounds were caught. Of course, not an everyday occurrence by any means, but many large ones were landed in those days.

At that time, there were brook trout along the shores and, until the pickerel got in, some were taken nearly every day. It was a sad day when the pickerel came into the lake. There was a man living along the Sacandaga River, into which the outlet of Piseco flows, who had a private pond stocked with them. The pond was made by a dam, and one day the dam broke. The escaping pickerel swam up the river into the lake . . . and then good-bye brook trout.

[Giving an added sidelight to life at Piseco, Mrs. Cooper wrote about the logging operations that took place close to Camp Tremaine.]

During my first years here, evergreen trees were being lumbered, and the bark was used for tanning at the Tannery in the village. There was a large log skid, and the lake was full of logs in the spring.

There were immense log skids, and booms which were towed down the lake by huge windlasses on large log rafts. The logs were towed to the outlet and floated down the Sacandaga River.

There was a high dam five miles down the river, and boards were put on that in the spring to raise the level of the lake and river, and three miles below that dam was another smaller one to keep the level high. After the logs were out of the lake, the boards were taken off gradually to let the lake return to its normal level.

It was exciting to watch the men ride the logs, and skip from one to another, while being towed across the lake and to see them separate the logs that had piled up on shore.

When Alice Tremaine was ten years of age, in 1891, Old Lobb began failing rapidly in health. He became seriously ill, and was transported on his last boat ride across Piseco to the home of Mrs. Rudes, where he could be cared for more suitably than in his small and destitute camp.

Evidently he had a premonition that his life was fast nearing its end, for he asked to have his friend, Charles Seavey, come from Poland to talk with him privately. Perhaps because of his fondness for fishing, or for some other reason known only to himself, Old Lobb made a very strange request, as Seavey many years later confided to me. In utter seriousness, Lobb had his friend promise faithfully to bury with him a complete outfit for fishing.

Thus, when this singular hermit was laid to rest in the tiny cemetery in back of Higgins Bay, his final wish was carried out to the letter. Beside him were placed a rod, reel, line, some hooks, and several of the trolling spoons that he had created and that had brought him so many splendid trout.

Old Lobb, then, went to the Happy Fishing Grounds of the Beyond prepared to explore the River Styx with his precious lure. Long may the memory of this inveterate angler live in the minds of sports fishermen who dip their baits into the waters of his beloved Piseco Lake!

"Nice fish!"
Photographed at
Piseco Lake by
Mortimer Norton.
COURTESY EDWARD
BLANKMAN (THE
LLOYD BLANKMAN
COLLECTION)

🌲 GEORGE PARDEE, SHARP SHOOTER
Lloyd Blankman

William Pardee was their father. He was born and raised at least partly in the Pardee clearing about two miles up across Little Black Creek, northwest of the Conklin clearing at Little Deer Lake. At one time this Pardee family lived somewhere near Northwood.

Will Pardee had eight boys, by name John, William, Charlie, Ernest, Alvin, Raymond, Edward and George. There were several girls in this family also. George and John married sisters, daughters of Burt Conklin. George died with pneumonia following the flu in 1920 at the age of forty.

George worked in the woods for Burt and together they guided hunting parties for several years. They hunted regularly for parties from Liberty, Oswego and Oneida. George guided steadily for Fred Ralph of the Oneida Brewing Company of Utica. Fred had a camp at the head of the Seabury Stillwater and probably spent half of his time there from the first of May until the middle of November.

George was a good shot. In fact he was a sharpshooter with either a rifle or a shotgun. Mr. Ralph would tip George $5 for every partridge he shot. Once, George shot a kingfisher with a 30-30 Winchester across the bay near the outlet of Black Creek Lake. The bird was sitting on a large rock. The gun that George used the most was a 30-30 Winchester Carbine.

Randolph Spears and George Pardee (left to right) COURTESY EDWARD BLANKMAN (THE LLOYD BLANKMAN COLLECTION)

MAYNARD PHELPS, THE OLD RANGER

Lloyd Blankman

Maynard Phelps (Ranger) took one of his first camping trips when the Gulf and Western R.R. was being surveyed. The summer of 1907 two of the surveyors took him on a fishing trip somewhere on Tug Hill, then mostly first growth timber.

The men sent him a picture of the trip, but the view was lost when Maynard's house burned in August 1916. A few years later the Ranger saw the picture in a sports magazine advertising shirts.

That [1907 camping trip] was the beginning of Maynard Phelps' life out of doors and as the years rolled around he was to spend much or all of his spare time in the woods and fields. There he began his nature study and he is still at it.

Game Protector Maynard Phelps at 36 years old in 1920.
COURTESY EDWARD BLANKMAN (THE LLOYD BLANKMAN COLLECTION)

Stamping Grounds

The old ranger's stomping ground was from the north side of Moose River to the Oswegatchie River, a vast territory. The Herkimer County line is 18 miles east of the Black River at Glenfield.

Maynard worked on the G.&W. Railroad for two summers, and that put him on the west side of the Black River. He also worked on the 32,000 acres of the Gould Tract plus the 8,000 acres on the Little John Tract in Oswego County.

Then followed an assignment as Game Protector on Tug Hill section, where he traveled the blamed forest North, West and South on snowshoes in over five feet of snow. Then he was sent to the Beaver River and the West Branch of the Oswegatchie River. Any tract he once traveled, he remembered and was learning all the time.

Everything is changed now. By 1916 all the big sugar bushes were being cut off and have now grown up to brush; the same has happened on Tug Hill. Never will be worth a cent again unless the brush is cut and the country is reforested. The ranger feels he has lived a little too long.

The Phelps family covers 171 years, 1797 to 1968, and has seen Lewis County almost from virgin timber to the now nearly worthless country except for a few dairy farms mostly along a three or four mile strip along Black River and a small portion of the town of Croghan on the east side of the river.

Maynard Phelps, a dapper camper at 42 years old in 1926.
COURTESY EDWARD BLANKMAN (THE LLOYD BLANKMAN COLLECTION)

🌲 FRENCH LOUIE

"The man who was most responsible for the promotion of French Louie was. . . Lloyd Blankman of Clinton. He did quite a number of lecture programs featuring French Louie."

> —*Maitland DeSormo, in his address titled*
> *"Hermits, Guides and Other Adirondack Characters."*
> *Author and owner of Adirondack Yesteryears.*
> *At the Sixth Annual St. Lawrence University Conference*
> *on the Adirondack Park, June 11, 1976*

Louis "French Louie" Seymour, at the back door of his West Canada Lake Camp in 1910. Louie was about 78 years old.
PHOTOGRAPH BY FRANCIS HARPER—COURTESY MAITLAND DESORMO

⁂ FRENCH LOUIE
Lloyd Blankman

The combined excerpts from two of Lloyd Blankman's articles, "French Louie" and "French Louie, As I Knew Him," form a nice introduction to the French Louie profiles that follow. Both articles appeared in *The Courier*, Clinton, N.Y.

It is almost impossible to believe that such a man as French Louie ever existed, but there he was, right in the middle of the scene, in Newton Corners two or three times a year for a spree that lasted two or three weeks. The old fellow couldn't even read or write his own name but what a man he was in the woods! Stories of Louie will be handed down for years to come.

Louie was a small, Vulcan-like man, a foot through from breast to back, stoop-shouldered a bit, but knit together with a powerful build. He moved about in his moccasins with the stillness of a cat, full of ambition in camp or on the trapline.

Elgie Spears wrote the following about French Louie in 1952. "Louie believed in freedom. He went alone deep into a wild country with forest and lake far and wide around him. There he could do as he pleased, a man in the wilderness. For the most part he wrested his living from woodlands, sparse clearings and waters, using but little of this and that from civilization. He rolled logs up into camps and used split planks and shakes for floors and roofs. He made his furniture. He made sleds for winter hauling, sap-buckets from birch bark, troughs from saplings and storage tubs from logs."

Mud Lake
It was just a twenty-minute walk by trail from Louie's place on Big West to Mud Lake. Mud Lake is a wild place any time of the year. Here the herons, helldivers, and loons cry at sunset; the deer splash in the lily pads. Sometimes at dusk fifteen or more deer are here at one time.

Brook Trout Lake
From Louie's place it is just a mile and a quarter across Big West and then just a twenty-minute walk to Brook Trout Lake. This lake is a wild place and it is rightly named. In Louie's day the place was so full of trout, when you caught one, it tasted fishy. Half way to Brook Trout you step over a small stream and your guide tells you, "this is the North Indian River."

Somebody Special
There was something about Louie that everybody had to like. He always had a twinkle in his eye. He was as hard as Laurentian Granite, as tough as Adirondack spruce. Out and around almost anybody is more or less like everybody else, but this fellow was different and worth writing a book about. Here is the story, therefore, of Louis Seymour of West Canada Lakes, better known as "French Louie."

❧ FRENCH LOUIE'S LIFE IN THE WEST CANADA "CRICK" COUNTRY

William J. O'Hern

French Louie's home territory was the West Canada Lakes. This one-of-a-kind trapper-hermit-woodsman could boast that he had lived over 40 years in the deep woods, northwest of Speculator, N.Y., as few others had. Eldridge Spears described Louie's existence as "a free life of private initiative in 'West Crick Country.'"

Louie wasn't a scribing man, not even to the extent of reading or writing his name. He was quite indifferent about how his name was spelled, which accounts for a variety of spellings. Spears said "the old man told me his name was Louis Seymour, but people called him French Louie. That was all right with him. Some spell it Louis, because he was a French-Canadian. Some spell it Loui. Others have it Lewey, because that is English and the way it sounds. In his quiet, gentle manner he said 'such things were for other people to bother with.'"

As a young man Louie had come down from Canada, where he had been traveling with a circus. He never told in any detail why he left Canada, but it is known that when he was a small boy, his biological mother died and his "tartar-like stepmother" ill-treated him. In his late teens he joined a traveling circus, eventually leaving it, preferring to hoof it to the center of the Adirondacks, where, deep within the forest, deeper than the earlier settlers decades before had gone, he hooked up with an old-timer who lived at Big West, the highest lake in that part of the mountains. No one followed him as other pioneers had been followed. And, unlike Noah John Rondeau, hermit of Cold River Flow, who had to give up living in the woods, Louie stuck it out to the end.

Louie believed in freedom. Elbow room amid the trees was what he sought. Living in a wild country surrounded with forest and lakes, he could do as he pleased. He came and went as he liked.

For the most part he squeezed his living from woodlands, poor clearings and waters, using but little of this and that from civilization. There was plenty of time to figure things out for himself and he had all the time in the world to carry out his projects. He rolled logs up into camps and used split planks and shakes for floors and roofs. He made his furniture. He made sleds for winter hauling, sap-buckets from birch bark, troughs from saplings and storage tubs from logs.

In 1906 Eldridge and John Spears, natives of Northwood, a little village now wiped out by Hinckley Reservoir, decided to explore the West Canada Lake country. Eldridge recalls the brothers' first meeting with Louie: "The first day we hiked to Black Creek Lake, where we stayed overnight with Bert Conkling and his brother, 'Rock,' of Wilmurt." The following day, "on the trail between Brook Trout Lake and Big West we came upon a rather short man, a bit stooped, grizzled and gray . . . and with arms and hands that seemed to reach gorilla-like almost to his knees. Rather old, yet plainly a man of great strength. Yes, it was French Louie."

Even at the age of 77, standing in moccasins, Louie's appearance was still that of a powerful man. Except for a little trembling of the hands, he could spring down with the grip of his fist a trap spring that would hold a bear.

"Louie was agreeable to our spending some time with him," Eldridge Spears remembered, "so we moved in."

One distinguishing thing about French Louie's camp was that it was a two-story log cabin. There was a combined living room and dining room where big-wig "city sports" hung out when they came up to hunt or to fish on the 5,000 acres owned by the Union Bag and Paper company they worked for.

In December 1951, Elijah W. Conklin, then in his 90th year, wrote this personal account of Louie's homestead learned a half century earlier on trips he made to Big West with his son George.

"The cabin was 12 by 12 feet and had a small lean-to made of spruce logs. It was built up against a huge rock that projected into the camp. The rock, heated by the stove, provided extra warmth in cold weather and coolness in the summer time. The roof was made of spruce shakes 2 feet long and 10 inches wide. The floor was made of split spruce, the logs planed smooth.

"The ceiling in the camp was seven feet high. We saw a large six-griddle stove in fine condition in the camp. His bed was the strangest: it was a 10-foot guide boat, square at both ends and hung on chains at each corner from the roof. It was filled with hen, partridge and duck feathers. At the head of the bed, a square hole was cut with a wooden plug in it. He shot deer from there at a deer lick outside—a stump with salt in it about a hundred feet distant. In the lean-to was a huge pile of empty jugs and bottles." It is assumed the cast-off bottles were emptied by other than Louie. He was known as a hard drinker *only* on his infrequent trips to a town or city.

"We saw some trousers hanging on the wall. You could not tell the original cloth because of the patches."

Over a period of years, Louie let in sunlight when he enlarged his clearing to make room for additions to his homestead. He also slashed off more space for a garden and a potato patch.

"Beyond the cabin," Conklin remembered, "was a garden 100 by 50 feet. The lower part had a three-foot retaining wall to make it level. He filled this with black muck from a swamp nearby and here he grew potatoes."

Louie even planted fruit trees. Eldridge tells: "Like Apple Seed Johnny, he planted an apple seed at the edge of the patch just beyond the back door of his cabin and the seed grew into a small tree. Then one season when Louie was wintering over in Moose River country, deer came along and browsed all the small twigs off, leaving only a stub of a tree, so Louie built a pole fence around the tree to keep the deer away."

"Below the garden," Conklin continues, "on a bench or lower level was his maple sugar house, 24 by 16 feet, with open sides. There was a sugar sap pan, 6 by 6 feet and a trough sap line about 400 feet long, to the center of a grove of maple trees. His sap buckets were made of birch bark, about a hundred of them in a little shelter. The wooden pins were pulled out and they were piled in a flat. Made into buckets, the four sides were turned up and pinned at each corner with the wooden pins. The sap ran into a 50-gallon barrel in the sap house, which was the most perfect carpenter work I ever saw, made with only an axe, a smooth plane and a slick."

Eldridge held, "Louie not only had the swellest of any trapper's camp in the whole Adirondack region, he had more camps as well." Louie recorded with pinpoint accuracy the locations of his 15 trapline camps on maps drawn on birch bark.

"Although Louie couldn't write or spell," Eldridge recalled when asked about the maps he had seen, he said the little Frenchman displayed several maps "which he said he had worked on for many years. Compared with a government topographic map, they were . . . remarkably accurate as far as the relative position of lakes and streams was concerned. But all the lakes were of the same size, too large, and all were round."

Louie said his "camps were here and there from Moose River to Lake Pleasant," according to Eldridge. "He said he had supplies at all of them and that he lived at first one or another, according to his requirements or desires. One of the requirements, he said, was to visit them to see that they were still there in proper shape. He said his best camp was really at Pillsbury Lake and that his best crop of potatoes was at the camp on a branch of Otter Brook."

Along with the camps, Louie owned 35 boats stashed at various bodies of water.

Conklin describes Louie's territory: "His trapline was about 50 miles long starting up Otter Brook. He had overnight camps every 10 miles. They were bark shelters 7 feet by 3 feet with a sheet iron stove, frying pan and tin pail in each one. His route was up the Otter, around Kitty Cobble Mountain, to Twin Ponds, over to West Canada Lake to Brook Trout Lake, down Wolf Creek to Indian River, Indian Lake, Squaw Lake, Falls Pond, down Falls Pond outlet. He had a halfway camp on Samson Pond. Also, there was a guideboat on each lake."

The Adirondack trapper of the nineteenth century encountered many hardships, not a few of which involved surviving in all kinds of weather. He left the woods twice a year. In the spring he brought out of the wilds his winter's catch of fur and hides. In the late fall he returned to town with venison, trout, maple sugar, and spruce gum. French Louie transported his forest products by a hand-pulled sled and on snowshoes. Speculator (known then as Newton Corners) was his usual destination for barter. There he exchanged his goods for supplies of corn meal and flour, tea, salt, sugar, beans and salt pork. After paying his bills and before returning with summer supplies in time to make his maple sugar, Louie would go on a drinking bat. This act of release from living back in the mountains where he would touch neither liquor nor tobacco was a splurge from the serious day-to-day business of survival.

Louie loved children and made a habit of speaking to all who flocked around him. They looked forward to the old man's stories and to pennies or candy he freely handed out.

Louie did most of his carrying of heavy supplies in the winter and spring before ice-out, using a homemade jumper—a sled. He told Spears in 1909, "I'm going to sled this stove over to Moose River next winter," pointing to a good-sized kitchen stove in his camp. "It is light. It don't weigh more than 200 pounds. I'm going to bring up a big one (wood-fueled kitchen range) from Speculator."

Louie was tough as nails. He told Eldridge and John Spears he wasn't much on carrying pack baskets when he guided for sports "as I am now 74," but in the same breath he allowed he was carrying "50 pounds of Moose River maple sugar" on his back when the brothers met up with him on the Brook Trout trail.

"Louie liked to talk," Eldridge told Harvey Dunham during one of the biographer's many interviews with Spears. But Louie "didn't kill deer only when someone was at camp who could eat it. With all his teeth in his upper jaw gone, he said he couldn't get away with much deer meat himself."

For several months during 1895, local rumors and reports in the magazine *Forest and Stream* "centered around the depredations of a couple of desperate characters who have been slaughtering deer" in the remote headwaters of West Canada Lakes. The magazine article went on to state, "These parties, one of whom is a Frenchman known as 'French Louis' and the other . . . a thoroughly bad egg . . . an Indian renegade (Johnny Leaf) from the St. Regis reservation, have been in the habit of killing large numbers of deer a day for several months past."

"Game protector Isaac Kenwell and Special Officer Lobdell went in after the pair." Under the pretext of wanting to purchase deer hides and furs, the officers attempted to get enough information to "convict the Canadian, but made only a partial success of it . Louis' case is one of 'I killed the dog but you must prove it,' and while there is little doubt of his having killed large numbers of deer illegally, the officers thought best to secure the Indian as the greater offender of the two and the stronger case for conviction. Leaf accompanied the officers back to his own camp, for the purpose of selling them his furs, and was there put under arrest, after having shown Messrs. K. and L. a carcass of fresh venison that had not been discovered by them during their first visit. He also brought to light the heads of three bucks that had been killed earlier than the latter part of December last. Louis, who seems to have mistrusted that all was not quite right, followed the party back to Leaf's Seabury country camp, and appeared very much frightened when he found the Indian a prisoner. He denied having killed any game out of season, or otherwise illegally, but it is safe to say that there will be sufficient evidence forthcoming in the near future to convict him on several counts unless he shall in the meantime leave the country."

To natives, it was a well-known fact that Louie and Johnny had been selling considerable quantities of deer skins to businesses in Fulton and Hamilton counties as well as unloading the venison at nearby lumber camps. However, it was difficult to convict on any evidence other than finding fresh skins, for the old excuse, "These skins were taken from deer killed by several hunting parties whom we guided during the deer season," would always be given for having any large number of skins on hand.

Eldridge said, "Louie once had a dog which he said he fed in the winter time by shooting cross-bills and 'summer canaries'—goldfinches. He sprinkled salt along a board, which cross-bills like. When a lot of them got on the board, Louie sighted a shotgun the length of it and mowed 'em down."

The previous winter Louie said he caught four bears, several fisher and some other furs. He sold about 30 deer skins a year "left at his camps by parties" and got $1.25 each. He got $15 to $20 for a bear skin.

Eldridge continued, "Louie had an eagle's wing in his kitchen which he used to sweep the crumbs from his board table. He had caught the eagle three years previously in a bear trap.

"Louie got a kick out of two men who had come up in the middle of winter to chase around after little birds the size of sparrows. One worked for the government and both made their living learning things about birds. Louie thought it was the funniest thing in the world.

"'They wanted me to take them around so they wouldn't get lost,' said Louie. I took them all over. They found owls nesting. After a while they found one of them small birds on her nest. They were happy. Ha, ha, ha.' Only Louie said it with a grin."

Elijah Conklin's written recollections record that Louie ". . . was the one who killed the last of the timber wolves in the Adirondacks. He killed five on Samson Lake. They killed his dog and he put arsenic in a doe's carcass and killed all five."

When Louie went hunting he took his dog, Old Cape, with him. Old Cape was trained to sit in a guide boat and at his master's command jump out of the boat, swim to shore, race up a mountainside, and drive the deer down to the lake where Louie could shoot them.

A March 1890 letter to the editor of *Forest and Stream* titled "Wolves in the Adirondacks," tells of deer-hounding parties in the West Canada Lakes that had lost dogs and of Louie's run-ins with a pack of wolves. Louie had frequently met the pack and had numerous stories to tell of their destruction of chickens, sheep, other game and the dogs of hounding parties they had killed—including some of his dogs. Louie cared a lot about his dogs. At first he thought many followed deer into territory far from camp, and then were taken in by guides finding the wayward animals. In 1888 and 1889, during which he lost ten dogs, he found solid evidence that they had been killed by wolves.

M. S. Northrup lived in Johnstown, New York. Each spring he fished in Louie's territory. The following report he attributes to Louie telling him "before the campfire."

Three years ago this winter, Louie, returning alone on snowshoes from his long line of traps—extending from Trout Lake outlet, around by Moose River Indian Clearing to Silver Run, thence back by the Cobbie's Stream to East Lake—reached the lake just at dusk, and rounding the point on a run so as to reach his shanty by dark, came suddenly on a large buck just run down by the wolves. They had cut his throat and drunk his blood when Louie's yelling scared them away. He was only armed with a club and bowie knife, and having no meat at his shanty he succeeded in keeping them off till he cut out a hindquarter, then he made for his shanty, got his gun and was gone but an hour. When he got back to the deer nothing but well-picked bones were left. Now, many will say Louie and his dog(s) would have eaten as many deer during the winter as the wolves, but that is nonsense. I have no doubt Louie has venison most of the time during the winter, but one deer would last him two weeks and a pack of wolves will average one or more per day. And I think our legislative committee to codify the game laws should put a sufficient bounty on wolves to exterminate them inside of one year.

[Northrup continues with evidence that a pack of wolves ranged in the vicinity of Big West.]

Now for my proof that wolves kill the dogs. A year ago last fall (better not name the exact date as probably it was after time for hounding) a guides' party was made up at Lake Pleasant to hunt at Big West, to lay in their winter supply of meat. Among them was Benage Paige, an old guide known to every one that ever was at Lake Pleasant. He had old Music, his famous deerhound, with him. Between Big West and South Lake is South Mountain. Landing at the old "Chi Phi Camp," Benage, in the swale back of camp, started Music on a fresh track. Snow was fresh and some three inches deep. The track swung right up the mountain through the open hardwood timber, which lay for nearly half a mile like a park, giving full view of the dog, which worked so fast, giving voice every few jumps, that Benage stood in admiration watching him. As he disappeared in a cleft of the mountain Benage started for his boat to await a chance of deer taking a turn to the lake, but stopped at hearing Music change his bay to a howl of pain. The day was as still as some fall days we can remember when sound can be heard miles away. Benage heard snarling and sharp barks, and then saw old Music with two wolves at his flanks come into view. Benage instantly yelled at the top of his voice and fired his gun, which scared the wolves away. The old dog came reeling down the mountain, dyeing the snow with his blood every jump. His strength gave out before he reached his master, who was hastening to him. Benage found him bitten through the back of his neck, but the cruel wound that was death to him was just back of the fore shoulder, where a chunk of meat as large as one's hand was torn out, laying the lungs bare. He lived but an hour. The party lost three dogs on the trip, and since that hunt no guide about those lakes has any doubt of the cause of the death of Louie's dogs.

One of the highlights in Louie's life was ". . . when he was entertained by Utica society at the Fort Schuyler Club on Genesee. No Less!" Eldridge Spears rapped out. Prominent among a party of men who took a trip to the West Canada Lakes "to see the country" in 1900 were Edward Munson, John W. Calder, Fred Ralph, and Frank E. Howell, head of Utica's Western Union.

They saw French Louie and they liked the soft-spoken, gentle man of the woods. Among other things he told them bear stories.

"Come down to Utica some time and bring some bear skin," said Ralph. "We'll buy them."

Louie said he would, and he did. He dropped in on Ralph at his place of business. He had a big roll of bear skins. They were prime, sleek and black. Ralph took him in tow, got hold of some friends and they gave French Louie a dinner at the Fort Schuyler Club.

There were more dishes and knives and forks and such for one man to eat with than Louie had ever seen or heard of and two or three fellers dressed in black were scurrying around to bring the grub and cart dishes away that could have just as well been used for new stuff brought in to eat. Louie answered yes and no. It was a queer way folks eat in cities.

After a long time, so it seemed, Louie was released with the cash for his bear skins. The relief was great, although he 'allowed' the boys meant all right. They certainly talked friendly and were nice to him. But it was great to get out. The open air was welcome. He headed for North Utica.

When Louie had come through North Utica he had seen some places that looked like Adirondack country. The road itself was a regular tote road in appearance, deep ruts in the mud, like the road over the hill from Speculator. There was a hotel or two that looked fitting. Louie stopped.

Some time after, a voice from the police station over the phone to Fred Ralph said: "We've got a feller down here who wants your help. He hit a man over the head with a shovel. He says his name is French Louie."

Ralph went to the rescue and learned that Louie had had a few drinks, got into a fight and thought he had killed the man. He had merely cut his head open. So he was freed. He headed right up Prospect, Hinckley and Wilmurt way. What a relief to be free and all alone in the center of the Adirondack Mountains!

French Louie didn't leave any great legacy for the benefit of mankind when he died, but still his life as one of the Adirondacks' last historical characters was significant.

If you are an adventurous person and are ever tempted to take a backpack trip into Louie's place, through a vast, wild country, do it. It is easier to walk the 16 miles into the wilderness—which is not as wild as it used to be. You will not find trout "packed to the bottom like sardines" as Eldrige Spears observed, but all who explore the "West Crick Country" will appreciate the efforts of many to protect the wilds for future generations of users.

In 1938, Harvey L. Dunham told a reporter for the Utica *Observer-Dispatch* newspaper that he had collected "some 20,000 words about Louie from various persons who knew, saw or heard of him." Dunham also said, "Some day I will lay before the public the results of my research into the life of the character of the West Canada Lakes." And so he did.

FRENCH LOUIE, AN AMERICAN CHARACTER
Harvey L. Dunham

As you speed over the more or less smooth highways through the Adirondack forest, you pass many small clearings, some near the road, some inhabited, some just a patch of lighter green on a distant slope. Each has its story. Follow up the West Canada Creek—"creek" by name, but larger than many rivers—which flows into the Mohawk River at Herkimer. You go first by car, through farm lands and into the beginning of the woods; then by tote road and trail, northward along a rocky stream, past wild, black, still waters, and, when the trails peter out, through tangled alders and leg-breaking windfalls.

If you go far enough up the old "West Crick" to its headwaters, you will come to the West Canada Lakes. On North Lake of these West Canadas is a clearing which has been a stopping place of hunters, trappers, and woodsmen for more than a hundred years. There, in the 1850s, were signs of rotting logs of an old cabin. So said the trappers Marinus Lawrence and Burr Sturges of Newton Corners, now Speculator. Soon after that date, they built a slab shanty against a large rock on the south side of the clearing.

In the 1870s, Louis Seymour, a French Canadian, better known as "French Louie," took over the slab shanty as his own and about ten years later built a new cabin that could accommodate his "guests," who were many. He lived at this clearing until he died in 1915.

Louis Seymour was born in Canada about 1830. As a boy, he ran away from home and came across to the United States where he worked with circuses and drove mules on the long Erie Canal towpath. It was not until the fall of 1868 that he climbed down from the big-wheeled buckboard stage from North Creek at the small Adirondack town of Indian Lake. He was stockily built, not tall but deep-chested, with broad shoulders, very long arms, and strong hands. He had a large head with light brown curly hair, and sparkling, blue-black eyes, narrow and smiling.

French Louie and Trume Haskell standing in front of Louie's camp at Big West. Lloyd wrote on the back of the picture: "Taken about 1900. Given to me by Trume Haskell. One of my best and rarest pictures."
COURTESY EDWARD BLANKMAN (THE LLOYD BLANKMAN COLLECTION)

A man of Louie's type blended with the surroundings, yet one native of Indian Lake Village looked curiously at this new Frenchman. Tall and wiry, Ike Kenwell, just past twenty, and about fifteen years Louie's junior, went out of his way to speak to him.

"Howdy," meeting Louie's squinting, friendly eyes.

"Work? She's plaintee?" Louie asked.

"Griffin's hirin' men. You want a job?"

"On de lumberwoods. Dees Griffin lumbercamp? W'ere she be?"

And so Louis Seymour came to the North Woods. He drifted from lumber jobs to trapping and had a cabin on Lewey Lake. His trapping took him to the Cedar Lakes and to Pillsbury Lake. From Pillsbury he went out to Newton Corners instead of to Indian Lake Village.

One season, he trapped with Burr Sturges in the West Canada section, and they made their headquarters at Burr's slab shanty in the clearing. The next season, in the '70s, Louie made the slab shanty and the clearing his home, and settled down to stay. He patched the roof, plugged the holes, and tightened the shack against the cold winters that were sure to come. In the spring he packed in a few chickens, built a coop and a small yard at one side of the shanty, and brought in some real windowlights to take the place of the oiled paper and cloth.

A few miles to the east, on the Cedar River, where a lumber company was operating, the boss of the lumber camp had been told by the superintendent, Isaac Kenwell, that whenever French Louie showed up, he was to be given anything he wanted, such as pork, flour, and beans. "If Louie comes in, treat him right."

During the cold winter months, Louie went often to the camp and was well taken care of. Late in the winter, those at the lumber camp saw him coming in pulling a sled with a couple of baskets on it. He went to the cookhouse door and unloaded nearly a bushel of eggs.

"My gosh," the boss cook said. "How much? How much do I owe you for the eggs, Louie?"

Louie answered: "No monee for flour. No monee for pork. No monee for bean"; and then added, with the same old twinkle in his eye, "no monee for egg."

But there was one thing that Louie did want. There was a good stove out in the settlements that he could buy, and he asked the boss if, sometime, when he had a tote team coming in, he would fetch in the stove.

"Sure thing," the boss said. The three-hundred-pound stove was bought, toted in, and Louie sledded it through the woods over a March crust to his camp at West Canada. This was the first real cookstove that anyone had ever had in there.

During the fall of 1886, Louie built a new camp on the clearing, with plenty of room for his "guest." In his part, the kitchen, where he lived, ate, and slept, his bunk was like a couple of sawbucks with a canvas between and then a blanket over some boughs or hay. He always slept with his clothes on, removing only his shoes. The stove was in the middle of the room, within easy reach of the bunk. The pancake griddle, the little tea pail, and the can of bear lard were on the back of the stove, handy. Everything was right there— the kindling, too—so that in the morning Louie could swing around, sit on his bunk, and start his fire.

He would get his little tea pail going, cut up some potatoes into the bear lard in the frying pan, and with a few pancakes and bear pork, he had enough for a satisfying breakfast. He ate with his fingers from the frying pan on the hearth-shelf of the stove, or with his tin plate on his lap. He could almost get his meal and eat it without moving off his bunk.

Louie had a garden that produced wonderful vegetables. Watching over it he had his own little army of "potato bug hunters," as he called his snakes. He would rap on a board, and they would come out to clean up all the fish entrails which he tossed to them. They kept his meat block clean. He found the snakes in his wanderings and brought them back in his pack, in his pockets, or inside his shirt. He made special trips to the sunny, grassy plains on the Moose River after the largest ones. Louie liked snakes, and gave them full credit for the mammoth potatoes that he raised.

The snakes did not deserve all the credit. Trout or the big suckers from the Mud Lake inlets in the spring made excellent fertilizer, and Louie did use fish. One can believe or not that he "planted half a ten-pound lake trout in each po- tato hill in his garden." If a deer was not too far away from camp when killed, Louie would pull the entrails in and put them into a pit to rot before they went onto his garden. Between the snakes and the fertilizer, the garden did well.

At the beginning of one hunting season, Trume Haskell, a young lad from Nobleboro, dropped his pack at Louie's back door. Louie was not at home, and Trume sat down to rest. In front of him, on a pile of deer bones, Trume saw a large snake, and on the packed dirt another, and still more. At least a half-dozen snakes were within a few feet of him. He picked up a strong stick.

"Look at 'em. Right at the door of the camp," Trume thought, as he went after them.

About an hour later, Louie came in, and Trume was quick to tell him what he had done.

"I killed four of them," he said. "Two got away."

Ye wolves and catamounts! Louie was the maddest Frenchman that Trume had ever seen.

"Boy, he'll never forgive me," ran through his mind. "That's the last of me and Louie."

Before they went to bed that night, Louie had stopped grunting to himself and said to Trume: "Wan ting nevaire do. Nevaire kill no more snake."

Louie was one who always minded his own business, and he wanted others to mind theirs. After he had been staying alone and had not seen anyone for a long time, he was always glad to see someone come in. At such a time, apparently thankful for companionship, he would talk freely at first, and then, suddenly, his social feelings satisfied, his uneasiness showed plainly that he wanted to be left alone. "Get out of my sight and leave me alone," his eyes seemed to say. One could then take a walk, and, upon returning, if one paid no attention to Louie, one got along with him all right.

When Louie disliked anyone, he wouldn't give him even a piece of string; he would not look at such a person, and money did not mean a thing in gaining his respect and friendship. He did not like those young sports who were always asking questions.

Louie learned a great deal of the lay of the West Canada country from a map that Marinus Lawrence of Newton Corners drew for him. It was drawn on brown paper pasted onto a piece of oil cloth and showed the main mountains and streams. With this map as a guide, Louie made maps of his own. These maps were drawn on paper birch in four sections, and took in a larger territory. They covered the country from Mud Lake to the forks of the Moose, and from the Cedars to the Indian River. They were about eighteen inches square, showing Louie's trails and camps, and many private marks such as traplines and sets; where he had seen plenty of deer and bear, or signs of marten, otter, or fisher. Distances were indicated by the time it took to travel between points. Few people ever saw these maps, but one who did said that the lakes were all drawn round and of equal size. Louie kept the maps in a large tin can with a tight cover.

Every fall Louie caught from two to five bears in his heavy bear traps. He cut up the meat and put it down in brine, the same as pork. The hides brought him eight or ten dollars each. He liked bear meat.

Louie was never lazy. He made sleds of split saplings, and with a harness that he got into, he pulled loads in through the snow from the outside. Often he pulled as much as two hundred pounds when leaving Newton Corners.

He also used a sled to pull venison into camp. Sometimes he pulled in the meat on a deer hide slung in a curved bough. The hide was laced between the ends of the bough so that, when pulled by the curved part, the bag, hair side out, was half dragging on the snow between the poles. It pulled easily with the two ends of the bough partly supporting the load and extending behind as runners. Wolf Creek Stillwater on the Indian River was a favorite hunting ground, and much of Louie's venison was pulled in from there in this way.

At least twice a year Louie went out to the Corners, where for two or three weeks, whooping it up until his money was gone, he amused and taxed the patience of the town. To Louie the furs meant liquor and a good time. He always paid all of his old bills as soon as he came to town, but there were plenty of furs and money left, and the first hotel man who sold him a few drinks took practically everything away from him. When Louie left to go back to the woods, some one of these men would buy a new team or build an addition to his business place.

Louie would not always come out of the woods when those on the outside thought he was due. They looked forward to his coming; they figured on it. There was rivalry for his trade, if it could be called "trade." At times, this was enough to start someone into the woods in search of Louie, to come out with him, and to steer him to the "right" place. Sometimes, he would turn all his money over to the bartender, who, pretending to mark the figures down in a book, told Louie when it was all gone.

Wilderness noises came from upstairs windows, from the barroom, or from the porch as Louie stuck out his head and emitted an awful, panther-like screech, or sent the howl of the wolf through the little town, or imitated the cry of an owl, loon, haw, or wildcat.

The children in school studying their three R's knew when Louie was in town. Some boy with sharp, sensitive ears would be the first to whisper loudly, "Louie!" and the children could hardly wait for school to be let out. Then they would rush to the village store and gather around him at the glass candy case as he spent his money; a dollar and a half or two dollars for candy all at one time. Nothing was too good for the kids: sugar hearts, and sticks with red and white spiral bands for the girls, and "likrish" drops for the boys.

On one of his return trips, Louie had some salt pork in his pack. He was quite unsteady, when, just before climbing Blue Ridge, he settled down on some matted grass in the sun. It was a good spot to rest. The spring air was quiet and warm, and Louie lay for a long time. When he reached around to adjust the shoulder straps, he thought he had lost his pack. The hedgehogs had eaten all of his salt pork, and even a good part of his basket! They had taken them right off his back.

Lloyd Blankman visited the site of Louie's West Canada Lake camp with a copy of Harvey Dunham's book Adirondack French Louie. *The caption beneath Dunham's picture of the fireplace reads: "The fireplace around which the room was never built." Thanks to Dunham's lobbying, the fireplace was preserved as a monument to Louie.*
COURTESY EDWARD BLANKMAN (THE LLOYD BLANKMAN COLLECTION)

Those going in to Louie's from Newton Corners had someone drive them to Perkins' Clearing, a few miles north on the Indian Lake Road. There they made a deal with Si Perkins to haul their duffel in on a wood-shod sled drawn by a span of mules. From Si Perkins' place they went by buckboard into the woods on the old Military Road as far as Sled Harbor, which was a grassy, open place in the trees at the beginning of rough traveling. Here they changed from buckboard to sled. The sleds were made of tough saplings strong enough to withstand the slamming and banging over the rocks and holes on the sled road that ended at Louie's clearing. Great quantities of fish and venison were carried out on these sleds.

Sometimes, when they would pick Louie up at Newton Corners on their way in, he would be in no condition to ride a buckboard. They would then tie him with ropes to the seat. He would not fall out and would be more secure than any of the other travelers when they went through holes and over the "bumpitty" corduroy.

What these guests of Louie's appreciated most was the rare privilege of simply being with him. He would often say, and mean it, "You owe me noting. Ah have good tam. Same lak you."

On Sunday afternoon, February 28, 1915, the town of Speculator was told that French Louie was dead. He had been out of the woods on one of his sprees and had died at the Brooks Hotel. The Corners felt it. Louie had belonged to them. "Old Louie's dead," they told one another in the stables, in the kitchens, on the roads.

Ernest Brooks, who had always been good to Louie, said he would pay for the burial. "Give him a decent funeral."

The school was closed on the day that the service was held in the little Methodist church, and the children sat in the two front rows of pews. Before the casket was closed, they filed slowly past it, and each laid a little spray of fragrant balsam on Louie's body. In the procession to the cemetery, about a third of a mile away, the children held branches of balsam in front of themselves as they walked. Louie was buried in the back corner of the town cemetery. He had gone over the last portage, taken the long, long trail in peaceful sleep.

JOHNNY MCCULLEN
Lloyd Blankman

Most of the men who worked in the woods had special talents. It was always open to argument as to which was the best man in his line of work. After years of practice and experience the men acquired knowledge and attainments they didn't even know they had.

Johnny McCullen always drove horses and everybody knew he was good. There wasn't ever much question about that.

Lumbering in the North Woods was at its height during the last century. There were no trucks or tractors then. Horses furnished the power.

They toted the supplies into the lumber camps in the deep woods on lumber wagons and bobsleds. They trailed logs to the skidways and hauled loaded logs to the stillwaters to await the spring drives down to the sawmills.

The mortality rate for the horses was high. Sometimes fewer than half of them survived when the drive started in the spring. All kinds of accidents befell them. There were sickness, trees falling, unseen holes and cliffs, icy roads, many occasions for trouble.

Johnny McCullen was a little fellow but strong and wiry, always good-natured, a likeable fellow, and ticklish. If one should point a finger at his ribs, feint a thrust and make a hissing noise, he invariably would jump and holler even if the finger didn't come nearer than two feet of him.

From boyhood Johnny always liked horses. He knew how to handle them. It was natural for him. He kept them fat and shining. He took good care of them in the stable, on the road, and in the woods.

He knew all a driver should know from skidding to hauling to toting. He didn't have to hang on to the load. He rolled with the wagon and never fell off.

One time, after Johnny had a drink or two under his belt, he took his little red dog, Snippy, into the dining room of a hotel, ordered and paid for a regular dinner for the dog, set him in a chair at the table with a napkin around his neck, and proceeded to show the people what a well-mannered little dog he was. Snip wouldn't eat until the others did and then nothing except what was put on this plate.

Johnny always drove horses, never did anything else in the woods. Sometimes he toted supplies or loaded logs or trailed to the skidways. He was always gentle with a team, always talking to his horses. He was a good driver, a hard drinker between trips but never on the road. He hardly ever tightened a line, yet he protected his horses from danger.

Johnny McCullen never married, never had any family or home. He lived mostly with private families, in lumber camps, and at hotels. He spent many years working for "Sol" Carnahan, one of the biggest jobbers on West Canada Creek.

At the height of his career as a teamster in 1900 he was about 50 years old. He drove teams from 1897 to 1902 for Burt Conklin, a contract lumberman except during the trapping season, when Burt was a dyed-in-the-fur trapper.

Very little is known of the latter years of Johnny McCullen's life. It is known, however, that he died in Jim Murphy's hotel in Prospect in 1935.

Johnny McCullen holding the reins. Photograph taken by Grotus Reising, 1899.
COURTESY EDWARD BLANKMAN (THE LLOYD BLANKMAN COLLECTION)

ALVAH DUNNING, HERMIT
Lloyd Blankman

The following account of the Adirondacks' most primitive man appeared in the
Utica Saturday Globe about 1897.

Alvah Dunning is a type of a fast-vanishing class of men. They may only
be found in a new country and disappear with the advance of civilization.
Cooper immortalized them in his character of Natty Bumppo, the hero of the
Leather-Stocking Tales. They are the men of the woods, the hunters and
trappers, simple, honest, hardy folk who live close to nature and who find
contentment in the solitudes of the forest, with the bear, the deer and the
panther for companions. You can find a few of them yet in the backwoods of
Maine, the Adirondacks and the Rocky Mountain wilderness, but before
another generation they will have passed away, as has the moose and the
buffalo.

Most Famous

Alvah Dunning is the most famous of Adirondack guides and hunters.
Famous men have followed him through the forests and streams of the great
New York wilderness and have slept in his cabin on Raquette Lake. The
snows of 83 winters have fallen upon him, but he is still hardy as the oak.
Dunning was born in the woods of Hamilton County, where his father was a
trapper. His home has always been among the trees. For years he lived on
Long Lake, but more than half a century ago he built a camp on an island in
beautiful Raquette Lake, and there he lives his simple, lonely life. Around
him, on the lake shores, are the luxurious cottages of the rich who come from
the cities to the woods in summer and bring their fashions with them. But,
though he mingles with these people, Alvah is uncontaminated by the habits
of civilization. He is the primitive child of nature, who knows every tree,
every flower, every animal of the forests, and who finds in them more to
satisfy him than in the arts of society.

Last Moose

Dunning killed the last moose in the Adirondacks 32 years ago. He killed
the last panther eight years ago. He may put a bullet through the last wolf, only
a few of which are left. Black bear are still quite common, but these and deer
are all that remain of the big animals that roamed through the Adirondacks in
Dunning's younger days. The number of beasts which his gun has brought
down, not counting smaller game like foxes, mink, otter and birds, will reach
far into the thousands. He killed 102 panthers in eight years. The biggest catch
of fish was made by him in 1833, when he pulled 96 pounds of salmon trout
out of Piseco Lake in two hours. The largest salmon trout on record was
caught by Alvah's hook and it weighed 27½ lbs.

Writer's Friend

Dunning was long the friend and guide of the famous writer, "Adirondack Murray," whose tales of life in the woods have fascinated many, and the old woodsman has been the original of some of his characters. A picture of Dunning seated beside his cabin door with his faithful dogs at his side and five dead deer in the background attracted much attention at the World's Fair.

Alvah Dunning, photograph by Seneca Ray Stoddard, 1891.
COURTESY OF THE ADIRONDACK MUSEUM, BLUE MOUNTAIN LAKE, NY.

ALVAH DUNNING
William J. O'Hern

As far as the hunters and fishermen around the Eighth Lake in Fulton Chain country of the Adirondacks were concerned, Alvah Dunning was a tad odd—all the same exceptionally honest, according to Dr. Arpad G. Gerster, a surgeon on the staff of the German Hospital of New York who remembered him in the October 1916 issue of *Medical Pickwick* magazine's article "Etching as a Diversion." Gerster said the American backwoodsman was "sober, industrious in a backwoods way, spent less than he earned, hence was never 'hard up.'"

Dunning was born at Lake Pleasant, in Hamilton County, on June 14, 1816, in a rough log cabin on state land, in the thick of the endless, unbroken wilderness. He spent his life as a squatter, at different tracts of land belonging to New York State.

Alvah was well liked by *some* sportsmen. Admiring sports he served referred to him as "Uncle Alvah." But Dunning also had his share of detractors, and among the Fulton Chain guides he was, for some reason, an unpopular man-in-the-woods. Famed Adirondack guide E. L. "Jack" Sheppard was an exception. Fred Mather, early twentieth century author of *My Angling Friends* (1901), said Sheppard, one of the best of the Adirondack guides, admired the old woodsman and in conversation with Mather said this: "I have known Alvah for thirty years, and he is an affable, hospitable man of the old style, all of whom looked on game laws as infringements on the rights of men who live in the woods. He is the last of a type that has passed. He kills a deer when he needs it, catches a trout out of season to bait his trap, firmly believes it a sin to kill wastefully, and destroys less game than many who cry out against him."

Mather first met Alvah in 1865. He hired the "tall, spare and wiry" man to take him trout fishing in Brown's Tract Inlet and Raquette Lake. Mather had traveled to the mountains to breathe the healing scent of balsam as a way of regaining lost health. Alvah helped him "put on the finishing touches" to his recovery. Mather wrote, "The old man—he was 'old' to me then—took good care of me, and I returned much improved. His talk of woods life was very entertaining, and it was only a few weeks afterward that I became acquainted with his mortal enemy, Ned Buntline, also a fishing companion, so that I got Alvah's story while it was fresh. Friends of each man have so mixed up the case that it resembles the history of Bonaparte as written by a French or an English pen."

Mather was referring to a confrontation that took place between Dunning and writer Edward Zane Carroll Judson, a.k.a. Ned Buntline. Buntline was living in the Blue Mountain Lake country and treated the territory as if he were lord and master of the acreage. Blue Mountain Lake had once been home to Alvah; he had fled to the area (the exact year is lost to history) following a grievous experience with his faithless wife. The water was then known as

Tallow Lake. When hotel-building men began to push into the woods, Dunning retreated to out-of-the-way Raquette Lake where the Wood family had dominated in unaccompanied glory. Dunning often returned to hunt in the Blue Mountain Lake area.

The cause of the feud between newcomer Buntline and Dunning, so the story goes, was that Dunning stole skins from Ned's traps—an evil deed, but not an uncommon act by a territorial trapper to attempt to discourage competitors. The climax came when Buntline confronted Dunning about his trap stealing and shooting holes into one of his Eagle Nest camp's boats.

Dunning could not stand men like Buntline. To the man-of-the-woods some city interlopers came into the forest dressed in velvet suits and marched around with pop guns. He believed not one of them could survive a week in the wilds on their own.

Buntline knew Dunning had no use for him. He also knew Alvah lived alone with his dogs, whom he loved, and recognized that his warning wouldn't settle well with the long-timer. In order to impress on the hermit-woodsman how serious was his threat to stay out of *his* territory and off of the waters of Eagle Lake, Buntline shot one of Dunning's favorite hounds that was sitting right by his owner's side.

Alvah was enraged. Once, he had told Dr. Gerster, "he drove out of his camp a whole party of hunters, his guests, because some of them had kicked and beaten one of his dogs. First, he gave them their breakfast, then ordered them off his island, unconditionally. When they threatened him with non-payment, his reply was: 'Get out and damn your money! I would not take money from such as you are.'"

Following the execution, Buntline warned Alvah that if he ever again trespassed on the lake or its shores he would kill him. Dunning got the message.

Harold K. Hochschild wrote in *Township 34* that Dunning related the incident to Allie Roblee, saying, "He [Ned] was the meanest damn man I ever knew." Seneca Ray Stoddard said of the occurrence in his 1874 guidebook that "Alvah was grieved thereby and threatened to set the 'Eagle's Nest' on fire, with a longing to indulge in cremation."

Buntline's reputation was well known. Alvah knew the dime-novel writer's past had included killing at least one man. However, his pride would not allow him to leave the territory on Buntline's terms. Dunning did leave immediately, going down the east inlet, or the Marion River as it is also called, to Raquette Lake—but with no intention of staying away forever. Shortly after Buntline's admonishing, Si Bennett spotted Dunning while rowing Buntline in his guideboat into Eagle Lake. Thinking quickly, Bennett pretended to have cracked his fingers as he crossed the oars. He yelled as if in pain. The deception worked—Dunning heard Si, recognizing it as a warning. By the time the guide had taken up the oars and renewed rowing into the lake, the old man and his boat had faded into the dark of nightfall.

Wanting his guidebook to offer more than maps and map nomenclature, distance and time, and types of routes, Stoddard included history of the region too. "When asked about the affair," he wrote, "Ned said, 'I drove him [Dunning] out of that section when I was there because he threatened my life. The old rip steered clear of me after he found that I was as ready to throw lead as he was *threats*.'"

Alvah's facial features were full of character. His face showed "determination, and it looks like a face that could not be developed outside the woods," Mather said.

"These woods is a-gittin' too full o' people fer comfort—that is, in summer time; fer they don't bother the trappin' in the winter; but they're a-runnin' all over here in summer a-shootin' an' a-fishin', but they don't kill much, nor catch many fish; but they git in the way, an' they ain't got no business here disturbin' the woods," Mather wrote that Dunning shared once they had built up a relationship. Dunning observed ". . . dudes get time to come up here . . . and sometime kill deer an' some of 'em leave a deer to rot in the woods, an' on'y take the horns ef it's a buck, or the tail ef it's a doe, just so's they can brag about it when they go home, an' they'd put me in jail ef I killed a deer when I needed meat. I dunno what we're a-coming to in this free country."

"They pay you well for work for them, don't they, Alvah?" Mather returned.

"Yes, they do, durn 'em; or I wouldn't bother with 'em; but I druther they'd stay out o' my woods. They'll come anyhow, an' I might as well guide 'em, fer ef I don't some un else will, but I druther they'd keep their money and stay out of the woods. I can make a livin' without 'em, an' they'd starve to death here without me. They're the durndest lot of cur'osities you ever seen; know more about guns an' killin' deer than any man in the woods, but when it comes to fishin' tackle you'd oughter see it."

Their friendly conversation came about after they had fished several days. Mather apologized: "I am very sorry to have disturbed you, and will go back home in the morning."

The old guide "looked up" and said: "I didn't mean you, 'cause you seem to know how to sit inter a boat an' to know the voices of the birds an' how to fish. Now don't you go an' take a meanin' outer my words that I didn't mean."

"All right, Alvah!" Mather answered. "But if these people don't kill much game or fish they can't disturb you much, and I'm a little curious to know why you object so much to their coming here. The woods belongs largely to the State, and they certainly have the right to come into them." Fred Mather's questioning had the wanted effect; it made Uncle Alvah seethe and "drew his fire."

"Yes," he said, after turning the thing over in his mind in the deliberate manner common to men of the woods, "that's the worst of it; they've got a right to come here and disturb men who've made their homes in these woods and their lives, and many of 'em's fools. I hate fools."

Mather simply repled, "I dunno; why?"

"Oh, they pester one so," Alvah went on. "A few years ago one came up here and tried to make me believe the world is round and turns over upside down in the night, and they all believe it, all of 'em, every durned one that I've spoke to about it. What d' ye think o' that?"

Mather had heard others tell of Alvah's nonscientific notion of the planet. Simply, the earth was flat and square. Any other point of view was wrong. He damned the public teaching of such blather as the earth was round like a ball. "Why, man," he used to say, "what would become of the fellows on the other side of the ball? They would stand on their heads, and then would drop off." To demonstrate and give credence to his theory he would fill a tin cup with water and turn it over. Another one of his doctrines was that every basin of water—lakes and ponds—had at least one inlet and an outlet. The ocean's basin was another matter. The great body of salt water had only inlets. No explorer had, so far, found its outlet, but such an opening he felt had to exist, otherwise the world would have undergone a second flood, like that in Noah's time.

Years later, Mather, speaking of Alvah with Ned Buntline, heard the less-than-scholary old man referred to as an "amaroogian." Mather said he was never able to find the word in a single dictionary but just knew ". . . it signifies a kind of unsophisticated woodsman, who cannot fraternize with a man of the world . . ."

He answered Alvah: "I think they're wrong, of course, for we can see that these lakes don't spill out in the night. Yet this world can't be as flat as a pancake . . . and as for turning over . . . ."

"You don't believe it?" Alvah solicited.

"Not a word of it!" Fred said he replied. "And we were friends."

In 1895 a New York *Sun* newspaper reporter traveled to Raquette Lake to interview the wilderness guide who held the reputation of having trapped the last beaver and killing the last moose, and to learn of his enterprises with fish, white-tailed deer and bear. No byline appeared over the June 6 *Sun* article. Eldridge A. Spears might possibly have been the reporter. Eldridge was a long-time writer for the *Sun* who vacationed at his Northwood camp (near Hinckley), knew the region well, wrote numerous articles, and raised his sons to be conservation-minded advocates for the protection the Adirondack Mountains. He maintained close connections to Adirondack characters including "French Louie."

A week after the *Sun's* "A Wilderness Guide" column appeared in the metropolitan newspaper, the Boonville *Herald* reprinted the interview under "Uncle Alva Dunning of the Fulton Chain of Lakes." The reporter described Dunning as, "still hale and hearty, with an eye so keen that he can shoot the head off a grouse at a hundred yards, and an ear so sharp that it can detect the bay of a hound a mile away."

The correspondent asked Alvah if he had seen any changes in the Adirondacks in his seventy-nine years, including sixty-eight years as a meat hunter, trapper, fisherman, and guide. And what about the animals now passed or fast passing from this region?

ALVAH: It's queer how sudden and mysterious the moose disappeared from the woods over south, younder [the Fulton Chain]. They were thick only thirty years ago. The last year of the war I was moose hunting, and the woods were full of them. It seemed to me as if I could shoot one at almost every turn. I killed eight monstrous big ones in five days. The signs showed that there were plenty more left, and I was counting on great sport again the next season.

The next season came and I tramped that whole country over for moose. All I got, and all I saw, was two, and the last one of those two, a big cow, was the last moose any one ever saw in that region or any other part of the Adirondacks except up north in the St. Regis country, where there are a few moose left yet. Where all the moose went to and what caused them all to leave the woods in one season, is a mystery I never could solve. They went, and they never came back.

My father, myself, and two others killed 100 moose one winter. I was in my twelfth year when I killed my first moose. Father had been out after it the day before, and it had got away. I told him that I'd like to go out and kill it. He laughed at me, and said it took a pretty good man to bag a moose, and he didn't think a boy stood much show with one. I stuck to it, though, and by and by he said I might go out with him and see him kill the moose. I shouldered my gun and went along. I led the dog, too. From all I had heard about moose, I concluded that they were mortal afraid of a man, and would flee and keep on fleeing as long as they knew that one was following them, but that they hated dogs so that they would stop on the trail to fight one.

On this moose hunt I was going along a few rods to one side of Father, but in sight of him. We hadn't gone more than a couple of miles when the dog began to lift his head, sniff the air, and prick up his ears. I resolved to act on my own responsibility. I believed that the dog had got scent of the moose. As we went on he pushed forward and tugged at his string, and I slipped his collar. Away he went, and I followed fast. Father hollered and wanted to know what I had let the dog go for, and I told him the dog had slipped his collar. I didn't stop, and was soon a good way ahead. I hadn't gone more than a quarter of a mile when I came upon the moose, which had turned to have a bout with the dog. The dog knew his business and kept the moose engaged. I got up to within safe shooting distance, aimed at the butt of the moose's ear and fired. The big beast dropped all in a heap in its tracks and never stirred. Pretty soon Father came hurrying up. I had one foot on the moose, and maybe I was grinning a little. Father looked a little surprised, but didn't let on.

"Well," he said, "you tumbled it, did you?"

"Yes," I said. "I thought I wouldn't wait for you to come up to let me see you kill it."

"He laughed, and went to skinning the moose out. As he skinned he kept examining the hide and carcass until he had skinned the moose clear up to the ears.

"There ain't any bullet mark anywhere," he said, "Where'd you shoot it?"

"Look under the butt of the ear," I said.

He looked under the butts of both ears, and all over the head, but not a sign of a bullet mark was there anywhere.

"This moose ain't been shot!" said father. "It's just been scared to death!"

This rather dampened my spirits for I couldn't bear to think that I had missed that moose. But the mystery was explained later, and I was redeemed as a marksman. The bullet had entered the moose's ear and gone on into the animal's brain without leaving a mark to show where it had gone in.

I hunted moose for a good many years and killed scores of them, but I never shot more than once at a moose to kill it. The first shot I always put it where it would do the business. Yet I shot a moose eleven times once before I killed it. I'll explain how that was. I was hunting on West Canada waters, over to the south yonder, and started two moose, a bull and a cow. They took to the creek. I shot the bull in the creek. The cow stopped. I didn't want to shoot her as she stood in the creek, so I tried to get her out on land. She wouldn't come out, nor she wouldn't go on.

"I'll have to get her mad, I see," said I.

I knew if I got her mad she'd come tearing out of the creek at me, so I fired a bullet into her nose. She shook her head but didn't move or show any temper. I shot another bullet into her nose. She didn't mind it any more than she had the first one. I kept on firing bullets into her nose until I had lodged eleven between her eyes and her nostrils, and still she stood still and kept her temper. It doesn't seem to me as if there ever could anything have been created that was half as contrary and not in its way as that cow moose was. I saw there was no use of wasting any more lead on her, even if there was room enough in her nose for any more, so I got mad myself, sent a bullet under her ear, and tumbled her in the creek.

It's amazing what chases moose used to give us. I followed a moose once for three days and three nights, and in all that it never stopped once to rest, eat, or drink. During the chase the moose brought me within a mile of my camp, but took me between thirty and forty miles away again before I came up with it and shot it, it still being on the move. The best time for hunting moose was during the month of February, but we used to get a good many when they came to the ponds and lakes in the summer. They would weigh from 800 to 1,200 pounds. The biggest moose, I think, that I ever saw I found dead in the woods one winter. I was breaking a road in the snow to get in a number of moose I had in the woods when I came to a tremendous mound of snow. I dug into it and found that the mound was caused by a dead moose. I suppose it had been shot and mortally wounded by some one in the fall, or before the snow had got very deep. I believe that moose would have weighed 1,600 pounds. Its horns were large in proportion, and I think they were the largest set of moose antlers ever secured. I cut the horns from the moose's head, and they made a good load for a cart. I could scarcely reach from tip to tip of the antlers. There were twelve points on one side and thirteen on the other. Squirrels had nibbled the points of the horns some, which damaged them, so that instead of getting $20 for them I had to let them go at $10. I sold them to a man from Utica, and they are still in that city, I hear.

THE *SUN*: Alvah Dunning camped, winter and summer, at Raquette Lake and the Fulton Chain. He has a snug camp on an island in Eighth Lake, and for nearly a quarter of a century was the only dweller on or about that lake.

ALVAH: I have lived through the years when deer actually ran in droves in the Adirondacks, but they haven't been as abundant in twenty years as they are today. All signs this spring show that the woods are full of deer. I had great luck with deer last year, although I started in with about as discouraging a hunt as ever made a hunter miserable. First I came out in sight of a buck near Seventh Lake, standing there pretty like for a nice, easy shot. I drew a bead on him, and to my dismay found that I couldn't pull the trigger of my gun. I put all the strength I had on it, but it was no use, and I was obliged to stand there and see that big, fat buck walk away and disappear in the woods. I came out into the carry between Seventh and Eighth Lakes, and saw a fat doe standing in the edge of the woods. I pulled up on her. I got the trigger to work, but the gun snapped. I tried once more, and it snapped again. It snapped a third time. The doe stood still, and I hastened to change the cartridge. In my haste I got a wrong sized cartridge, and before I could get it out and a right one in the doe concluded to go away, and she did. She had hardly disappeared when another one came loping along and stopped. The gun snapped on her, and had snapped the second time, when a third deer came along. The gun snapped every time I tried to shoot, and the deer got tired, I guess, and bounded away. There were four deer I should have had, and I didn't get one. I had a notion to break the gun around a tree, but it was a new one, and I took it apart and found there was something the matter with the tumbler of the lock. A man over at Blue Mountain Lake fixed it for me, and I was glad I hadn't broken it, for in a very short time I made a $15 shot with it. I shot a big otter before I got home, and I've shot two with it since, and they're worth $15 apiece. Otters are quite plentiful along the Fulton Chain waters yet. I get several every winter in traps and by shooting.

Alvah never tired of telling the story of how many years earlier he trapped the last beaver in the Adirondacks at that time:

Sixty years ago I trapped the last beaver that ever was caught in the lower Adirondacks. I was over on Piseco waters. I was prospecting around early one spring and I discovered a beaver dam. These things had long been rare, and beaver pelts in prime condition were worth from $20 to $25. I kept mum about this discovery, for I thought maybe I had run against a colony of beaver, and I didn't care to divide the profits with anybody.

I didn't trap the beaver that spring, and there was where I made a mistake. A man I boarded with, known as Uncle Enos, was an old beaver trapper. There was a cranberry marsh near where I had discovered the beaver dam, and one day when cranberry picking came 'round Enos went to gather some in the marsh with a man named Gilmore. He found the marsh all under water, and he knew what it meant in a minute.

"A beaver dam had done this," said he, and he wasn't long in finding it.

I found out about this from Gilmore two or three weeks later, and that Enos was keeping his eye on the beaver dam and intended to set a trap by and by, when the season got right. I didn't take any chances, and put in my trap right away. I got a beaver the second night, and I guess as big a one as ever was caught in the Adirondacks. It weighed fifty pounds. It was the only tenant the dam had and the last one. If I had only trapped it the spring before, or if Uncle Enos hadn't forced me to catch it in self-protection, the last beaver would have brought me $25. As it was I only got $5 for it.

There never were a great number of bears in this part of the Adirondacks. There isn't enough shack—beechnuts, acorns, and the like—to draw them here. There are some bears though, and just as many as there ever were, I guess.

The queerest thing I ever knew a bear to do was to play 'possum. Bill Ballard and I once set a trap for a bear and caught him. When we found him in the trap I blazed away at him with my rifle, not ten yards away, and he tumbled where he stood and never moved. That he was as dead as dead could be there seemed nothing surer. I went up to him to cut his throat and let the blood out of him, as some folks like bear meat to eat. He lay there perfectly motionless, but I noticed that his eyes were half open and looked as if they were watching me. I thought it was the death glare in his eyes and I bent forward to cut his throat. As I did so I noticed the big sides of the bear swell out slowly, but as if he were taking in a long breath. That saved my life, I believe, for I straightened up, and as I did so the bear sprang to his feet and grabbed at me with his claws. They did not miss my face more than two inches. I tumbled back, got my gun, and put a bullet in the bear's brain that settled him. The funny part of it is that the first shot I fired at the bear never touched him anywhere. There was not a mark on him, as we found when we dressed him. The bear had simply tumbled when I shot, and lay there as if dead on purpose to seize me and avenge himself when I walked up to him. My first bullet hit a sapling and was turned from its course. That was the narrowest escape I ever had. I never knew [up to then] a bear [to] play 'possum.

I have killed and trapped a good many bears, but I guess I never killed any in quite such a queer way as I did the two that Joe Mitchell and I found in a hollow hemlock once, over near Piseco Lake. It was in the spring, and we were building a camp. There was a lot of brush growing out of the stub, and I was chopping it away, when I saw a big bear paw thrust out of the hollow. I whacked it off with one blow of the axe. The bear that owned it jerked the pawless leg back into the stub and instantly thrust the other paw out. I chopped that one off, and it fell to the ground by the side of the other one. The bear pulled that leg in and then, as if to see what was going on outside, stuck its head out almost to the shoulder. The head never got back into the hollow again, for I chopped it off, and the rest of the bear fell back. Almost immediately another bear came to the front and stuck one it its paws out. I chopped it off. The second paw was put forward, and that was promptly chopped off. Then the bear shoved its head out to investigate and the head was chopped off at once. I don't think two bears were ever killed like that before.

THE *SUN*: Alvah is no longer monarch of all he surveys thereabout, for a few months ago a family put up a house at the foot of Eighth Lake and Uncle Alvah says he feels crowded. He has another camp at the head of Raquette Lake, near John Brown's inlet. He lives entirely alone, and divides his time between his two camps.

Harry V. Radford, himself a great lover of the woods and editor of *Woods and Waters*, a paper devoted to the Adirondacks, fancied Alvah. Radford wrote in "Adirondack Department" of the October 1901 issue of *Field & Stream* that Alvah "had a wonderful reputation as a woodsman. During his life he killed or trapped every animal in this region whose hide or carcass had any value." This was during the days when there were "no restraining laws and men had not yet come to consider the subject of game preservation."

He showed the stock he came from by starting with his father[2] as a hunter and trapper himself at the age of six. A tireless "meat hunter," he fished, hunted and trapped for the commercial market continually, making it a business for over seventy years. His reputation as a woodsman and success in the pursuit of game made him a conspicuous figure throughout the Adirondacks. He guided noted writer Rev. W. H. H. Murray and Superintendent Colvin of the Adirondack Survey.

Alvah spent immeasurable hours pulling on oars, carrying his guideboat, or cutting, splitting and stacking wood for fuel. Sleeping in a shanty, fighting off clouds of mosquitoes and black flies, and eating wild meat and edible plants, he was always impeccably clean-shaven as a young man and dressed for cleanliness when J. R. Stoddard took his photograph.

Dr. Arpad Gerster's private practice on New York City's East Side, he recalled in his memoirs, ". . . was not very lucrative, it was steady, picturesque, and full of movement." Having an interest in woodcraft and American forests, he came to the Adirondacks. North Woods visits were a "refreshing diversion from the exhausting tension of busy professional life." In 1883 he bought a camp site adjoining the deserted Hemlocks Hotel from Edward Bennett. The following year he erected a log cottage dubbed Camp Oteetiwi. "Raquette Lake was a gem of solitude in its unspoiled bloom of freshness," and Alvah Dunning was one of his more interesting neighbors.

---

[2]Alfred L. Donaldson recorded in *A History of the Adirondacks, Vol. II*, that "Scout Dunning had served under Sir William Johnson, and was accounted almost as skilled and ruthless an Indian warrior as the more renowned Nick Stoner. Scout Dunning was just one of many men during the American Revolutionary War who hated Indians because they had had members of their family murdered in Indian raids in the Mohawk Valley."

Dr. Gerster said Alvah "loved to talk with those that did not laugh at him, and the freshness and mobility of his intellect, and the phraseology he used, were wonderful in a man who had spent most of his life in solitude. He was a fierce enemy, but a loyal and steadfast friend of those to whom he took a shining. At age 69 he was no longer a young man in the woods but still plied his services over long hours even though he had long suffered from pain in both wrists. He said that his wrists were once dislocated by the fall of a tree. When one of his hearers expressed some surprise that his arms had not been broken, Alvah promptly replied that they undoubtedly would have been had his bones not been stronger than the tree. Instead of his arms having been broken by the wallop, he said, the tree that had fallen across them smashed in two! The teller of that story said he witnessed the two guides in his party each hold a forefinger to the side of their noses while Uncle Alvah was relating his experience with the tree."

Alvah Dunning was an awesomely skilled rifle shot in his day. Many stories epitomize his impeccable marksmanship. Harry Radford's recounting of a contest between him and Caleb Chase, of Newcomb, who was also an acknowledged marksman of unusual ability, is typical of the stories. In the winter 1901–02 issue of *Woods & Waters,* Radford wrote of the contest in "Other Adirondack Matters."

"A small iron carpet-tack was inserted in a smooth, whitened plank, as a target, at a distance of forty yards, and each contestant was to have five shots. So fine, indeed, was the mark that only the clear, practiced vision of the woodsmen could detect the tack at that distance. Dunning had placed four bullets within a hair's breath of the tack, but had not hit it; and Chase's five shots were equally well located. It looked as if the contest would have to be re-shot, when Dunning, who was using a superb rifle made by C. Steward, of Painted Post, New York, placed his fifth and last shot directly on the head of the tack, driving it deep into the plank.

"The contest was held on Murray's Island, in Raquette Lake, twenty odd year ago, when Dunning was over sixty years of age."

Alvah Dunning stories passed among guides and sports as frequently as a bear paws a honey comb in a bee tree. Allie Roblee's recollection told in *Township 34*, and reiterated in many articles about Alvah, is a classic example of the kind told. Once asked by Roblee, "What does the earth rest on?," Alvah answered, "It sets on a big rock." Roblee picked up, "And what does the rock rest on?" "Another big rock, ye damn fool," boomed Alvah, setting closure to the conversation. There were also stories of his doubt of the usefulness of soap and warm water; his actions to keep city sports from camping on Brown's Tract Inlet, property he considered his own sacred land; and his skeptical reading of Genesis, Chapter 7.

One grand lost opportunity to Adirondack history may be the anecdotes Judge Edgar P. Glass and his sons Joseph and Ned of Syracuse might have been able to set down about Alvah Dunning. In 1875, Alvah built a cabin on the island in Eighth Lake. At that time campers called the area the "Hinderland," perhaps because of its remoteness. The island camp was one of two shanties Alvah maintained. The other was near the mouth of Brown's Tract Inlet, Raquette Lake. Both locations allowed the hermit easy access to Eagle and Bug lakes and the region around Shallow Lake and the Upper and Lower Brown's Tract Ponds—his favored range. Judge Glass was one of the "sports" Alvah guided, and on the first of April, 1896, Dunning sold the camp to Judge Glass for $100. In 1899 New York State got title to the island via a tax sale.

Edgar's grandson, Joseph J. Glass Jr., an attorney in Syracuse, N.Y., provided me with a copy of the Quit-Claim Deed Alvah signed, giving his grandfather possession of the approximate one-acre parcel of land Alvah had occupied "for the past 21 years or more." Joseph said his father told him very little about the island camp and Alvah. The camp was on an admirable location but fishing and hunting adventures were just commonplace activities. The stories didn't seem important. Joseph did recall his father remembering, "Alvah could see no more of the world than what was around him, which of course was flat. For that reason he thought the world was perfectly flat and the moon, sun and stars rose and set. Alvah told my father and Uncle Ned a good deal of woodcraft."

In the latter half of the 1890s, Alvah's hardened reputation grew a little softer and his name even more a legend thanks to a truly generous present Dr. Gerster offered. The woods and quietude of Raquette Lake were a natural medium for his artistic side; Dr. Gerster enjoyed etching and the freedom artistic expression provided. Etching in copper was also a relaxing diversion from the demands of a surgeon. In his book *Recollections of a New York Surgeon* (1917) he tells of a particularly tasteful piece of work that attracted some intense interest: "There is little to be said about my own etchings, for they amount to no more than most amateurs' work. Proofs of one plate only were sold. It was the portrait of Alvah Dunning, the famous guide and sage of Raquette Lake. Once, while hauling a large trout into the boat, his silver watch dropped overboard. Alvah grieved pitifully. Soon after, the idea was conceived of etching a plate from a photograph of the old man, taken by Stoddard. When the church fair at St. Hubert's on Raquette Lake was held, two proofs were given, to be sold for not less than $5 each. They were picked up immediately. Thus at Raquette—and later on in New York—twenty proofs were disposed of, netting the sum of $100. With this, a gold watch was brought at Benedict's, where the proprietor added (as his contribution) a super gorgeous gold chain. At the Christmas celebration at Camp Pine Knot, Raquette Lake, the gift was placed in Alvah's palm by Mr. Durant. The old man toppled over in a dead faint. He soon revived, however, and lived to enjoy the use of his new timepiece for many years . . . ."

So much more might have been written of Alvah Dunning. Had an industrious writer spent a month in his cabin and jotted down his stories and made a character study of one of the most interesting men in the mountains, we all might be able to look back on the tales and feel the enjoyment of his company, for a little bit of Alvah Dunning lives in the heart of every sportsman.

Fortunately for history, Edward Bennett wrote a series of articles titled "Reminiscences of the Adirondacks," in *The Post-Star* (Glens Falls, N.Y.) over a ten-week period in 1929. Bennett was a longtime resident of Raquette Lake and owner of Under the Hemlock Hotel. He was one of the locals who knew Dunning best.

Alvah Dunning was "truly a child of the woods," he said. "He cared nothing for the news of the outside world. A newspaper a year old was just as good to him as one a day old. He could not tell you who was governor of the state or who was president. But he did know how to hunt and trap. I knew him longest and best of the old guides. I can relate a few anecdotes about him.

When Governor Cleveland was elected president [of the United States], the Fort Orange Club of Albany wished to give him a farewell dinner. One of its members wrote to Isaac Kenwell who had a small log home on Raquette Lake, for the accommodation of sportsmen, to get them 25 pounds of brook trout and get them to Albany by a certain date no matter about the price.

This was the last of February and against the law to catch trout. Kenwell was not well at the time so he sent for Alvah and told him what he wanted, and to be sure to get them by a certain date. Alvah said all right. He went up to Shallow Lake and got the trout. When he brought them, Kenwell asked him how much they were. Alvah said, 'That's all right, I'll take it out in provisions.' Kenwell said, 'Oh, no, I will get the cash for them and I want to pay you.' But Alvah went away and did not take the money.

Kenwell took the trout to Blue Mountain Lake and they arrived at Albany on time. Shortly after, Alvah heard something that Kenwell said about him and got miffed at it and would not go near Kenwell. So one day he sat down and wrote the following letter to Mr. Cleveland. I have seen the letter in the Fort Orange Club.

Mr. Cleveland:

Some time ago, Ike Kenill [*sic*] asked me to catch you some lake trout. I done so. He offered to pay me but I did not take any pay. Just now I am out of baking powder and if you would send me some I would be very much obliged to you.

A. Dunning

Alvah could write after a fashion, but his spelling was amusing. Mr. Cleveland got the letter and of course did not know what to make of it, but someone in the office knew Alvah and told him all about it, and what a character Alvah was. It amused Mr. Cleveland very much, and he sent him two cases of one-pound boxes of Cleveland's baking powder.

One fall when I was working at Camp Pine Knot for W.W. Durant, and he had gone out for a short time, he told me that whenever Alvah came to the camp, to take him in, feed him, and let him stay as long as he wanted. He came one night in November, 1878, just as I was sitting down to supper, so I told him to get ready and have some supper with me and stay all night.

After supper I read and smoked awhile and left Alvah sitting at the table. There was a Bible there that Mr. Durant's mother had left for me. Alvah picked it up and began to read it. I was nearly asleep when I heard Alvah say, "That's a damn lie." I was awake in a minute and said, "What's that, Alvah, you reading the Bible and saying it's a damn lie?" "Yes sir, yes sir, it say here that the Lord opened the flood gates of heaven and it rained down 40 days and 40 nights and drowned the earth to the tops of the highest mountains. Why," he said, "I've seen it rain here for 40 days and 40 nights and it never raised Raquette lake more than a foot."

I let it pass and did not try to enlighten him.

The following year, Mr. W.A. Bockes, a cashier of the First National Bank of Saratoga, stayed at Raquette Lake as a guest of Mr. Durant. He asked Bennett if he knew anyone in the vicinity who had any otter skins. Ed said, "Yes, Alvah Dunning has 10."

Hearing that, Bockes asked to be taken to Alvah's camp. "I did so," Bennett recalled, "and introduced Bockes to Alvah. Bockes told Alvah what he was after and the old man went into his camp, turned down the tick he slept on and brought out the otter skins. It was very warm then, and the odor was not very pleasant. But a little thing like that did not bother Alvah.

"Bockes asked Alvah how much he wanted for the skins. He said, 'Ten dollars each.' Mr. Bockes said he would take the lot and took out his check book and drew a check for $100 and handed it to Alvah. He said, 'What's that Mr. Bockes?' 'Why,' he said, 'it's a check for $100.' Alvah said, 'No sir, no sir, don't want it, won't take it. I sell my fur for cash.' 'But.' I said, 'Alvah , this gentleman is the cashier of the First National Bank of Saratoga.' 'Don't care, don't care, if he's the governor of the state. I will not take it.' So we had to go back and we told Mr. Durant about it and we all had a good laugh. He let Mr. Bockes have the money and that evening we went over and got the otter skins. That shows what type of a man Alvah was. He was a child of the wilderness."

By 1895, technology and change were taking place all over the Adirondacks. To once-isolated Alvah Dunning, who guided his first party of hunters when he was only 11 years old and the mountainous region was virtually unknown, the invasion of the wilderness by summer tourists, railroads, steamboats, hotels, and cottages was just too much.

In "Alvah Dunning," a March 22, 1902, *Forest and Stream* article, Fred Mather reported that the old woodsman had been "filled with a spirit of misgiving for his future comfort and welfare. He saw the site upon which had once stood his hut, and in which he had entertained Grover Cleveland, occupied by a bustling railroad yard." The railway paid Alvah $600 to relocate amicably. Alvah accepted the offer. Mather continued: "The waters where he had caught trout, hunted moose and deer, and trapped beaver and otter, were frequented by pleasure boats, and so he turned his face toward the setting sun and started for the Rocky Mountains, in hope of enjoying the solitude which was no longer to be found in the Adirondacks. For a time he hunted and fished in the Dakotas and Michigan, but he failed to find the seclusion which he desired, and it was not long before he returned to his former haunts. Broken in spirit, he once more camped about Raquette Lake, and guided hunting and fishing parties for such men as Collis P. Huntington, William West Durant, Lieut. Gov. Woodruff, J. Pierpont Morgan and others. He came out of the woods every winter of late years and for a time last winter boarded with friends in Utica."

Although not quite erect of form as he was once, but still tireless of foot and bright of eye, his weathered face betraying his years, he accepted an offer in March 1902 to attend a sportsmen's show in New York City. On his way home he stopped in Utica for the night, putting up at the old Dudley House, on Whitesboro Street. The trip was to have been a way to look back on his decades of eventful and active life in the wilderness and forward to many years more among the animals and forests he loved. Byron E. Cool, a long-time North Lake resident, said, "Alvah had but very little use for the advancement of civilization as he could live in the woods without any help from outsiders." He told Cool: "guess I've lived too long. I used to hope I could die in peace in the wilderness where I was born."

Alvah, however, was not to leave this world in the wilderness but through the accidental inhalation of illuminating gas. Dr. Gerster, who can be counted among the early sportsmen to camp at Raquette Lake, tells of Alvah's sad death. "Stopping at a little hotel at Utica, N.Y. , he was aroused by a pert hall boy's warning not to blow out the gas. The stop of the cock of the gas fixture in his bedroom had been broken off by someone else. When he retired to bed, he turned off and turned on again the flow of the deadly gas, and was found the next morning dead in bed. A gold watch and $213.00 were found in his clothes.

Newspapers all over the state and East Coast published lengthy obituaries of 'The Last of the Old Adirondack Guides.'"

Learning of the death of Alvah Dunning, Isaac T. Norris of Baltimore, Maryland, recalled a meeting with "Uncle Alvah" in the March 22, 1902, issue of *Forest and Stream*:

In July 1869, coming down the Marion River from Blue Mountain Lake, our party of four, with two guides met suddenly on a trail over a short carry, two splendid hounds, and in a few moments a tall, slender, weather-beaten man appeared, carrying a pack basket and a three-barreled muzzle loading gun. The two shot barrels, of about 16 gauge, on top, the rifle barrel under, with a ramrod lying along the side in the groove. The hammer of the rifle struck upward.

The whole get-up meant business. His comment upon his gun, 'She do throw buckshot wicked,' I well remember.

His pack contained trout for a well-known sporting resort in Saratoga, so he informed us.

We bargained for a few lake trout for supper (as we had nothing), and when he estimated their weight at eight pounds, one of our guides said, "Ain't that a leetle hefty, Alvy?" He replied, "Maybe," and added another fish.

He accepted our silver with thanks, but declined the flask with the remark, "You can't get none of that truck down my throat."

And so we parted. I wonder what has become of that gun.

We slept that night at the "Old Wood Place" on Raquette lake, and heard rounds of revelry by night from the island near by, where "Adirondack Murray" had as guests that night Miss Kate Field and her mother.

So many guide stories. So many tales. And yet, so many additional recollections of "Uncle" Alvah Dunning have gone untold. I have visited Eighth Lake Island for fifty-six years. The paddle across the green-blue spring fed water has never lost its appeal. I've told my children and grandchildren about old Alvah. I think Alvah's life would be a subject for an entire book. Until more is assembled about him I'll be content to let my mind wander as I push my canoe through the sandy-bottom outlet between Eighth and Seventh Lakes. "Alvah," I might say if I lived in an earlier era and had hired him as my guide as we waded down the shallow mile stretch of water toward the Uncas Road that spans Eighth Lake's outlet, "I usually fish with the fly for trout. I'm fond on this sort of fishing. The trouble with the Seventh Lake country is that the rainbows and natives are driving the speckled trout out of the streams."

My sage guide would reply that indeed the rainbows are game fighters, and he would suspect I would find it rather difficult to get them of much size with the fly. "I kin goyd ya to more'n half a dozen trout-filled waters within the sound of a mating call of a panther from camp and you know when a cat wants to find one of its kind it can get up a good loud screech. It's got to, for they ain't plenty and that call has got to go miles through the woods. About the beginnin' of July last year a party I goyded had 'em a fair time fly-fishing at these places."

My anticipation would build as we waded toward our destination. I should think it quite worth trying. Alvah would know.

As we continued through the forest-lined outlet I would tap him for information about the wilds. "How long since there were any wolves in the Adirondacks, Alvah?"

"Wall, I don't know azackly. When I was a boy they was common an' you could hear 'em howl o' nights along the lakes or up the mountains, an' we used to shoot 'em an' trap 'em, but never did no poisonin' like they do out West. Let's see! They was plenty up to about the time General Taylor died."

"When was that?"

"The wolves went off about that time; some said they went into Canada an' some thought they died. I guess if they'd a died we'd a seen some o' their bones som'ers, but a few was around here durin' the war, in the '60s, and I killed a big one then, but ain't seen none since. Some men say they've seen 'em o' late years off toward the Saranacs, but I can't say. While the war was goin' on there wa'n't so many men comin' to the woods an' things picked up a little."

There is a little of the old-time sportsman in me. I would have wanted the opinion of the wise guide. "Alvah, some folks say that a panther screams and others say it never does. What's your opinion?"

AMAZIAH D. (DUT) BARBER
Lloyd Blankman

It is unclear who is recalling past times to Lloyd in this interview.

I well remember Dut Barber. My first meeting with him occurred during a vacation at Nobleboro, in 1885, as I remember. While DePeyster Lynch, a school mate at the Utica Academy, and I were summering at Griff Evans' we decided to hike to Jocks Lake for a packbasket sight-seeing tour. [Jocks Lake is now referred to as Honnedaga.]

When we arrived at the lake, the ancient log cabin known as Herkimer Camp in which we had planned to camp was found to have been recently occupied as a stable and was quite uninhabitable. Camp Raymond, along shore a mile to the west was also found to be ruinous but serviceable for a limited stay.

Jocks Lake was the most beautiful sheet of water we had ever seen or could imagine, with low rounded hills clothed with virgin forest to the water's edge, and the water as clear as the air itself.

In the early evening, from the camp across the lake, came a solitary boatman who proved to be Dut Barber, and who invited us to be his guests as long as we would like. He was wearing a white cork 'lion-hunter's' helmet which was his habitual head gear, and held the habitual cigar between his teeth.

Although neither of us had ever met him, he was known by reputation to us as well as to every native and visitor in all Wilmurt. His invitation to us revealed his outstanding characteristic, hospitality. Lynch and I received no exceptional welcome; every woodsman who approached his camp was a welcome guest. It had no latch string.

Our stay extended into the fourth day; we were furnished guns and ammunition to participate in a deer hunt, along with other guests who were by chance friends. Fishing tackle and boat were also at our disposal. Nothing was too good or too choice for his guests.

After Camp Barber had been developed into a modest tourist hotel, I enjoyed many outings with Jocks Lake as a center. It seemed to me that ultimately away down deep in his heart Dut Barber must have conceived that Jocks Lake was his very own—he loved it so. He was familiar with every feature and phase of the landscape. He built lean-to camps in a dozen roundabout localities convenient to fishing waters and run ways; close by each of them was hidden a row boat well secured. He maintained a pack of hounds—deer hounding being then an accredited sport. Woodsmen can appreciate such facilities. The guides in his service were able and companionable—the best. A Sportsman's Paradise indeed! A Happy Hunting Ground! No wonder that in boyish enthusiasm I seriously considered becoming a North Woods guide—just like Dut Barber! Imitation is the sincerest flattery.

My most memorable hikes up North Woods way were made in company with Dut, putting out the dogs in hunting season. The party would be under way shortly after sunrise, with half a dozen dogs in leash, off trail, up hill and down, fording streams, sighting a lake down below, up mountain sides, always on the lookout for a fresh deer track, releasing the dogs one by one. That was the life!

Dut had a real sense of humor. During this tenderfoot's outing with him to the West Canada stillwaters on a fishing trip, Louis Seymour (a well-known semi-hermit) had a two story house at which we would stop for the night. I envisioned in anticipation a rustic lodge with boulder chimney, living room decorated with deer heads and carpeted with bear skins. The reality proved to be a shack with two bunks, one above the other, which accounted for the two stories. When we arrived we all laughed together—at me.

Dut was a born gambler. On the trail he would take a silver dollar from his pocket, toss it to the ground a few yards in advance, and challenge his nearest companion with a "Head or tail?" And in the evening, with no drinking water in the cabin, he would cut the cards with his guides to decide who would be the victim to fetch a bucketful from the spring.

Dut appeared to be at all times a happy person. City born and bred but coming into dislike for city life, he sought the freedom of a new environment in the wilderness. I came to classify him as a new type Thoreau. In the surroundings in which as a boy I knew him, he was, above all, immeasurably likable. An altruist, he shared whatever he had.

⚘ WILL LEWIS

Lloyd Blankman

Will Lewis at the age of 19 was 6 ft. 1 in. tall and weighed 140 pounds. He was always thin and from a young man had a mustache. His left shoulder was noticeably lower than his right, caused by his daily carrying of a gun. His calm manner and his knack of getting "pretty tickled" made all who were lucky enough to know him, like him.

His voice was low and quiet with one exception. That was on the rifle range when his deep, booming "Pull" carried over the countryside. In the many decisions of life he thought things over pretty carefully and acted to the best of his ability. He did not spend time on regrets and worries. Each day he did the best he could and when he went to bed he went to sleep.

Will Lewis loved the woods. He felt the same call of the forest that French Louie and Nessmuk did. Time and geography made being another French Louie impossible. Maybe he even said to himself, "I'm born 50 years too late." His literary ability prevented him from being immortal like Nessmuk. But somewhere in between he found his place in the sun.

He was born in Central New York near Norwich and died in that town 86 years later. The following note was written by him at the age of 85: "I was born in 1870. At the age of five years my parents moved in the lumber woods on the banks of the Genesee River. I began shooting small game with a bow and

Will Lewis (age 36) poses proudly on Decoration Day 1906—also his birthday—with his "world record" catch of 62 woodchuck tails.
COURTESY EDWARD BLANKMAN
(THE LLOYD BLANKMAN
COLLECTION)

arrow at the age of six years, was using firearms at age of eight years. Small game was very plentiful so I had lots of practice. At 12 years of age I was using breech loading rifles and shotgun. In 1891 I became acquainted with Henry J. Borden who had a cheese and butter factory and rifle range near North Pharsalia, where I began learning the fine points of rifle and pistol shooting."

The great deal of trapping he did along the Genesee River is not mentioned. Neither are the years of 1885 through 1890 when he lived on a large farm near Bath, New York. There he built a crow-bow gun and became an expert with it.

The country's financial panic in 1893 brought the Lewis family back to the sawmill and lumber business on the homestead farm near Norwich. Here he learned his father's trade which he did the rest of his life. There was little work for him in 1894. Previously his cousin, Clarence Curnalia, having asthma, had gone to St. Regis Falls to live for his health. So Will learned of the great North Woods wilderness. Alone with his new 45-70 Winchester on August 31, 1894 he took the 9:00 a.m. train for Utica and points north. This same year New York State voters declared the Adirondack Forest Preserve (all state-owned lands in the Adirondacks) "forever wild."

The years 1898 and 1900 Will traveled north with horse and wagon, spending a month or so at a time and living in the wagon, make-shift shelters and old buildings. After that every year and sometimes several times a year he journeyed to his happy hunting grounds. The experiences and deer he got he kept track of with notes he made on the spot.

Bill Potter and his daughter Iva at his Rochester or High Falls Camp
COURTESY EDWARD BLANKMAN (THE LLOYD BLANKMAN COLLECTION)

Outdoorsman Bill Potter at remote Northrup Lake in 1932.
COURTESY EDWARD BLANKMAN (THE LLOYD BLANKMAN COLLECTION)

BILL POTTER
Lloyd Blankman

The subject of this account was a rugged outdoor character in a frontier settlement called Wilmurt. He lived in the days when hunting, fishing, and trapping were leading occupations, and he was an expert at all three.

He guided many to the runways of the deer and the lurking places of the trout. As a trapper he was without a peer at catching an otter. According to Trume Haskell of Barneveld, Bill would trap otter in habitats no one else would suspect the animal to be inhabiting.

Bill Potter was a native of the West Canada Creek country, having been born and raised there, and many are the stories of his exploits in the woods. He spent all of his time in the forest, summer and winter, and he always carried his rifle with him, a 303 Savage. Severe weather conditions meant nothing to him; in the open spaces he was as much at home as the animals themselves. He knew how to take care of himself in the woods.

Striking in appearance, he was six feet tall, weighed 200 pounds, and was as straight as a balsam tree. His distinctive garb was a red plaid jacket surmounted by a broad brimmed black felt hat with the brim turned up, front and back, in typical lumberjack style.

In 1911 some Rochester men formed a club and built a camp on the outlet of Jocks Lake, just below a beautiful 30-foot waterfall called High Falls. The club engaged Bill to act as caretaker of the property and guide for the members. For more than forty years, even after all the original club members had passed on, this place, known as Rochester Camp or High Falls, was Bill's home in the wilderness.

Occasionally Potter came out of the woods to the frontier after supplies. Here he stayed in a log cabin made by himself on the woods side of the hard road. West Canada Creek was on the opposite side. The cabin was hidden in a clump of spruce trees, but he could hear the steady roar of the creek rushing by the rocks and boulders.

Let it be said that, like many others, Bill was considered to be a game violator on occasion. It is probably true that Bill caught and kept short trout and killed venison out of season, but he lived in the woods the year round and depended on the creatures of the forest for food. Little was thought of this at the time. Many others did the same and were probably justified in doing so.

This native-born Adirondacker was a member of the Atwell Fish and Game Club of North Lake and of the North Star Grange at Ohio (Herkimer County). He suffered a stroke in the summer of 1954 while on his way into the woods. He died a few days later at the age of 74 and was buried in the foothills of the mountains he loved.

BILLY "MOLEY" CROZIER
Lloyd Blankman

Last names are often misspelled on historical documents or mispronounced during recollections, as exemplified by this story.

Someone recalled an old hermit, called "Moley" Cronizer, who had a shanty back in the woods, off on a side road.

Yes, two more memories coincide, there was a Crozier, old Billy Crozier, a hermit who lived in the woods. Maybe you know where Wells is. Take the dirt road off the main road to the west and soon you come to an old house and barn. From there the road is abandoned and soon you see the shack of the old recluse. He was a little, rather short fellow, and kind of peculiar.

A good old friend who can put his image into focus is Josie Bowker. She lives not far from where she grew up. In recalling her girlhood, old Billy Crozier is a vivid memory.

Josie was one of a large family. Sometimes on a summer Saturday afternoon, her father let the children go berrypicking. This was a reward for doing their work all week. They would take their pails, walk down the dirt track, cross the iron bridge and start climbing up a hill.

After the steep climb they came on to the old road that led to the berry patch. A large pasture was full of blackberry bushes. There the berries were thick and large. Filling their pails was fun.

Beside the berry patch lived old Bill Crozier with his horse and his dog. He had a shack, a garden, and a barn (of sorts) for his horse. Josie says, "It was the horse that held the shelter up when he was in there. Old Billy had a fence to keep his horse from roaming afar. The fence had to be crossed to get to the berry patch. The children were allowed to use the gate and always told, "Keep the gate shut." But boys being boys, they would sometimes purposely leave the gate swinging. Old Crozier being a good old gentleman didn't stop permission into the berry patch.

Then Josie remembers old Billy's trips to town for provisions. She says, "he would never be arrested for cruelty to animals; he never harmed his horse." Billy "perched on his old wagon box, the old black horse chose the pace, and his little black dog trotted under the wagon." Thus they headed for home, down Birdsall street and when they came to York Knoll, Old Billy could be heard singing all the way down the road, and the song was about a little dog that walked under the wagon.

One November, years later, people heard the hermit froze to death and wasn't found for days. According to Josie, back then, anyone could freeze in November. November 14, 1900 "Billy" William Crozier became a statistic when Coroner Harris arrived at 3:00 p.m.

The record reads: Name - William J. Crozier

Died: November 11 (probably) found dead. Cause: Exposure

Is this the hermit "Moley" Cronizer or is it "old Billy" Crozier? We may never know. The original caption on this old postcard provided a third spelling of old Billy's last name: "The Late William Cozier, of Norwich. A Veteran of the Civil War and an Eccentric Character."
COURTESY EDWARD BLANKMAN (THE LLOYD BLANKMAN COLLECTION)

Collection 3
The Conklins of Wilmurt, a Pioneering North Woods Family

THERE EXISTS A CONSIDERABLE literature devoted to the financiers and industrialists who sought to escape the teeming, polluted cities to find peace and tranquility in the mountains. The sportsmen came to camp, hunt, and fish, accompanied by their guides.

Missing, however, is a book dealing with an Adirondack pioneer family who settled in the woods and raised their sons and daughters in a woodland setting before "The Gilded Age"—the period after the end of the Civil War that brought intense development and tourism to the Adirondacks, including railroad and steamboat transportation and the growth of fashionable hotels and inns. There, in the largely unmapped, lightly explored wilderness of the Adirondack Mountains, the pioneer husband and wife lived a commonplace yet event-filled life of survival with their family.

Such a story was penned in 1891, by Henry Conklin, while he was care-taker in charge of the Snyder Camp at Jocks Lake. Henry called the story of his life "Through Poverty's Vale, or Sixty Years in the Wilderness of Want."

Conklin and his family lived in a log cabin, became an important part of Wilmurt and raised a large family. Lloyd Blankman came to learn about this pioneering family through interviewing Conklin clan members at their annual Conklin family reunions. Most informative were the older members: Harriet, Ruth, and notably Lyman Conklin, 90 years of age in 1970, the last surviving Conklin nuclear family member who talked with the amateur folklorist about his family's life and Lyman's nephew Roy, Burt Conklin's son. Before leaving, Lyman handed Blankman a favorite photograph of himself and his brother taken in 1898 by local photographer Grotus Reising. Both boys are shown in the picture making maple syrup and sugar. Lyman was 18. His brother Milo was 41.

Lyman disclosed that Milo was a trapper for a few years and then became a lumberman and logger. He was married twice, had six children and died in 1927.

Honey and maple sugar products are the oldest known sweets in the North Woods. Lyman and Milo's sugarbush was located at Wolf Hollow, two miles in the woods, north of the Conklin family homestead. The enterprise was a family rather than a commercial operation. Usually two holes were bored into a maple tree. Spiles made of sumac wood were inserted—one end sharpened to fit the auger hole in the tree. About 100 wooden buckets were hung on trees to catch the sap, usually in March, that dripped through the hollow pith of the stem into the buckets. Filled sap buckets were carried with a shoulder yoke and poured into a big tub for storage until the sap could be boiled down in large iron kettles holding 100 to 150 gallons. The large kettles were suspended on poles over an outdoor fire like a well sweep and could be raised or lowered or swung away from the fire to keep the syrup from boiling over.

Two dippers were used in processing the syrup. One dipper, hanging on the stump in the photograph above and resembling a frying pan, was used to remove the scum of froth that forms on the boiling sap. The other, above it, was used to dip the syrup and pour it into a mold to solidify into cake sugar. The mold was sometimes in the form of a maple leaf.

Many items used in early life in the North Woods may be seen in the picture given to Blankman. Sugar-making was hard work, a 24-hour-per-day operation, but it paid off in the household. The sugar was used in place of cane sugar and on pancakes, which were served at least once almost every day in the year.

As a result of my experiences with old-timers who had spent a lifetime working in the lumber woods, I can imagine many of Lyman's experiences, ordinary for his time—everyday, if you will—that he shared, yet facts Lloyd Blankman would choose not to record. One of the woodcraft skills lost today in this country is one my grandfather and his peers possessed—that of handling an axe and a cross-cut saw. When you think of it, those two hand tools are almost as responsible for settling America as was the iron plow. It was an enormous task to clear the forests of America! Old-timers have said to me that if I want to know what hard work is, I should get down on my knees in the snow and help saw down a large tree with a cross-cut saw. I don't know if Lyman's older brother was long-armed; but if he was I might have joshed with him, teasing if the longer-armed brother ever tried to pull the saw through the log farther than the shorter-armed brother could reach. It was a common joke back then to trade a sarcastic remark like, "I don't mind your riding the saw, if you wouldn't drag your feet."

As Blankman dug deeper into the history of the pioneering families past, the Conklin family's history became an important factor in shaping his weekly "Adirondack Characters" column and lectures about early life in the North Woods. Blankman was intrigued by the rugged life, how people improvised and made day-by-day decisions that affected the welfare of the entire family.

Burt, the eldest of the children, was dominating the scene. Rugged in spirit, full of boyish energy, individualist beyond his age, resourceful in ideas, seemingly everywhere in the remote wilderness out of choice, he more than

Lyman and Milo Conklin (left to right) boiling sap for maple syrup.
COURTESY EDWARD BLANKMAN (THE LLOYD BLANKMAN COLLECTION)

any other dominated the spirit of the family. Born in 1861, Burt was the darling of the forest. Here the whole panorama of life in the wilderness unfolded: the drama of spring log drives, the work of trapping, wood-cutting and ice-cutting; the zest of hunting and fishing when one is dependent on the results for food; the excitement of selling a load of furs he would convert into Christmas presents for his children. I am positive Blankman found amusing sidelights in everyday events—an impromptu ice-fishing venture when a fisherman broke through the ice in the vicinity of a spring—the Sundays when his father's brothers would go hounding for deer—Burt's 40-mile-long traplines near Little Deer Lake—the winter night Burt and his son Roy got turned around and had to spend a long, exposed night under a cold star-studded sky— the time Burt played hide-and-seek with an officer of the state.

As Burt Conklin grew, he eagerly absorbed the techniques of lumbering. When not trapping, he operated a lumber business and maintained camps where he guided sportsmen in remote sections along the West Canada Creek. At a young age he had become an accomplished rider of logs and was patiently teaching Lyman the finer points of the art. With him, Lyman and their brothers were shooting squirrels, rabbits, deer and bear long before children today pick up a rifle. And they joined together in watching out for each other's well-being in the deep-woods country they learned so well.

Blankman's recordings are a true record of the Conklin experiment at pioneering and the accounts are based upon simple but sure sources. First are memories, which have not dimmed with the years. Then is meeting and correspondence with principals in their Adirondack life; correspondence and conversation with sisters, and with brothers and sisters-in-law and siblings. Visits to the Wilmurt and Pardee clearing scenes were made by Lloyd Blankman in company with his son Edward and friends at intervals during the summer and fall until 1970, and then more rarely as Lloyd's health deteriorated. Many who in any manner helped, and others who could do little more than point Lloyd in a direction, contributed to Blankman's quest, so that his writings of the Conklin family and the manner in which they lived are rather complete.

Lloyd's most fruitful writing period was the 1950s and '60s. His stories occasionally press the recurring Conklin theme, or at least intertwine the family with related subjects. I believe in interviews he struck it off well with the usually close-mouthed natives because he compared how and where he grew up to the difficulties they had experienced.

Those who travel the woods and back roads north and south of Route 8 today will not see the Conklins' log cabins, or Burt's family-owned sawmill along the West Canada Creek. There is a cemetery along the highway in the Town of Ohio and a Wilmurt Corners down over the West Canada Creek. No softwood logs are floated down the river. Today's fishermen and paddlers will see the water and might notice where water-driven mills once stood. Fortunately, a number of Grotus Reising's photographs survive to illustrate how they looked long before the mills became inoperative and decayed.

Organizing these stories has been a rewarding experience and it is my hope that readers of this book will gain a simple and refreshing picture of the Conklin's and their life in the Adirondacks.

The Conklin Homestead near Nobleboro. Grotus Reising, photographer.
COURTESY EDWARD BLANKMAN (THE LLOYD BLANKMAN COLLECTION)

Mr. and Mrs. Henry Conklin and much of their extended family
COURTESY EDWARD BLANKMAN (THE LLOYD BLANKMAN COLLECTION)

🌿 HENRY CONKLIN
Lloyd Blankman   .

The following article by Lloyd Blankman was originally called "North Woods Profile." It appeared in *York State Tradition magazine*, Vol. 19, No. 4, Fall 1965. It includes details found in two of Blankman's "Adirondack Characters" columns, "Henry Conklin—Pioneer" and "Early Life in the North Woods."

Henry Conklin spent his boyhood in Blenheim, Schoharie County, and then, about 1845, went with his parents and brothers and sisters by oxen team and bobsled to a frontier post called Wilmurt in the southern Adirondacks.

Here, amidst the struggle for existence in an environment where hunting, trapping, and fishing were the leading occupations, Henry grew to manhood. In 1856 he married a neighborhood sweetheart, Elizabeth Flansburg, and proceeded to raise a family of six boys and three girls. Henry made shingles for the market in Utica, ran a trapline, and hunted big and small game to provide fresh meat for the family.

In 1861 Henry and some of his neighbors enlisted to fight in the War Between the States. About a year later, he was wounded in the Battle of Fair Gap and six months later was discharged from the service.

About this time he purchased 500 acres of land lying east of where the Haskell Inn is now located, gave a plot of land for a school, and built a frame house on the north side of Route 8 just east of a cold spring brook. The house became known as "The Homestead."

Strangely enough, Henry Conklin was more of a farmer than a woodsman. He maintained a large kitchen garden with all kinds of vegetables and a patch of peas. The corn and buckwheat raised were taken to the grist mill and ground into cornmeal and pancake flour.

"Grandpa" Conklin, as he was called, [by siblings interviewed], must have loved flowers, too, because there were wild flowers in his yard, brought in from distant places, for they were not native to the foothills. There were such flowers as cranesbill, wild geraniums, wild phlox, bounding Bets, blue vetches, and down by the brook, spearmint and peppermint.

Henry was a quiet man, known locally for his trade as a shinglemaker. No one ever knew him to quarrel with anyone. The forest was regarded as something to contend with and to furnish something for existence. Grandpa and Grandma never used profanity nor kept any alcoholic beverages in the house, although Grandpa always had his tonic, a bottle of gin and juniper berries, from which he drank an ounce each morning. The doctor prescribed this tonic for Bright's disease.

As Henry grew older, he pieced quilts in winter and often peeled potatoes and other vegetables with his jackknife.

This grand old man with bright blue eyes and a twinkle in them was beloved by all who knew him. He reserved his sly sense of humor until all were seated at the dinner table, believing that laughter was good for the digestion.

In 1915 he died in his home in the rolling hills he loved, where the meadows are always green and the trout always rising.

THE CONKLIN SISTERS - EXCERPT
Lloyd Blankman

The Conklin family of Wilmurt consisted of three girls and six boys. Five of the six boys and one of the three girls were trappers. They were a family of trappers.

Harriet Conklin Youngs was born in 1871 and died in 1947 at the age of 76. She was perhaps the only Adirondack trapper of her sex, smoked a clay pipe, and drank some whiskey at times. She was an attractive girl, married William Youngs, and they were childless. She lived in a cabin way back in the woods.

Lillian Conklin married a man by the name of Evans and they lived in Herkimer until her death in 1902 at the age of 39. Lillian was a good house-wife. They had four children; one daughter, Mrs. Jennie Coakley, now resides in Herkimer.

Ruth Conklin Shepard was born in 1873 and died in 1964 at the age of 91. She married Nat Shepard, one of the early guides and hunters. The Shepards raised a family of six children. She was a Gold Star Mother. The writer met her on several occasions at the annual Conklin family reunion.

❧ MERRY GO ROUND LETTERS
Lloyd Blankman

The Merry Go Round Letters of the Conklin family of 1901 through 1903 was quite an idea. It was a chain letter system. One member of the family started a letter on its way to another. The recipient wrote a letter to another and included the one just received. If each person did his part in the course of a week or two, every member of the family had heard from all the rest of the family. One letter answered for communication with all the family. Unless the chain was broken, it kept going in a circle.

Henry Conklin, Pioneer, to his wife. May 30, 1901. Wilmurt

Dear Wife:

I seat myself this rainy afternoon to write you a letter. I am well today and hope this will find you the same. Thirty-nine years ago today in the morning I sat down in my tent to write you a similar love letter on the battle ground at Fair Oaks just before the battle began. Today they are strewing flowers on the soldiers graves all over the country. My heart goes out today with the boys and friends who are honoring my comrades that have heard the last roll call.

Last Monday I started a letter the other way round and if they all are prompt you will get it by Saturday. You see I can't write so many letters to all and I have got up this plan so we can hear from all once a week. All you will have to do is to write your page and put it in another envelope and forward it.

I suppose you would like to hear how I am getting along. I have lots of work to do, the chickens to feed and hens and calves. Have lost two chickens. It has been so wet. The calves are doing well but your Jersey calf is very delicate and sometimes quite contrary. She makes me climb the fence every time with a pail of milk and I have to put my arm around her neck and pat her on the neck before she will drink. I don't want no more Jerseys.

Well my planting is done and will sow my oats for fodder tomorrow. I have got my fence done on the hill. Have had Frank Van Court to help me this week. I will have a little rest now in a few days and then will go fishing every afternoon a few hours. Have had a few messes of trout. I can't get away to go to Black Creek Lake nor over to Woodhull as I know of now.

Well Gramma is real smart. She has worked up a whole set of sheets and pillow cases for camp. Cass, George and Gramma are alone now as Albert, Anna and Merle are up to Big Brook in a log job with Will Tedlock.

Nat's folks are well and they are clearing land. Henry and Ward stayed with me last night coming around by the bridge. The surveyors are there running out Nat's farm. Burt and Aurey's folks are well. Rock got home all right. Edna and Edith are home now.

Well it seems so very strange and silent to stay here all alone on the old farm after the racket we have had in the years of the past and sometimes when it gets too silent I open the piano and play, *Sweet Home Rest For The Weary*, and *Bear Me Away On Your Snowy Wings*. Well I am glad you like it over there and hope you and Jack and Maggie will have good times and keep well. You need not worry about my being at home for as old Mag said, "I will let you know I am here."

One letter from Lyman, and one from Hattie. All are well. Got yours of the 24 yesterday. Would like to come over and fish but work before pleasure. Send this to Milo and he will send it on. I send my love, my prayers such as they be and best wishes to all on this merry go around page.

I can't write but two letters a week so please excuse me and write soon and think how different it is today, to what it was 39 years ago. I have forgot all the hardships I have went through in trying to do my duty to you all.

As ever your loving husband,
Henry Conklin

☙ MILO D. CONKLIN'S MERRY GO ROUND LETTER TO HIS PARENTS (1901)

Lloyd Blankman

Dear Mother and Father and Sisters and brothers:

I will try the merry-go-round letters and if it don't make me sick, I can write her again. We are all well and hope this will find you the same. I can't write very well because the dog is under the table bumping his head against it. Marian has gone to Camp. We have had a nice week and things are growing very fast here. I have been cultivating corn sand potatoes. Will begin my haying Monday. We have 80 acres of grass to cut and have 25 acres of late corn. I milk 20 cows and get 450 lbs. of milk per day. The cows are most of them blooded stock, the red poled breed and they have no horns. I have got to work on the road tomorrow and don't have much time myself. A dam bull herd is going by now.

I hope you will all be well when this reaches you.
Milo D. Conklin

 FOREST RUNES
Lloyd Blankman

Burt Conklin remembers his first ride: Dad had a yoke of oxen and a lumber wagon with only one board called a reach, from axle to axle. We all sat on the board and went down the road, forded the West Canada Creek at the crossing, as there was no bridge then, and did our shopping at a hamlet called Ohio. Then we returned home before nightfall.

Fishing

Just across the road, below where we lived, was Little Deer Lake. Before the dam was built, this spring fed lake was a spawning ground for trout from the West Canada Creek. Dad used to take us fishing at the spring hole here, and we always got a basket full of trout.

One time my sister's husband, George Pardee, went fishing with Dad to Black Creek Lake and they came home with a tub full of big trout.

Hounding

On Sunday, Dad's brothers would come and bring their deer hounds with them. Dad would take the hounds into the woods, put them on deer tracks and let them drive the deer to the West Canada Creek. Then everybody would sit beside the runways to the creek ready to shoot the animals as they came down the hills. For miles up and down the road people were watching for the deer to come down from the woods.

Our "Dad"

Dad was always a great hunter, trapper and fisherman. He was an instinctive woodsman. One winter he went all alone into the North Woods and got $300 worth of fur before Christmas. We stayed at Grandpa's one whole summer while our mother and father worked at the Wilmurt Lake Club known as Tarnesda. We all had chores to do; we had to feed the calves, go after the cows, carry in the wood and pans of chips, help make the hay by hand and so on. If we got too noisy in the evening, Grandpa would say, "Dang it, guess I'll have to get my strap," and things quieted down in a hurry.

THE FINCH-CONKLIN FEUD

Lloyd Blankman

When Burt Conklin finished paying for his place he secured an option to buy the remainder of the lot unsold which contained Little Deer Lake.

About a year later Finch eyed the lake and tried to buy it but couldn't because of the option. He promised to buy the lot and sell Burt that portion of the lot north of the road for a stated price.

Burt signed over the option to Finch who immediately purchased the lot and built a dam below the lake.

Six months later Burt requested that papers be drawn for the north portion. Mr. Finch replied, "I have found the north portion is worth more than I thought and I have decided to keep it." Thus the Finch-Conklin feud was begun, and it carried on for years.

Never a week went by that countless large trout weren't taken from Little Deer Lake. To counter this loss Finch built a barbed wire fence about eight feet high with wire drawn tight only four inches apart. It extended all around the Lake property south of the road with the gates padlocked.

He also bought the largest dog he could find. In fact he didn't have good luck keeping them so he purchased several. Some of them turned out to be gentle and cowardly and never bothered anyone.

Burt loved to fish at Little Deer Lake. Photograph by Grotus Reising, 1897.
COURTESY EDWARD BLANKMAN (THE LLOYD BLANKMAN COLLECTION)

The Conklins' Hard Road Homestead built in 1887 near Little Deer Lake.
COURTESY EDWARD BLANKMAN (THE LLOYD BLANKMAN COLLECTION)

Later on Finch tried to protect the pond with a shotgun loaded with birdshot. Burt Conklin carried one in his back until he died. Then one time the keeper found the fence cut one morning. Every strand of wire from top to bottom was cut in around forty or fifty places. No one ever learned who did it but Burt owned a long-handled bolt cutter.

Finch owned the acid factory in Northwood and five fish ponds. He once lost a valuable boat from one of the ponds. It was later discovered on the Twin Lake reservoir. Thus the feud ended.

THE LOST BABY
Lloyd Blankman

On the road between Hinckley and Wilmurt about a mile beyond a place called Northwood, there is a little grocery shop on the north side of the road, with a small pond in the back of it. A mile north of this place on a high hill in the woods is a large abandoned farm. Here in this long-deserted clearing the Basfields raised a large family of nine children mostly without the benefit of schooling.

The cows had the run of the forest for their pasture, as there were no fences in those days. A cowbell was fastened by a strap around a cow's neck so the animals could be found in the morning, and at the close of day.

On busy days when the father and boys were at work, Mrs. Basfield often rounded up and brought the cows in from the woods at night. One day she started after the cows with a baby in her arms.

She was somewhat frail and soon tired, as the animals had wandered far in the woods that day. To ease her task she placed the baby on the ground in the hole of a large hollow standing tree. Then she went on and planned to stop for the child when she came back with the cows. However on her return she became confused and could not find the tree where the baby was.

Upon returning home, an alarm was spread, a search party was formed and started at daylight. They combed the woods for two days without success. They never found the baby.

Roy Conklin's mother told him the story of the lost child. She heard the story from her sister-in-law, Stira Cummings, who was a sister of the lost baby. About 1909 Roy remembers seeing the baby's mother who was visiting their home. She was in her nineties at the time, probably born in the 1820's. They built their home in the dense forest. The story is true but almost unbelievable.

Today this area is wild and forested for miles around. No visible signs of the buildings remain here now, although there is a small clearing in the woods where the farm buildings may have stood.

A pair of maple trees in the forest near Wilmurt, one with a shelter tree cave in its trunk. Photograph by Lloyd Blankman
COURTESY EDWARD BLANKMAN (THE LLOYD BLANKMAN COLLECTION)

Roscoe Conklin, bear hunter. Grotus Reising, photographer.
COURTESY EDWARD BLANKMAN (THE LLOYD BLANKMAN COLLECTION)

ROSCOE AND THE BEARS

Lloyd Blankman

The unique Conklin family of Wilmurt consisted of nine children. There were six boys and three girls. Roscoe, better known as "Roc," was the fourth child and the third son in the family.

Roscoe was the storyteller but most of his stories were figments of the imagination. Roc was tall, strong and rugged. He did some trapping, drank more than the others, hunted and fished in and out of season.

He married Katie Withers of North Wilmurt, but they had no children. He was born in 1864 and died in 1950 at the age of 86 near the family homestead.

"Roc's" best known story, on "Bears," was first published in the Utica *Saturday Globe* back at the turn of the century.

Roc was hunting in the woods with a repeater slung over his arm. He had five cartridges in the gun and five more in his pocket. All at once bears started to converge on him from all directions. He dropped two bears at once with two shots between the eyes of each. Then the whole woods seemed to blossom with bears. They came from all directions. Before it was over Roc had ten bears with ten shots and he was out of ammunition.

He ran to camp for more shells but when he got back the bears were gone. Roc concluded if he had had the ammunition he might have had a real mess of bears.

(An award winning account titled "Roc Hated Bears" is included in Howard Thomas' collection of stories, *Folklore from the Adirondack Foothills*.)

JACK CONKLIN'S MOONSHINE
Lloyd Blankman

Adirondack guides "Red" Jack Conklin (sitting) and Ed Robertson.
Photograph by Grotus Reising, about 1898.
COURTESY EDWARD BLANKMAN (THE LLOYD BLANKMAN COLLECTION)

Everybody up around Wilmurt knew "Red" Jack Conklin. He was youthful, strong and rugged. He liked to hunt, fish and trap and was good at all three sports, mostly for pleasure. Both Jack and his brother "Roc" the bear hunter, story teller and trapper liked their whiskey.

When the Volstead Act was passed by Congress, for a time whiskey was hard to get. Soon, however, moonshine became available at a high price. It was then Jack conceived the idea that it would be cheaper to make it than to buy it.

After searching through Utica, Herkimer and other places, he gathered enough materials and instructions to make a small still of sorts. It held only about three gallons of mash but did quite well in providing enough moonshine to drink.

Soon his friends began tapping this supply and buying some from him. He kept his still running most of the time and sold several hundred gallons. Of course, there were other stills, and markets began to shrink.

One day word came through by the grapevine that the revenue men were coming. This called for action. Out to the woods behind a log covered with brush went the still. Down the brook went the mash. The moonshine on hand was too good to be wasted, but there was more than they could drink, so why not bottle it?

Somewhat woozy but able to walk and carry a load, Jack gathered up the bottles, filled and corked them, and in some way carried them back into a swamp formed by springs. Here he pushed all the bottles down into the mire out of sight.

His work and precaution was all in vain, for the revenue officers never appeared. However, he never set up his still again.

After everything quieted down a day or two, Jack decided it was time to have another drink. He went out to the swamp after a bottle, but to his dismay, not one bottle of moonshine could he find. He searched and searched but to no avail.

Many years later, toward the close of his life, Jack was ailing and thought some cowslip greens would make him feel better. So Jack went to the swamp with a large pan and started to pick some marsh marigolds, or cowslips.

After getting his pan partially filled, while reaching for a bunch of greens, he spied a cork sticking out of the water. Reaching down into the water, he found a bottle of his long-lost moonshine. Out of the pan went the greens into their place went bottle after bottle of luscious liquid. For many days thereafter Jack Conklin was a happy man.

"Red" Jack Conklin's camp was a popular gathering place. Red is standing to the far right with his hands in his pockets.
COURTESY EDWARD BLANKMAN (THE LLOYD BLANKMAN COLLECTION)

RAYMOND SPEARS KNEW BURT CONKLIN
Raymond Spears

Raymond S. Spears started his career for New York State as a game enforcement officer in 1949. After many positions in the Conservation Department, he wrote the following letter in reaction to reading "Burt Conklin, the Greatest Trapper," which appeared in *New York Folklore Quarterly.*

Of all the woodsmen from Grant to Haskell's, Burt Conklin was the most "typical!" I knew dozens of the natives—became one, in fact, myself. . . . I followed [many] . . . over winter and summer trails, notebook in hand. . . . [Burt Conklin's] ears [were] alert to every woods sound, his eyes watchful for every sign. He spent his time in the woods. He took a small logging contract on the Webb Preserve. While [he was] on this small job, Orlando Dexter was bushwhacked in Franklin County and a $50,000 reward[3] stimulated the hunt for the killer. One day a man came to Burt's camp, carrying a rifle, looking for a job. He was good. He stayed all winter on the job, but none of the visitors ever saw him. In the spring he retrieved his rifle from the gun grease and blanket wrapping in a hollow tree, and slipped away to Utica and "went west."

"I bet, Ray, that feller knowed the answer to who killed Dexter!" Burt said. "Course, I never thought nothing 'til after he'd gone. Fifty thousand? Whoo-op!"

Burt ran traplines through five or six camps through Black River and West Canada headwaters. On occasion I tramped with him on snowshoes over the line and Loops. I fished from Spruce Lake Mountain to Moose River with him; he knew the runways of individual fisher, certain bucks, mother bears and their cubs, haunts of foxes, marten, where the otter ran.

"Now what's he worried about?" he would say, peering at tracks in the sand of a brook bar or in the snow in a balsam swamp—fox, Pekin, or bear.

"His restless curiosity embraced the whole region of his range. When he set a trap in Twin Lakes Outlet I asked him, "Won't it freeze in, Burt?" "Sure!" he said, "But it'll thaw out early, next spring. Mebby I'll get a bull otter that always comes this way. The winter'll wash out our sign—he's a suspicious old devil!" Thus he set traps in November to catch an otter in

---

[3] Two inaccuracies have come to light since this account was published 1949. Orlando Dexter's name was really Orrando, and there is no evidence of a reward above $5,000 until the 1930s, when it was $10,000. It may have been raised above $5,000 in the months following the killing, but it was certainly never $50,000.

March. He set traps for foxes early and when the fur came prime, he'd bait the traps, dropping the bait along the runways.

When I became fire patrol in the Forest, Fish & Game Commission under the reform administration, I was on the spot for I knew woodsmen from Big Moose to the Fulton County line. I lived in Little Falls, and the word was that a "city man can't catch anybody." The boys forgot I was one of them, but not Burt Conklin. If he violated I didn't know it, though I spent nights in his hidden camps. I followed snowshoe tracks into and out of the woods.

"Been to Mill Creek?" Burt asked me one day. I found a camp there, and bones thrown out. I measured the snowshoe trail to Little Jack's house. A crowd was there. On hooks hung a dozen pairs of snowshoes. I drew my 4-foot ruler and began measuring, consulting my notes, counting meshes. I turned the case over to the game warden who brought the culprits to court, "the two Pennsylvanians" and two Wilmurt boys. In two winters they had swapped 72 deer for liquor and a little money.

It was at this time I came in the spring to Burt's place. Always he had a big team of horses, five or six head of cattle, a hundred chickens, a dog or two. But now the barn was empty; no dogs were around; there were no chickens— just a few hens.

"What happened, Burt?" I asked.

"I'll tell you, Ray!" he laughed. "I brought out better than $700 fur this winter. I sold it, an' turned around to pay the feed bills for those damned chickens, cows and horses!"

"I'd worked all winter to support a lot of livestock! I sold the whole caboodle! Been doing it all my life! Support a team of horses all the year around to get $10 worth of plowin' out of them come spring, and hauling feed for those hens!"

Burt Conklin belonged to the tribe of real woodsmen, his viewpoint from the woods looking out. He refused to be a guide, and seldom worked for logger wages. He disliked the trapping that caught wild pelts before the fur was prime and that kept over into the spring when fades, rubs, and sheds were caught. As he passed his prime and saw the effects of Conservation law, he nodded his approval. But when the lug through loose snow became too much, Burt opened a little store in Wilmurt and lived through his last years there.

Burt knew wildlife. He would stop in his tracks, listening to the music of a grouse drumming, an owl calling by moonlight, and to bandy jeers with a flock of blue jays. A woodsman, he belonged to the kind who were common before the Civil War.

The mountains owed him a living—and paid him many values.

BURT CONKLIN – THE GREATEST TRAPPER
Lloyd Blankman

Burton (Burt) Conklin (1861–1947)

In a moss-covered log cabin, standing about where today the east end of the Flansburg Bridge on Highway 8 crosses the West Canada Creek above its "Broadwaters" sweep, where trout lurked, Burton James Conklin was born on January 22, 1861. Bundled in furs and comforted by the flames of the wide fireplace, the infant rested peacefully in the isolated hut. Six boys and three girls were born to Henry and Elizabeth (Flansburg) Conklin. With their surroundings in the dense Adirondack forest, it was inevitable that five of the sons would become trappers. Among them, Burt became far and away the best; indeed, it would be no exaggeration to claim that he became the greatest in the North Woods since the days of Jock Wright, Nat Foster and Nick Stoner.

Burt's first extensive trapping experience came in 1880, probably in the month of February, when he and an uncle shouldered their equipment and hiked in to Jocks Lake. They stayed in a camp near Herkimer Landing, but after a couple of days the uncle departed, leaving the neophyte to trap and hunt alone. By that time, or at least soon after, Burt loved nothing better than to explore the haunts of wildlife deep in the Adirondack wilderness.

The trapper encounters many hardships, but gains pleasure in even the roughest experiences. After two or three years on the trapline, the spell of its appeal becomes so strong that it is impossible for him to give up the rough, free life. Fortunately, Burt's great strength and agility permitted him to carry more equipment and pelts on his back and to travel farther in the woods than any other man of his age or weight. Whenever he and his son, Roy, were in the woods, together, Burt would supervise setting the traps and take care of all furs, while Roy did the cooking and other camp chores.

Burt's Traplines

The territory, almost centrally located in Herkimer and Hamilton Counties, comprised the principal arena for Burt's actions during the peak of his fur-gathering career, a period which spanned the years from 1906 to 1919. During most of those years, he had for a companion his son, Roy, who had acquired a post-graduate course in trapping techniques from the "chief engineer" himself. The "school term," and best season for collecting pelts in prime condition, covered the months of November through February, and, sometimes if the weather were favorable, extended well into March.

From their head camp at Black Creek Lake, which they reached after nearly a day of hard traveling, burdened by their weighty packs of food and clothing, Burt and Roy busied tending the traps staked out along different lines touching many streams, lakes, and ponds in a wide area embracing one of the richest fur centers in the North Woods.

Burt Conklin at the peak of his trapping career.
COURTESY EDWARD BLANKMAN (THE LLOYD BLANKMAN COLLECTION)

An example of their typical routine indicates the extent of their campaigns in touring the traplines.

On the first day out from Black Creek Lake, Roy devoted himself to inspecting the line leading around and over the mountains east of Big Brook, while his father went to the Twin Lakes region.

The next day they snowshoed to South Lake, remaining overnight in a State camp at the dam. Here Burt had a branch line up to Little Salmon Lake and the foot of Honnedaga Lake which he investigated while Roy struck off westward.

The next morning, they continued on the trail of traps to about a mile from the head of Honnedaga, thence along the lake to the head of North Lake and on up to Canachagala. After a night's stay in another State camp, they followed a route that took them easterly to Horn Lake, and, the following day, they tramped over the branch lines to Jones Lake and the south side of Ice Cave Mountain and Goose Neck Lake.

After a night's slumber in a log and shingle camp at Horn Lake, the two trappers bore north to the Moose River at Natural Hatchery Stream, thence up the Moose River to Indian River and upstream to the foot of the First Stillwater. Here they rested in camp for the night, then traveled on to Indian Lake and to Louie Stillwater on Indian River, up that to Wolf Creek, and then south to Northrup Lake.

Relaxing for the night at Northrup, Burt and Roy then tramped on through the forest to the foot of Buck Pond Stillwater, south to Belden Fly Stream, down that waterway, and then to their camp on Shirttail Creek. At this point they had established a headquarters, and from here two branch lines led away.

Still another trunk line extended over to Metcalf Lake, and thence to the East Branch of the West Canada Creek, where a rude hut was situated. Yet another trapline stretched over to Pine and G Lakes, easterly to T Lake and down its outlet to the high and famous T Lake Falls, then back to camp. Circling in another direction, they would return by way of Big Rock Lake and a chain of ponds to the Shirttail Creek camp.

An additional line went over the mountains and valleys to Bear and Little Rock Lakes, down Metcalf Stream and the West Canada to the head of the Seabury Stillwater, then up and along the south slope of Ragwheel Mountain westerly to Big Brook and Black Creek Lake.

This was a vast zone of operations, in the wildest section of the Adirondacks, and it provided an enormous quantity of superb furs. The two men did not reckon up the number of miles they plodded over the winding routes, but they knew they had to have approximately 300 traps to supply the lines. After one complete circuit, the partners came back home lugging 40 mink, 10 raccoons, 25 pine marten, 4 otter, 30 foxes, 25 fisher, and 150 weasels—a bundle of pelts that netted them close to $700!

Traps

Traps were seldom brought out of the woods but were cached in some place, usually near a camping spot, where they would keep dry and not rust. There were too many of them and they weighed too much to try to carry them, along with rations, clothing, and other gear, on the long trail from Black Creek Lake to Wilmurt.

In his early life, Roy described his father's preferences for and techniques with traps:

> My father used any kind of trap he could get, carefully setting the weaker ones to catch the weaker animals. Many animals were taken in deadfalls.
>
> When he and I were trapping together, we used mostly a No. 2 Oneida Community jump trap. As near as I can remember, this had a jaw spread when set of about four and one-half inches by about six inches, with the springs on the bottom of the trap. This would catch and hold foxes, fisher, coons, mink, weasels, marten, and otter.
>
> The most durable and lasting trap of all was the Newhouse. I remember once while setting a line of fisher traps we happened to notice a large spruce tree that showed marks of having had pieces of slabs cut from it, such as some old time trappers used to build cubby houses with.
>
> We started pawing with our hands in the leaves and dirt in the most likely place that seemed to us such a trap might have been set. We found part of a trap chain, pulled on it, and out came a No. 1 Newhouse single-spring trap, black with age but not rusty. We tried the spring and it seemed to be as strong as when new.

Burt Conklin's son Roy Conklin,
80 years old in 1969.
COURTESY EDWARD BLANKMAN
(THE LLOYD BLANKMAN
COLLECTION)

I have an idea that the trap may have been preserved by boiling it in hemlock boughs and then dipping it in hot deer tallow. Sometimes we did this to some of our traps, but usually we merely hid them somewhere where they would stay dry until another season. We always took up our traps on the last trip around the line.

Well Sweep and Cubby House

When preparing a trap for fisher, Burt would choose a large spruce on a rise of ground so that during hard snowfalls the boughs would cause the snow to drop away from the trunk and then work downward to the lower level. As a result, snow around the trap would be less deep. In addition, he always tried to find a tree with a hole or hollow space between two large roots, which would become part of the "cubby house" and which also helped to protect the bait from extreme cold. When less cold, the bait gave off its maximum odor to attract hungry or curious animals. Sometimes, a long, slim, hardwood stick was jammed into the ground at a 60-degree angle, enabling the heavy end of the well sweep to slide down and swing the trap end out free from the tree against which the cubby house was built.

If the trap chain became entangled and prevented the sweep from working, or if the fisher could reach the tree, it would climb and pull the sweep up until the pole cleared the crotched stake. When that happened, the fisher stood on the ground, and the vicious frenzied demon became a whirlwind of devastating behavior. Everything . . . but *everything*! . . . within reach of its razor-sharp claws and teeth would be shredded – the cubby house leveled as though it had never been built, the well sweep chewed off, and whatever the trap chain was fastened to would be splintered. The resulting damage from an angered or fear-filled fisher is incredible. Eventually it will either escape by leaving part of its foot in the trap, or else become exhausted and die from the strain of the struggle.

If a fisher escaped it was difficult to locate it, particularly if new snow covered its tracks. To find the trail, the loose snow was scraped away where the fisher might have been detained by small brush, fallen tree tops or anything else that might impede its progress. Wherever the fiendish animal had been there was certain to be plenty of wood splinters or bits of chewed brush beneath the snow.

If these efforts were unsuccessful, Burt and Roy continued their search for the fisher by following fox tracks, for a fox can scent a dead animal for a considerable distance. When approaching within a foot or two of the quarry, the fox would smell the human odor on the trap, stop, then retreat. There the trapper would dig away the loose snow and come upon the fisher with the chain caught on something too tough for the animal to destroy.

The cubby house, erected to attract the cunning fisher, was usually three feet high, six inches wide, and two and one-half or three feet deep from the front opening to the rear end of the space between the tree roots. It was constructed by placing lengths of strong wood crossways between two crotched stakes driven into the ground to support the front bar. Lengthwise to the cubby house, hemlock bark was laid over these short poles, or, if bark was unavailable, dead sticks were used to form a sort of rafter for the roof made of spruce boughs. Generally, four or five chunks of wood were set on end to form each wall of the cubby house, leaving an opening six inches wide from front to rear. About a foot inside the house, a little mound of snow and brush was made, on which was seated the trap. The trap and its bait were screened by balsam or hemlock tips, or dirt and leaves, with a hedgehog hide and quills on top for prying eyes to discover. The mound would keep the trap free of snow if any should sift into the cubby house during a heavy storm. A short, weak twig was set upright under the trap pan to prevent squirrels from springing the jaws.

The main pole of the well sweep was cut from a spruce about three inches in diameter. Boughs from this tree formed the cubby house sheathing. The top portion of the tree had all its limbs chopped off close to the stem, except one which was left an inch long on the thicker end.

The stem was driven into the ground, leaving the big end a foot or more high. The ring on the trap chain was fastened to the light end of the pole, usually with a fence staple. The chain held the narrow end down by means of a link that was slipped over the stub of the limb on top of the stake. When a fisher was caught and tried to tear loose, it pulled the chain off the stub so that the heavy end of the pole would lower and force the wriggling victim up into the air, where it was helpless to escape.

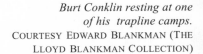

Burt Conklin resting at one of his trapline camps.
COURTESY EDWARD BLANKMAN (THE LLOYD BLANKMAN COLLECTION)

Shelter Rock

Burt's intimate knowledge of the forest and of traits of its furred and feathered inhabitants and his ability to outwit them made him one of the most illustrious outdoorsmen of the North Country. His knowledge of the lore of the wild plus an innate knack of turning it into profitable account won for him the title of "the greatest trapper" in the region.

Throughout the woods are numerous natural shelters provided by over-hanging rocks and ledges where hunters and trappers like Jock Wright, Nat Foster, and Burt Conklin have found refuge over the years. One of them was about six miles in the forest from the route leading to the road from Wilmurt to Hinckley, at the foot of a stillwater on the Middle Branch of Little Black Creek. There a boulder furnished cover for many men caught too far back in the forest after dark to make their way safely out to the settlements. The boulder rests in the ground like a huge, blunt wedge on top of a knoll at the end of Tamarack Marsh. From the ground it slopes outward and upward on two sides, providing dry shelter ten to fifteen feet wide. It was put to good use by early hunters, fishermen, trappers and often by the Indians. Burt Conklin was a shrewd trapper who rarely came out on the slim end of a deal, especially when it concerned furs, for he knew the market and the qualities of prime pelts as did few other men, and he could hang up more skins in one season than anyone else in the Adirondacks.

In truth, due to this remarkable but justly earned reputation, there were ripples of jealousy among the natives of the West Canada Creek Valley over the quantity of pelts which the canny trapper was able to separate from their four-footed owners. And, occasionally, this jealousy fomented suspicion of his methods.

The Tamarack Marsh near Little Black Creek.
COURTESY EDWARD BLANKMAN (THE LLOYD BLANKMAN COLLECTION)

Evidence of such mistrust crystallized when, through the subtle wireless of the wilderness, Burt got wind that someone had entered a complaint to the authorities in Albany that "everything about his trapping is not legal."

In the winter of 1918, Burt and his brother, Jack, were running lines on private and state-owned lands well up into Herkimer County. Of course, when they heard that the game protectors had been "sicked" on their trail, the pair had no idea where the officers were going to strike, but they guessed it would be at Honnedaga Lake. And they were right!

Their trapline crossed about the middle of the lake, and they could not pass over the frozen surface without leaving snowshoe tracks. On this particular trip they carefully checked every trap beyond the lake for anything that the state men could pounce upon. After marching over Honnedaga the first evening, they continued on to the camp at Snyder Lake; the next day they stayed in a cabin on a paper company's tract at the head of Louie Stillwater.

At this place, Burt and Jack had a long circle trapline that brought them back to the same camp at night. Then the next day they would follow this line again for about a mile. Burt planned intentionally to travel in the same direction the first day that they would on the one following.

When wearing snowshoes, ten men could pass through an area on the webbed feet, and no one could tell how many had gone by, from the single track they had made. To take advantage of that condition, Burt and Jack set out on the circle trapline toward the point where their main line branched off.

Burt knew of a well-worn deer runway near this junction. When he came to it, he removed the snowshoe from his forward foot and laid a wooden paddle about five feet long on the hard-packed runway. He stepped on it, unfastened the other snowshoe and placed that foot on the paddle without breaking any of the markings of the snowshoe trail.

By changing in this fashion, both men succeeded in getting several feet away from their snowshoe tracks without leaving any marks. They followed the deer runway in their hunting packs for three or four hundred feet beyond the snowshoe trail. At that spot they put on their rawhide snowshoes and circled until they returned to the main line without coming near where their tracks could be seen.

That night the game protectors arrived at the camp the two men had left in the morning. The next day they traced every snowshoe track leading away from the cabin, but all circled back to the spot where they had departed. The state men were stymied and returned, disgruntled, to the lodge at Honnedaga Lake.

Burt and Jack lingered at a friend's hunting camp to await developments, but nothing happened. They heard that the protectors had remarked, "Those trappers must have wings. We'll never try to chase them again."

Indeed, there was no need to, for they conformed to the outdoorsman's code in vogue those days, and the only unfavorable element was the distaste in the minds of those who envied Burt's competence on the trapline. However, knowing they were under surveillance, they had an intriguing challenge to play the cunning games of "fox and geese" with their stalkers.

The Lost Cabin

In the fall of 1909, Roy was teaching in grade school, and when the term ended at Christmas time, he teamed up with his father to run the traplines. Burt figured that together the two of them could cover a much broader range than he could alone, so they trudged into the remote tracts toting five dozen fisher traps.

One morning the partners began stringing a new line of traps. They turned northward from Jones Lake and tramped to the Cobblestone, then down the Indian River to Horn Lake outlet. The area was unfamiliar to them, and they moved along with considerable interest, thinking about the prospects for fur there. They remembered the general layout of lakes and streams from examining topographic maps on previous occasions, so had some idea of the region.

They arrived at Horn Lake around three o'clock. The tired trappers began searching for a camp but did not find any. On the south side, they came upon a well-blazed trail and decided this would take them to Snyder Lake, four miles farther south. The men hid one of their Adirondack type, split-willow packbaskets containing the duffel they would not need immediately and set out for Snyder Lake where they had been told a good hunting camp was located.

The woodsmen traveled as fast as possible, but darkness was closing in just as they reached the lake's shore. They scouted everywhere in the dim light but could discover no camp. Another blazed trail led from the lake at the point where the one they had followed touched the shore, and this pathway had fooled them.

A hurried survey revealed a rock with a small mound a few feet away; nearby was a dry spruce stub about 15 inches thick and 12 feet high. Tipping the stub toward the rock, Burt started a campfire at the base of the boulder, then chopped a small spruce for boughs. Roy collected as much dry wood as he could find to last for a long, exposed night under a star-studded sky.

Using their tailed snowshoes to scoop some of the four-foot deep snow from between the low mound and the fire, they heaped it on the sides. They next erected a crotched stick on each flank with a pole across the top, and placed thin limbs along this bar back to the mound. They laid spruce boughs over the limbs and on the sides and piled a few more on the snow inside the lean-to to make a seat before the fire.

The half-frozen trappers, who had had nothing to eat since breakfast, now ate chunks of heated jerked venison and biscuits, moistened with steaming black tea, while they huddled in the open-face camp, surrounded by the quiet gloom of the forest.

With the long-handled, small-bladed trapping axes, the men cut wood from the spruce stub as well as dry, soft maple poles to keep the fire burning and to maintain some warmth in the sub-zero weather. They had failed to bring a blanket as they were confident of finding a cabin by the lake, in which there would be bedding and food as was the custom in all trapper's cabins. Burt always left his own camps with an adequate pile of dry wood, blankets, and food, so he would have something for himself on a return trip or unplanned visit, as well as for some other trapper who might be caught in the woods without adequate provisions. Such was the unwritten code of the wilderness: the wayfarer was welcome to enter a cabin and make use of its conveniences, but he was expected to take proper care of the equipment, replenish the wood supply, leave the hut clean when he departed, and "pass the good deed on" to someone else in need whenever the chance arose.

Twice that night, our friends had to take up the seat boughs and dig out the snow in order to be even with the campfire as it melted the snow below and settled. The mound behind them proved to be another rock, which sloped forward and, as they dug, crowded them towards the fire.

Towards early morning, the two men drifted off into slumber. They awoke to find the life-sustaining fire nearly extinguished. Stiff from their cramped positions, they made a strenuous effort to move about to stimulate blood circulation so they could chop more wood and restore the flames.

When daylight at last broke, they struggled to their feet. Burt shouldered the packbasket, and the weary pair started along the trail that had baffled them the evening before. They soon learned it led only to a pond on the shoulder of a small mountain.

As the men lacked food, they resolved to retrace their steps to Snyder Lake and to retrieve the hidden packbasket with its provisions at Horn Lake. But as they turned to leave the pond, they saw their breakfast standing 300 feet away on a knoll . . . a deer staring at them quizzically. They killed it, dressed out the hind quarters, lugged the meat back to the camping place and feasted on roast venison.

Burt's Cabin

After that adventure, Burt and Roy snowshoed to Horn Lake to locate a suitable site on which to build a hut for future trapping expeditions. For that purpose, they required a spot with spring water nearby, an ample wood supply, and a clump of spruce trees to furnish logs for the sides and ends of the cabin. Preferably, this site should be away from the beaten paths where there would be slight chance of being molested by intruders.

One of Burt Conklin's "green timber" camps along his trapline.
COURTESY EDWARD BLANKMAN (THE LLOYD BLANKMAN COLLECTION)

After a thorough survey, they selected a spot southeast of Horn Lake, a short distance up an inlet stream. It seemed to be away from all the known trails. So the next day, loaded with all the skins, an axe, cross cut saw and other equipment they returned to start construction.

They dug trenches in the snow down to the earth for the foundation of the camp. Then they cut spruce trees and trimmed out the logs. They burned the discarded brush in a fire in the center of the plot, and by evening most of the snow within the enclosure had melted.

In the morning they brought the stove and roofing to Horn Lake. Working steadily, they built all but the roof during the day, and slept there at night. The following day the camp was completed except for some refinements.

Measuring about 10 by 13 feet inside, the cabin was sufficiently roomy to accommodate a couple of trappers, hunters, or fishermen. The surplus roofing spread over the rafters only far enough to shield the bunk, so brush temporarily had to be laid on the remainder of the roof. When they returned to put on the finishing touches, they brought in a frow, drawing knife, and shingle nails. In one day Burt rived and shaved enough shingles to cover the roof, while Roy nailed them on. The proficient wood-chopper turned out shingles so rapidly that his son had to hustle to keep up with them.

From that setting they caught many pine marten and fisher.

Hide and Seek

Natives along West Canada Creek killed deer to eat whenever they hungered for meat—winter or summer. Laws even then regulated deer shooting, but few people paid much attention to them except to be careful about not being caught with the goods. They were not wasteful hunters and, except for the obnoxious "market hunters," did not slay more than they could consume. At the time, when a person killed a deer, he generously passed out hunks of meat to relatives or friends. The size of the fit chunks depended on the number in the family.

One day, it is told, an "officer of the State," known as a game warden, sought out Burt. He asked him a series of pointed questions and then produced a search warrant to look for illegal meat. He did not succeed in accusing the hunter of any violations. But Burt knew such a visit was the result of someone's hushed complaint. He probed his memory to recall persons who might have knowledge of his doings, and to try to identify the squealer. But he never found out.

At that time in the Adirondacks, gathering hemlock bark for tanning was a booming industry and was particularly extensive throughout the upper West Canada Valley and into the Piseco Lake district. One wintry day Burt was helping a neighbor load bark several miles back in the forest beside a sleigh road used by bark-peelers. The snow was quite deep, and, on the way out, but still far from the clearing, the keen-eyed mountain man saw where a deer had recently crossed the road. It was too late then to pursue it in the lowering darkness. Early the next morning, however, Burt took his rifle and snowshoes and went after the whitetail, arriving at the place where the tracks traversed the forest road about daybreak. It was not until the afternoon that he located and shot the deer.

Deftly he dressed the carcass and cut it into two parts—the neck and fore quarters in one part, the hind quarters in the other. After deciding which way he would proceed, he seized the front section and tossed it into the snow in the direction he was going. Then, heaving the hind quarters over his shoulders, he started away, stepping about in order to scuff a little snow over the front quarters, at the same time leaving behind a trail that looked like a natural snowshoe track—with no part of the venison visible above the snow.

Burt had some fisher traps set in the region so he decided to inspect them on his way home. He had dogged the deer in such a zigzag course that he was finally six miles back into the woods at the spot where he had dressed the buck. When he arrived at the trap, he pitched the hind quarters behind a ridge of snow piled up on a large fallen hemlock trunk. He re-set his trap and, when nearly finished, his trained ears caught the crunchy sound of snowshoes. Glancing up, Burt saw his uncle, who lived near him, trudging along the trail.

"Where's your deer?" the uncle asked.

"I don't see any, do you?" replied Burt.

"No, I don't," the other answered.

His uncle told how he had followed his tracks all the way from the sleigh road and knew he had killed a deer but could not figure out what had become of it. The cagey hunter determined not to admit slaying the deer and not to give his uncle any of the meat. They chatted for some time until Burt broke away with an excuse and headed homeward. The baffled relative trailed along for about a mile, then turned off to go toward his own home by way of the sleigh road after Burt had told him he had a few more traps to examine. When out of sight, Conklin circled to see what his uncle would do, and found he had gone on toward the road. Retracing his tracks, Burt retrieved the hind quarters from where he had tossed them behind the snow on the log. With a cunning smirk on his face, he snowshoed back home.

Adhering to the code of the trapper, Burt never took fur from another man's set, but he lost many pelts to less honest woodsmen. One time when he and Roy were walking together in the woods, the dog with them dashed to the edge of a stream and began barking furiously. A big raccoon was in a trap, and its foot was almost severed by the biting jaws. When the two hikers reached the coon, it broke loose. Burt grabbed a stick and knocked it senseless before the animal could hobble away. He hung it on an overhead limb and left the trap with the foot still clenched in it. The trapper never came back, and the coon hung on the limb until it rotted away.

The "Dead" Bear

One time on another deer hunt, Burt shot a big black bear. The animal appeared to be dead when he approached, but by now Burt had learned not to trust in appearances. With his rifle in one hand, he grasped a front leg and pulled the bear over on its back. Bruin was not breathing, and gave every evidence of being lifeless. Burt was confident the animal was dead and that he could safely begin to dress it out to relieve body heat, remove the innards and blood, thus saving the edible flesh. Burt laid his firearm on the ground within reach and with his skinning knife began to cut around the rectum so that part of the beast could be drawn inward and removed through the opening in the belly along with the main portion of the entrails. Spreading the bear's hind legs, Burt got down on his knees to begin cutting. As he inserted the knife blade into the thick hide, the bear came to life.

Terrified, Burt sat back on his haunches. The bear started drawing itself together, like rolling into a ball. It opened its mouth and let out a hideous roar. Then the brute lunged and grabbed with its mouth at the half-petrified man. How Burt ever avoided the ferocious animal is a mystery, but the threat of the bear's fierceness must have unlocked his reflexes immediately and enabled him to escape from the gnashing teeth.

Barely conscious of what he was doing, Burt leaped to his feet in an instant, clutched the rifle, and fired without putting it to his shoulder. A moment later the bear was really dead from the bullet crashing into its head. Several minutes passed before the solitary hunter, whose knees were too weak to let him stand, could recover and stop shaking.

Shaving Shingles

The trapping season covered four months only—November, December, February and March, but not January when there was too much snow. In the other months, Burt became a contract lumberman, never a lumberjack or a guide. He bought and paid for considerable property, mostly farms. He built a barn, piped in spring water and among many chores made shingles. Shingle-making was one of the occupations Burt followed, whenever there was spare time, to bring in extra income. He had an extra log room on the north end of his house for shingle manufacturing. Shingles for his trapline cabins were made there, and he turned out a great quantity to sell.

Spruce trees provided the raw materials, but select trees had to be 18 inches or larger in diameter, straight-grained and with loose, shelly bark. On an average, only about one tree in 100 would produce first-quality shingles. Only that part of the trunk up to the first limbs was used for shingles.

Coonradt Reising of Wilmurt making spruce shingles
COURTESY EDWARD BLANKMAN (THE LLOYD BLANKMAN COLLECTION)

Much care had to be taken with a crosscut saw to make certain the shingle blocks were square on the ends, or they would not be square on the butts. Shingles were never split with an axe but were split, or riven, with a froe (or frow) and with a wooden mall (or maul), from the top down, in the same direction as in the original growth of the tree. They were then shaved or smoothed with a drawing-knife. Usually six strokes of the knife were required. The shaving was done on a shaving-horse, a horizontal vise-like arrangement operated by the feet.

When packing shingles, a form was used to keep each batch uniform both in size and in the number of layers. Two pieces of flattened spruce about three inches in diameter, before dressing, held together each bunch of shingles. The spruce pieces, at top and bottom, were secured by pins, resembling ladder rungs, extending through holes and wedged with a wooden cleat at each end. Enough shingles were packed in a bundle to cover 50 square feet of roof, and each bundle sold for one dollar. Four bundles was considered to be a big day's work . . . and good pay!

Trout Fishing

Native brook trout fishing was excellent at points along the rocky course of West Canada Creek, and one of those was right in the Conklins' front yard, where a cabin Burt built across the highway from his frame house stood on the bank above Broadwaters. Here, in early morning or late afternoon, it was not difficult to get a fine string of speckled trout almost any day of the season. Some of them weighed up to around three pounds.

Then there were always trout in Black Creek Lake. Even though the fishing was not spectacular, limit catches could be creeled repeatedly. Seldom did the trout caught there weigh less than a pound, and usually they were much more. There was good fishing at the Crosby Vly below the lake and also in Big Brook.

Far-away waters held appeal as well, and one summer Burt and Roy got a chance to test their luck in Northrup Lake. They were on a jaunt up into the mountains to examine fur-producing grounds not tried before, and part of their paraphernalia consisted of two fishing rods brought to help augment and vary their forest fare. After prying into every part of this tract for more than a week, one evening, as they ate supper on the south shore of Indian Lake, below the Indian clearing, they wondered if the food supply would last until they reached home. Fishing had been poor, and there would have been no trouble in devouring many more trout than they had landed. An idea occurred to Roy.

"Why go home empty-handed?" he spoke to his father. "Why not take out a mess of trout to sell, so we can have something for our effort?"

"That would be good, but where can we get them?"

"How about Northrup Lake?" Roy queried. "I've heard you say that a fellow could always catch plenty there."

"Yes, we could," agreed Burt, "but it's an awful long ways there, and we don't have enough food."

"Let's look in some camps for abandoned food," proposed Roy. "If we can find a little, I'm game to try the lake if you are."

"OK, let's do it."

As the sun streamed over Indian Lake the next morning, the two explorers packed their duffel and started hiking. The first camp they came to was an open-face log lean-to. It yielded a few slices of dry bread, about two cups of corn meal, half a pound of ham, half a pound of sugar, and some coffee. Pushing on for five miles more, another shelter loomed in their path, and from it they added two pounds of flour and some miscellaneous food stuffs. They reaped nothing more as they trudged up and down grueling grades until night.

As soon as light permitted, they moved on the following morning, and, about ten o'clock, they were gazing upon the placid surface of Northrup Lake, one of the best natural locations for speckled trout in the North Country.

Roy repaired an old bark lean-to and rustled up something to eat. Meanwhile, Burt searched the shore line for a raft, finally stumbling upon one that was rickety and water-soaked, but which proved to be seaworthy enough to keep them afloat.

The shore was marshy, with buck brush growing to the water's edge. At this point the muddy bottom was about a foot deep.

Burt cut two light, dry spruce poles 12 feet long. He used them for shoving out the raft, and for anchoring it by jabbing the poles down between the middle logs into the mud. The anglers cautiously boarded the unsteady raft, set two chunks of rotten wood on the flooring for seats, and placed one packbasket in the center to hold any fish they might catch.

After poling out about fifty feet from shore, the men began fishing. But they had not a nibble for almost an hour; they tried several other spots with similar results.

"There's a gravel bar somewhere along the shore about this far out in the lake," Burt finally remarked. "If we can find it, I think we may catch some fish."

Up came the anchor poles, and the raft was pushed gently along. Testing the bottom as they moved, Burt exclaimed, "Here it is! My pole hit gravel!"

They urged the raft slowly toward shore where the mud was deep enough to hold the poles and commenced to try the new grounds. Not a single trout touched the bait, but the men sat quietly, dangling their lines close to the bottom. Half an hour later, Burt felt a bite and drew up a seven-inch scrapper. After dropping it into the basket, he tossed the bait back in the same place. The hook had barely lowered two feet before the line began cutting through the water, and soon another spotted fish, a bit larger than the first, was flopping on the raft. About then, Roy snagged into one. The fish had suddenly started to feed, and from then on there was plenty of action and excitement.

Trout after trout was hauled out, and the fishermen paid no heed to time or to how many "catchees" were going into the packbasket. Not, that is, until Burt threw a plump ten-incher on the pile and, as he turned to cast his hook in again, there sounded a thump on the raft and a splash in the water. The basket was shaking with wriggling fish, and they were spilling over. Burt glanced around and hollered, "Whoa! Don't catch any more. We have too many now."

Roy looked at his watch. It was 4:30. Seldom had they struck such brisk fishing or landed so many fine trout in an afternoon. Northrup Lake had treated them royally.

Burt dressed the entire lot while Roy prepared supper. After eating all they could they packed the rest in damp moss and placed them beside a cold spring brook.

They relished for breakfast the next morning a few more delicious, pink-fleshed, dark-sided mountain speckled trout. The remainder were evenly distributed in the two packbaskets, and the satisfied anglers headed for home at daybreak. Burt knew this part of the woods well and did not have to consult his compass at any time during the day to keep on the right course. However, like all other wise trappers, Burt never entered the forest without a compass, together with plenty of matches in some kind of container in which they would stay dry in any weather.

Burt and Roy finally reached home at midnight after a steady, tiresome hike. Even so, after resting a while, Burt hitched up the horse and buggy and drove off with the fish. At nine in the morning, he was back . . . with $40!

Burt Conklin's Rustic Inn near Speculator, 1934.
COURTESY EDWARD BLANKMAN (THE LLOYD BLANKMAN COLLECTION)

The End of the Trapline

A turning point for Burt came on May 11, 1911, when he moved from his house by the West Canada Creek to a farm near Hamden in Delaware County. For eight years, he planted crops and raised cattle for the market from spring to fall, but every winter season found him treading the old trapline trails of the Adirondacks, in a trade he was unable to give up. But once more Burt pulled stakes and, in 1919, moved to a farm in Terry Clove, near where Roy and his family were farming. At one time, Burt operated a sawmill on this Terry Clove farm, doing sawing for neighbors as well as for himself. Farming, though, at last, told on the constitution of this son of the forest, and in 1928, Burt sold the place and bunked in with Roy until he finished a log cabin on his son's farm at Broadwaters, on the north bank of West Canada Creek. There he was content with catching a few more pelts in the vicinity of his camp at Black Creek Lake. Finally, the culmination of many years bore down on this great woodsman, and he was compelled to abandon the rigors of the trapline. He was satisfied to tarry for longer spells by the fireside or to fish for sassy brook trout in front of his cabin.

Burt Conklin wrote on the back of a photograph of the Rustic Inn "I am well and doing business at the same old rate." He was 73 in this picture dated 1934.
COURTESY EDWARD BLANKMAN (THE LLOYD BLANKMAN COLLECTION)

The last season that Burt set out his traps was in the fall of 1935, when he strung a few at Black Creek Lake in company with his grandson, Lloyd. In the same year, the old trapper purchased the Rustic Inn, near Morehouseville, for two of his grandsons to operate as a road stand. That project did not appear very promising, so they gave it up after a year or two. Believing the inn would flourish under his own supervision, Burt decided to take over the management himself. He made a success of the venture until he passed away there on January 31, 1947, having traveled the Trails of Life for eighty-six years.

In the small McIntosh cemetery at Ohio, New York, in the shade of the mountains he loved, Burt Conklin, greatest of all trappers of the Golden Age, laid down his packbasket to rest awhile from the toil of the trail.

Eldridge (Elgie) Spears who, with his brother Randolph and father, was one of the famous writers on outdoor subjects at the turn of the century, knew Burt for 60 years and traveled in the woods with him. Elgie prepared the obituary, published in the Utica *Observer-Dispatch*, which summed up, briefly but accurately, Burt's career:

> Burt Conklin, man of the woods, who died last week at his home in Morehouseville, used to do a little farming in the summer time at his home near Little Deer Lake, then when the frost swept the leaves from the trees, he headed deep into the woods to set his traps.
>
> Conklin was a wiry little man who carried a heavy pack on his back, walked miles and didn't get tired. He had overnight camps along his traplines. His lines were far flung across Black Creek to Twin Lakes and Hobart V. Roberts' South Lake country thence over to what Burt preferred to call Jack's Lake (Honnedaga) and into the Indian River Region, then far to the east to Spruce Lake. He had a cabin on Shirttail Creek near another Indian River and he reached down to Metcalf Lake, looping all the way with side lines to cover a vast section of the Southwestern Adirondacks.
>
> Conklin knew the habits of marten, fisher and other rare and most valuable furs, not to mention the mink, fox and lesser animals. It is reported he had as many as 500 traps baited and set at one time. In good snowshoeing, it required a week to go the rounds, removing the catches, resetting the traps and digging out those that may have been snowed under. At the end of the day in his 'Cubby Camp' he skinned the animals, and in the morning was ready to start all over again at the break of day.
>
> It was a hard life, but an interesting one to Burt Conklin, who could read the tracks and the signs of the woods. It was a profitable winter, too, when furs were plentiful and prices were right.

🌿 BURT CONKLIN'S CHRISTMAS PRESENT
Lloyd Blankman

Burt Conklin, the trapper, had a poor year in 1906. It was the month of November. Christmas was coming on, money was scarce, and it was a family of five. So, Burt got his traps and supplies ready, said goodbye to his wife and three children, and disappeared into the forest.

In three hours, after an uphill march, he reached his Green Timber Camp near the Tamarack Marsh. From here his main and loop traplines crossed and crisscrossed in all directions reaching even as far as the Moose River. Now he proceeded to set his traps and collect his fur pelt harvest.

He didn't see his family again until just before Christmas. With his son, Roy, he took his furs to the Herkimer market and collected $125, a considerable sum for those days. His catch consisted of mink, otter, fisher, martin, 'coon, and foxes.

The Conklins had a nice Christmas.

Burt Conklin (right) provided his family with a Merry Christmas back in 1914. Ray Milks (left) was one of Burt's trapping partners.
COURTESY EDWARD BLANKMAN (THE LLOYD BLANKMAN COLLECTION)

✿ HUNTING - OR NO HORNS
Lloyd Blankman

Hunters, like poets, are born, not made. Wear clothes for hunting, a neutral color, like a decayed stump. In hunting silence is golden. Go quietly, slowly and silently. Remember that the woodfolk can hear, see, and smell, with keener faculties than your own. While you lumber through the woods you will never know how many animals leave your path as they glide away unseen.

But there is an art, little known and practiced, that succeeds in outflanking most wild animals. This is the art of sitting on a log. Few can do this. It includes a deal of patience with cold feet and chattering teeth. But used faithfully and patiently it is quite as successful as chasing deer all day on tracking snow. It can be used when the leaves are dry; many hunters have their best luck by waiting patiently hour after hour on runways. The large droves of deer in the Adirondacks are a thing of the past.

Roy Conklin, son of a great woodsman and trapper, and one also himself, didn't hunt in 1959, and so didn't get a deer. He might not have gotten one anyway. Success in hunting is mostly luck anyhow. It is necessary to be in the right place at the right time, together with other complicating factors.

1957 Hunt

In 1957, the day before doe day, he was hunting on a mountain that had been completely cleared of trees years before for acid wood. The new forest was composed of tall trees with limbs on the top. There was practically no underbrush. The view was about as unobstructed as it would have been had the trees been telephone poles. The mountainside stood at about 45 per cent. There were depressions and elevations.

Approaching the crest of an elevation he looked into a depression below. There was about six inches of loose snow on the ground and so any object uncovered by snow was very conspicuous. Directly below him at about 100 yards lay a large doe with ears extended and head up on a long neck looking directly away from him. No horns between the ears! Roy stood still and looked around over to the left—probably fifty feet away lay a smaller deer with head up, ears extended, looking away also. No horns. He scanned the ground all around close and over to the right was another deer, larger than either of the others. Its head was behind some trees out of sight. He looked at his watch. It was eleven thirty. About thirty feet in front of him was a log about a foot through crosswise. He got down on his hands and knees, crawled up to the log and sat there watching. The noon whistle in town blew, later the whistle at one p.m.

Conklin men pose with other family members after a successful hunt.
Grotus Reising, photographer.
COURTESY EDWARD BLANKMAN (THE LLOYD BLANKMAN COLLECTION)

Disappointment

A few minutes later the large deer moved its head around from behind the trees. There were no horns on this deer either! Using the scope on his rifle, he could see single hairs through it on the deer heads. No horns. He crept back out of sight and went on hunting. Saw more deer but no horns. Before leaving the hill just before dusk he went back to where he had seen the three deer. They were still there. Of course the next day, doe day, they could not be found.

In 1958 he went hunting the first day of the season, sat on a stump on top of the hill not far from where he had seen the three deer the year before. In a half hour he saw what he thought was a doe about a hundred yards away, walking and eating from the ground. Through the scope on his rifle he spied two horns. He soon had venison to eat!

ROY CONKLIN'S TROUT
Lloyd Blankman

A West Canada Creek Brook Trout.
Photograph by Roy Reehil. COURTESY ROY REEHIL

Roy Conklin, on the twelfth of June, fished the West Canada Creek and caught three fish about 7, 9, and 11½ inches respectively. The largest was a native descended from Canadian stock, while the others were from the state hatchery.

The following theory is advanced to explain how the Canadian strain populated the West Canada Creek, which is in the Mohawk River watershed. Certainly they could never have ascended the drop at Trenton Falls.

Little Black Creek, which is in the St. Lawrence watershed, was densely populated by the Canadian strain of brook trout. The coloring is different, being red along the sides next the belly, the flesh is firm and pink, while the state hatchery trout are much lighter in color without the red coloring along the sides; the flesh is white and oily.

State Held Off
Years ago sportsmen tried to get the state to raise the Canadian strain, but the Conservation Department contended there was no difference. Now the department has recently purchased some breeding trout from Canada.

Thousands of years before the white man came, beavers thrived in the Adirondacks and had dams on most streams and ponds in the woods, for example on Little Black Creek.

Floods and high water would come, washing out the beaver dams and private ponds, and in the process the trout would reach a stream in a different watershed, that is from Little Black Creek, to Conkling Brook and thence the West Canada Creek.

Honnedaga Lake was probably populated with trout in much the same manner. Trout could never have ascended the sheer drop here on the outlet after the ice age.

Trout Haven

Just below Honnedaga Lake on its outlet is a swamp leading to a beaver meadow on the head of a stream that empties into the outlet below the falls. This meadow was always full of trout.

Sol Carnahan built a dam on the outlet just below Baby Lake. He had to dam up the beaver meadow to keep the water from running that way out of his reservoir. Beavers making this pond enabled the trout to swim into Baby Lake and then ascend two hundred feet up a gentle rift to get into Honnedaga Lake.

At the turn of the century there were no other trout but Canadian strain in the West Canada Creek and no other fish except suckers and minnows.

The above may be nonsense, but it is certain that the Canadian strain got into the West Canada Creek by some means or other.

Swanson Dam and the fishing hole below it. Photo by Jack Miller. COURTESY EDWARD BLANKMAN (THE LLOYD BLANKMAN COLLECTION)

II
Adirondack Traditions

Collection 4
Frontier Occupations
and Recreation

Grotus Reising (right) takes a break from his work as a traveling photographer
to relax and go fishing. Photograph by "Mrs. Brady" of Newport, NY.
COURTESY EDWARD BLANKMAN (THE LLOYD BLANKMAN COLLECTION)

🌲PEDDLERS & ITINERANT PHOTOGRAPHERS
William J. O'Hern

"MA! THE PEDDLER'S WAGON is coming up the road," might have been the excited cry heard from children as they rushed into their cabin home to announce the coming of a familiar salesman whose horse bells made a distinctive ring in the mountain air.

In the backwoods communities of the Adirondack Mountains any caller was welcome. Peddlers with their wares were doubly welcome. Those outfits that might pass through, during good weather, could be dispensers of notions in exchange for old rags, tin peddlers, or book salesmen hawking books "just off the press" from a New York City publishing company. With no hesitation in his spiel as he lifted a book from his bag, the peddler would claim it was a true and exciting account of the discovery and rescue of so-and-so, or that the publisher had pulled out all the stops to produce a volume "every red-blooded American should place on the front-room table where no visitor's eye could miss it."

All the traffickers brought dashes of the outside world, often furnished needed goods, and provided bits of social amenities and neighborly news or some word of more widespread country or state happenings to the isolated families. Whomever the salesperson, a warm greeting was always delivered.

Today we look disapprovingly at the door-to-door salesman, but at one time no one questioned the reliability, honestly, and character of the traveling merchant. Housewives were never too busy to go over the peddler's wares. Colorful bolts of cloths, jewelry, pots and pans, thread, pins and needles, buttons and hats, and other doodads all came out of the seller's one-horse wagon.

The salesman could count on at least one trade for old clothes and rags the children had retrieved from nearby lumber camp shanties, where a considerable quantity of castoff garments left by departing jacks could always be found. These he would pack into burlap bags that were attached to the wagon in easy-to-see places. The deal necessitated a good deal of haggling. Since mother had washed the worn clothing for the express purpose of exchanging it for finery such as the peddler's wagon displayed, the deal took time.

A courteous peddler was also sure of an offer to eat lunch wherever he chanced to be at 12 o'clock. In trade for the free noontime meal he would exchange the few remaining feet of a bolt of muslin.

There were other peddlers too. The itinerant photographer was one of them. Some came a-calling unannounced. Others would arrive having first been met in a far-off town weeks earlier when someone would arrange for them to come for a special occasion or a family photograph to be taken.

The photographer would most often arrive with a light wagon bearing a light-proof space into which he would seek cover when darkroom work was required to develop negatives. Intriguing to the curious were the contents of a large wooden case clasped with a lock. It was filled with glass plates, printing equipment and chemicals called for by his trade.

The photographer would set up his square box camera and then direct people after discussing location and position. Everyone dressed in clothing kept for Sunday finery and special occasions. Women wore shiny satin and bengaline dresses with crisp taffeta and frills. Little girls spread their starched skirts wide; the boys in their knee breeches and starched collars wore self-conscious grins. Men stood stiff and proud in their Prince Albert coats and wide-brimmed hats as they stared into the lens. A favorite horse might be included. So too were various objects placed promiscuously for *atmosphere.*

After much bustling around, the photographer would drape a black shawl over his head and tell everyone "Still, please." As surely as the thread sold by the peddler went into the shaping of a much-needed garment, the photographs of old, taken by the traveling photographer, capture images of rural mountain life long forgotten.

Today, the computerized digital camera has replaced the big box camera and long black shawl as the symbols of photography. Discarded because of changing times, the cameras of the past have been transformed into conversational knickknacks and antiques.

Motivated by many old photos collected over the years, Lloyd Blankman sought out information about two prolific Adirondack photographers, Grotus Reising and Fred "Adirondack" Hodges. The information he gathered formed the basis of a series of columns written by Blankman that appeared in *The Courier,* Clinton, N.Y. newspaper during the 1960s.

🌲 GROTUS REISING
Lloyd Blankman

Just before and after the turn of the twentieth century, the foothills of the Adirondacks were almost all solid forest land, and here the people worked the marginal lands and harvested lumber from the extensive tracts of virgin timber.

There were no pocket cameras then, to record the interesting events of everyday life, no movies, radios or television sets. Pictures of families and friends were scarce and therefore made good entertainment to break the monotony of life on the farm or in the lumber camp.

Satisfying the need for entertainment in the Wilmurt region was Grotus Reising, a short thickset man of German ancestry, who came to this frontier settlement as a child with his parents.

Photographer Grotus Reising. The markings on the photo indicate that Grotus probably sat for the portrait in the studio of a photographer named Fowler in Herkimer, NY
COURTESY EDWARD BLANKMAN
(THE LLOYD BLANKMAN COLLECTION)

Although hunting, fishing, farming, and lumbering were the common occupations, Grotus fell in love with photography and set out on a career of recording the scenes and people with the cumbersome equipment of that time. He took pictures whenever an opportunity for a sale occurred. He took most of the family pictures of early life around Wilmurt, some animal pictures, and all of the Conklin lumber camps. He attended neighborhood dances and took pictures using flashlight powder. Many of his old glass negatives may be found today and prints may still be made from them.

Later on he bought an old Edison phonograph and several hundred records, and with these he gave entertainment at lumber camps, village meetings, or wherever a congregation could be assembled. He advertised in advance and took up a collection. One of his neighbors today remembers two things in connection with this man – the hooded camera and the phonograph with the large horn. He recalls also his voice, which sounded as though he were talking through a thickness of cloth.

Grotus at one time was tax collector and in 1901 took the census in the area. He never did his own driving. He rode all over the North Country with Louis Fagan, who operated a livery out of Poland and who now resides in Gloversville.

Photography remained his chief interest in life. At various times, however, he sold Winchester rifles and did some painting, carpenter work, gardening, and odd jobs. He was honest, sober, industrious, and dependable. He never married and he maintained a keen interest in community affairs, serving many years as school trustee for the Reising and Star school districts in the town of Wilmurt.

The declining years of his life were spent at the home of his brother Conrad in Cold Brook. Here he died in 1940 at the age of 80. He is buried in the old cemetery at Ohio City (called Ohio City to distinguish the hamlet from the township and state of the same name).

🌲 FRED HODGES
Lloyd Blankman

One product of the many acts of kindness that has survived over the decades is the original draft titled "'Adirondack' Hodges (1888–1958)," handed to Lloyd Blankman by author Maitland DeSormo. On the back of the thirteen-page document is scribed "Biography written by Maitland C. DeSormo (Hodges, Son-in-Law). Presented to Lloyd Blankman by the Author May 11, 1963, with permission to use in his work, "Adirondack Characters."

A revised version of the original story appeared in Vol. 18 No. 2 of the 1964 *York State Tradition* magazine. The following article from *The Courier,* Clinton, NY, is a recapitulation of Hodges' life. DeSormo's complete story also appears in his 1974 book, *The Heydays of the Adirondacks.*

Fred Hodges at age 41.
COURTESY EDWARD BLANKMAN (THE LLOYD BLANKMAN COLLECTION)

Only three men have ever been accorded the rare distinction of prefixing the word Adirondack to their names. All three deserved the title. The first two gained their fame by writing and the lecture platform, the third by his work in photography.

Who were these men? William H.H. Murray, the minister and writer; Harry Radford, the editor and explorer; and Frederick A. Hodges, the camera artist and gun expert. The Adirondacks exerted an irresistible attraction to all three men.

During All Seasons

For more than thirty years, during every season of the year Hodges roamed the Adirondacks taking pictures of the forest peaks, the lakes and the streams, trails, flowers and the morning and sunset skies. He went back into distant places, that few people ever see, and he liked everything he saw.

His collection of negatives, numbering over 8,000, is the largest and one of the two finest in existence.

He was also acknowledged to be one of the best men in the country with both the rifle and the pistol, and was a respected and effective firearm instructor.

Sharpshooter

A hunter came out of the woods at Glade's place one time with a jammed cartridge in the barrel of his rifle. Fred Hodges was there and removed the cartridge from the rifle. He knew how to do it.

Then the subject of marksmanship came up. The stranger asked Fred if he could shoot. Fred allowed that he had done some at times. Upon request to see what he could do, this Adirondack man stepped up to a stump and pushed a live cartridge into the soft wood of the stump. He then turned and walked about twenty paces from the target. He now faced the stump and slowly raised his pistol, aimed, and without hesitation, fired.

Demonstration

To the amazement of the hunter, the reports of the pistol and the cartridge in the stump were almost simultaneous. The hunter later learned that this man was one of the best pistol shots in the world.

During his life, Fred built two camps, one of them at Blue Mountain Lake, which he named Meeko or Squirrel Inn. The other one, called Partridge Camp, he located on a wooded ridge overlooking North Brookfield.

In these camps he could escape from the pressures of trying to wrest a modest living from what was considered to be an unprofitable profession. Summers he toured the hotels and resorts in the woods, showing and selling his pictures to the guests, but there wasn't much profit in this.

Quiet Man

Fred was a quiet, unassuming, even a shy man, who never spoke very often, but when he did, he had something to say and was worth listening to. He had many friends, but being the way he was, only two or three in whom he thought he could confide. They all testify to the respect and admiration they had for him.

In the words of one, "He was a man of great depth, many times the man he appeared to be. He always kept Bibles in his home and camps. He read them and put their precepts into daily practice."

In the woods his reflexes, his walk, his actions were like an Indian's. His garb in the woods was often gray wool clothing and Cree Indian moose hide moccasins. Everything about him was convincing proof that Fred Hodges

Big Moose Cedars, by Fred A. Hodges.
COURTESY GEORGE R. CATALDO

"Adirondack Hodges" was quite a man, and for good reason the North Country folks long ago, nicknamed him, "Adirondack."

Fred died suddenly at the Adirondack Museum in 1958.

*   *   *

Lloyd Blankman, living in the company of published writers who were willing to help his own historical writing projects thrive, was indebted for their thoughtful offers. Maitland DeSormo made the following commentaries that further illuminate his father-in-law. The remarks do not appear in DeSormo's final version.

For more than thirty years and during every season of the year Hodges roamed the Adirondacks, recording on film and in his yet-unpublished notebooks the varying moods and scenes of its forested peaks, its lakes and streams, its trail vistas, morning and sunset skies. He knew as thoroughly as a sensitive man can know a vast area of the central and southern Adirondacks. He knew as well as the average man knows his own hometown the populated portions and the country back of beyond—the places few people ever see.

His collection of negatives, which eventually numbered more than 8,000, is unquestionably the largest as well as one of the two finest in existence. Only the Stoddard trove can match it for quality and falls far short of being its equal in quantity.

Furthermore, the value of many of Fred's photos was enhanced by tinting, an effective combination of two kinds of artistry, a skill which he learned from his father.

To further justify the inclusion of the name of Hodges on the honor roll of the mountains it should be pointed out that he had an early phenomenal ability as a hunter and fisherman. He was also acknowledged to be of the country's top-ranking experts with both the rifle and pistol. His proficiency with that notoriously inaccurate weapon was very impressive. His match scores, carefully posted in his journals, and the stack of perforated targets fully attest to his superior skill with his favorite handgun, a .38 Special. Even at ranges as long as 100 yards, he could frequently put four out of five shots into a paper deer. As Remington knew the horse Hodges knew the pistol!

🌲 BERRYPICKING: THE BLUEBERRY GIRLS
Lloyd Blankman

Nora Courtney and Mary Hubbard were neighbors. One day in August in 1900 they went after blueberries in the woods. When they returned Grotus Reising was on hand to take their pictures. They were proud of the berries and they tipped their pails slightly toward the picture taker.

Dee Courtney and his wife Nora lived in a house on a high bank overlooking the West Canada Creek. The Burt Conklins could see their place from where they lived at Broadwaters.

The Courtneys had two children, Bernhard and Agnes, born in 1894 and 1896. Agnes died in 1907 of pneumonia. This was a sad loss to the family and to the community.

Dee and Nora worked lumbercamps as cooks for "Sol" Carnahan, the big lumberman, contractor and builder of

*The Blueberry Girls (left to right)
Nora Courtney and Mary Hubbard.
Photograph by Grotus Reising, 1900.*
COURTESY EDWARD BLANKMAN
(THE LLOYD BLANKMAN COLLECTION)

dams and bridges. The Courtneys lived at one time on the knoll just east of Haskell's Inn. Dee died of the flu during the epidemic after World War One.

Mary Hubbard's maiden name was McPhillips. She and her husband, Fred, did a flourishing business in what is now Haskell's Inn catering to hunting and fishing parties, since Mary was an excellent cook. She was tall and slender, very pretty with kinky auburn hair, a typical Irish lass.

There were three children, Ed, Minnie and Ray.

Jerry Flansburg built what is now the Haskell Inn for his bride when he was discharged from the army after the Civil War.

Most of the women up in the woods wore cotton stockings for everyday and had a silk pair for good or dress-up affairs. Nylons weren't even heard of in those days.

The old cotton stockings were used on the arms for picking berries in July and August. They reached from the upper arms to the fingertips. They protected the wearer from fly and mosquito bites, from scratches by prickers and branches on the bushes and from sunburn on hot summer days. It was fun to pick berries in the woods and the berries made excellent pies.

❦ GUM PICKING: A FORGOTTEN ART
William J. O'Hern

Gum picking, like bushwhacking, is another tradition in the Adirondack forests. A century ago it was a means to supplement one's livelihood. Spruce gum, the forerunner of chewing gum, provided woodsmen a profitable sideline from 1880 to 1915.

High-quality gum would bring one to two dollars per pound from a processing plant, and on a good day five pounds could be collected. Kenneth Goldthwaite writes in a 1906 *Country Life* magazine article that he found spruce gum picking to be "an unusually interesting and novel vocation in the North Woods in February and March." Goldthwaite and his partner sounded hearty—unaffected by the weather conditions: ". . . one cold windy morning brought my friend Philip Doty and myself . . . [to] Rainbow Lake [in Franklin County]. . . . I was clothed to meet all the blasts of the north wind, . . . I was so bundled in flannels that I could hardly bend." The duo protected their bodies in the typical clothing of the period—wool Mackinac jackets and woodsmen's knickers, double-width leggings and deer hide moccasins.

The partners headed out over the ice toward Wardner Flow inlet, on snowshoes pulling a toboggan loaded " . . . high with camp provisions . . . pulling like beasts of burden while particles of snow and ice stung the face."

Under stress and in demanding winter conditions the soon-to-be-gum pickers followed the "devious [stream] windings" to its headwater source, a spruce swamp, where previously on a knoll, Doty had built a "roomy and comfortable" log and tar paper camp at a cost of $25.65.

For two weeks the men "got close to Nature." They hunted rabbits for the camp stew pot, trapped marten, otter and mink, "tramped through the woods

Clarence Williams demonstrated how he used his homemade gum spud for Lloyd Blankman. Photograph by Lloyd Blankman, 1956.
COURTESY EDWARD BLANKMAN (THE LLOYD BLANKMAN COLLECTION)

on snowshoes," experienced a "healthful and wholesome" outdoor life, enjoyed the novelty, "and came out fully repaid, financially as well as physically, for the amber resin of the spruce that we sold to a Plattsburgh, N.Y., druggist paid the expenses of the trip."

There isn't one particular season that is best to pick gum. Goldthwaite chose winter. Had he gone in the summer he could have gathered the 18 pounds of blister gum (first quality was worth $1.50 a pound) and the 22 pounds of "seconds" (worth 85 cents a pound) with less labor and expense and found a greater variety of wild food to eat.

Profitability is the bottom line for gumpickers. Choosing a good district for a base of operations was important. Goldthwaite's choice wasn't the best. He covered the eastern edge of the swamp that extended to the Osgood River and northward to the Sable Mountains. It was an average location dotted with small ponds and wet places, and timbered with spruce, tamarack, and pine. (This region is where the North Branch of the Saranac River has its origin.) It is very likely he would have found more spruce gum had be canvassed the western side, along the Osgood River.

Gum pickers looked for three varieties of spruce trees: white, red, and black. The best quality (and most valuable) gum comes from the white spruce. It has a thicker sapwood in proportion to its size and age than the pitch-bearing red and black spruce trees. It is common knowledge that trees growing in the warmth of the southern exposure grow the fastest. Gum will also ooze out in the greatest quantity on the south side.

Spruce gum can be described, as Goldthwaite understood it, as "the healing salve of the tree." He recorded his understanding:

"The high wind that whirls through the forest twists and bends the trunks, on account of the density of the upper branches, and sometimes opens a seam. Some morning in March following a night of extremely low temperatures you will hear the crack of a tree trunk like the explosion of a rifle, under the contending forces of frost and the warmth of the rising sun. Again, a bird in the search for a grub beneath the bark may make a hole in the wood, or a woodsman chip out the side of the tree to establish his trail. It requires about four years to cover the wound to nature's satisfaction, and after that moss and bark may accumulate over or mingle with the salve, to form peculiar lumps, which may hang down or fill a seam. At first these lumps may not convey anything, but to the practiced eye they have a value according to their quality, which is usually determined by their age."

Since Kenneth Goldthwaite labored all day outside, harvesting the bulk of the gum with a gum tunnel, or a gum spud, reaching high, far above the reach of a man, I assume the information he wrote about gum formation and variety is accurate. He knew the effort needed to reap $1.50 a pound of first-quality spruce gum. Not only did a prospector have to collect the gum, it then required labor-intensive cleaning of bark and other foreign substances, and only then was it sorted or graded.

On cold days, gummers would collect spruce sap by chipping it from the trees with a special type of picker called a gum spud. The least expensive was home-made, put together when the pointed end of a metal file was driven into the end of a stick about five feet long. The file's broad end was ground into a chisel and a tin can was attached to catch the gum.

Edward Blankman showed me a long-handled gum spud once owned by Tim Crowley. Crowley and French Louie both picked gum, but as Harvey Dunham emphasized, "Louie was never what one would call a real gum picker."

Clarence Williams reaches to collect spruce gum using his gum tunnel. Photograph by Lloyd Blankman, 1956. COURTESY EDWARD BLANKMAN (THE LLOYD BLANKMAN COLLECTION)

Ed demonstrated to me how his father had told him the long-handled, galvanized iron, funnel-shaped end was used. The gum spud is one of many old-time Adirondack artifacts his father, Lloyd, had collected. The funnel is about six inches deep, three inches in diameter at the top and tapering to one inch in diameter at the bottom. Into the bottom is soldered a ferrule. This metal device is slid on the end of a straight, light, dry pole. The length is decided by the picker's height and how one expected to use it. It could be lengthened by adding sections of pole spliced to the first length with the aid of galvanized iron ferrules about six inches in length. Holding the spud against a door jamb to take the place of a tree trunk, Ed demonstrated how the sharp edge of the tunnel is forced against a lump of gum, which drops into it and is later transferred to a canvas gum sack tied to one's waist.

Gum spuds (also known as gum tunnels) were never a mass-manufactured tool. Gum pickers either made their own or hired a local tinsmith to make one to their specifications. A strong pocket knife is all that is needed to gather the gum when it is within reach.

Goldthwaite said, "Medical men sought" new, clear and translucent gum for use as an antidote in pulmonary troubles. Chewing gum manufacturers also sought the first-quality gum. Druggists paid less. They bought the lower-grade "seam gum, old gum and that found clinging to blazed spots."

Gum pickers Goldthwaite and Doty were amateurs. They were aware spruce gum didn't grow in paying quantities in one's backyard. A week or two on foot or snowshoes through the heart of the tall timber was necessary to harvest paying amounts. Henry Melvin, a professional who joined the men for a few days, showed his skill at finding three pounds of first-quality a day. "Occasionally, in a country that has not been gummed recently," Goldthwaite learned, "one may get ten pounds in one day." Once, partner Daniel Doty "brought into his camp at Rainbow Lake a bushel of gum weighing twenty-three pounds, which when cleaned netted eighteen pounds."

With the aid of map, compass, and his "sense of direction," Goldthwaite made his way "suggested by Nature's signs and guide posts," through the headwater country of the North Branch of the Saranac River. The work, the harvest, the winter's sun, the lofty evergreens and the "still unsurveyed" swamp were satisfaction enough for Kenneth Goldthwaite and Daniel Doty. His article's title stated it best: "A Winter Vacation That Paid for Itself."

In one "Adirondack Character" column, Lloyd Blankman wrote of Tim Crowley, a professional gum picker and buyer. Crowley's mountain territory was expansive. His home was in Piseco yet he covered territory from "as far north as Big Moose and Twitchell Lake." Crowley would also pick gum from logs in yards, rollways, skidways, booms—anywhere logs came from the forests. He was known to pick gum from all directions, whether down the Moose or Black Rivers, down West Canada Creek, or down the Jessup and Hudson Rivers.

TIM CROWLEY, SPRUCE GUM PICKER
Lloyd Blankman

Tim Crowley
COURTESY EDWARD
BLANKMAN (THE
LLOYD BLANKMAN
COLLECTION)

The dense evergreens and wet shoreline that ring Spruce Lake are a part of history. In the winter of 1885 Tim Crowley began picking spruce gum along the lake's shore. Around 1910, when gum picking became unprofitable, Crowley turned to trapping and guiding. He built a large camp, an unpolished hostelry of sorts, at Spruce Lake to accommodate guiding parties. It was built of logs and shingled with shingles made by hand on site. Inside were a stove, table, some camp stools and bunks fastened to the walls. Sometimes when Crowley had a warm fire it would get quite hot in the upper bunks and campers would have to throw off their blankets or come down to cool off. Lloyd Blankman's profile of Crowley adds to recorded history this long forgotten Adirondacker.

This little fellow who picked the spruce gum in the Adirondacks more than anyone else was born into a poor family, near Osceola in Lewis County in early 1861. His father worked as a farm laborer. His mother died when "Tim" was seven years old.

At an early age, Tim was bound out to a farm family. Among his duties on a dairy farm, he had to milk four cows and he had to take care of the milk utensils.

After he became of age he left this place of hard toil and worked at other jobs. For a while he drove mules along the Erie Canal. He returned to farm work on property which belonged to Mr. Daniels, who one day, discovered a source of spruce gum. Tim Crowley and Daniels, while in partnership, traveled about Lewis County gathering spruce gum until the supply became quite scarce.

Back to the Farm

The Daniels' eventually returned to their farm while Tim Crowley went down the Mohawk Valley and up to Glens Falls. While enroute to Glens Falls, he stopped at a drug store for a supply of spruce gum. He was told that a lumberjack from North Creek supplied him. Once he obtained the lumberjack's name, he started out for North Creek. When he met the lumberjack, he offered to buy all of the spruce gum that could be obtained in that area.

Tim Crowley stayed in the vicinity of North Creek collecting a new supply of spruce gum which was shipped to Boston. He contacted Mr. Daniels of Lewis county and invited him to come to North Creek and help pick gum. They gathered spruce gum until the supply became meager. Then Tim Crowley moved on to Speculator in Hamilton county seeking a new source of gum.

Good Supply

In the vicinity of Dug Mountain near Speculator, Tim Crowley found an excellent supply of gum. The first day he picked sixty pounds of gum within several hours. This would indicate that he found a valuable source. There were times when he was able to gather one hundred pounds in one day. He sold the gum at one dollar a pound on the Boston market.

About 1885 he came to Piseco. Tim came during the winter and went along Spruce Lake looking for gum. He stayed at Sealon Clark's camp at Spruce Lake. When Sealon Clark left the area, Tim took the camp over and continued to pick gum. Sometimes he would have a partner who assisted him with the work. Some of his partners were: John Leaf, an Indian; Floyd Abrams; Floyd's two sons, George and Bill; and Demice Abrams. All of them were from Piseco.

Tim killed his first bear while gum picking. The bear was in his den, which was located under an upturned root on a shelf high upon the ledge. He killed this bear by chopping it in the head with an old ax. After this incident Tim killed many bears and soon became known as "The Bear."

Tim could not remember the exact number of bears he killed, but he knew that he had killed more than forty-five.

About the year 1896 Tim married Josephine Curtis of North Creek. The Crowleys' had one child, a girl, who died in infancy.

In 1897 Tim bought a piece of land from Floyd Abrams. On this land he built a log house. Mrs. Ila Simons of Piseco lived about where the house stood.

Art Declines

Around 1910 gum picking became unprofitable. Tim Crowley turned to trapping and guiding. He built a large log camp at Spruce Lake to accommodate guiding parties. A few years later the State Conservation Department made him move the log camp. Tim sold the large cabin to William Courtney, who with the help of his sons moved it to its present location.

In 1913, Tim Crowley came back into the village of Piseco and bought the Courtney Hotel. Tim remodeled the hotel and tried running it for two years. In 1915, he rented it to Leon Anibal who ran it for five years. Tim sold the hotel.

Tim did most of his trapping alone until 1925. In 1925, Clarence Williams trapped with him for one season. The late Cecil Cotts.

Tim Crowley gave up his trapping career in 1935 and retired to the house that he bought from Ben Parslow. The late Clarence Williams stayed with Tim and took care of him during his declining years.

Tim Crowley died at the age of eight-two in the hospital at Gloversville. Tim died of infirmities that are associated with old age.

He was buried beside his daughter's grave in the Higgins Bay Cemetery near Piseco Lake Village.

LOGGERS CIRCA 1900
William J. O'Hern

*A dam building crew at Mill Creek Lake outlet, 1900. Tom Grimes
(far right) and "Mr. Young" (on horseback) are the only two identified.*
COURTESY EDWARD BLANKMAN (THE LLOYD BLANKMAN COLLECTION)

The days of the log drive in the Adirondacks are over. Lumbering,
of course, is still going on. The difference is in the extent of the cutting,
modern techniques and equipment and the total disappearance of the old-
time company-owned lumber camp shanties.

The mountains are still the same today as when the old-time lumberjacks
left the woods. The land supports rich robes of spruce and hemlock, patterned
with stands of hardwoods. On mountain and hill is the same breathless beauty
that must have thrilled the lumber companies' never-ending appetite for wood.

My interest in the Adirondack logging culture stems from my own work
in the Crockett's sawmill early in my adult life. There I learned hard work—
enjoyable but demanding. Talking to old-timers started me down a path of
personal research. Seeing my interest, one veteran of the lumber woods after
another steered me to friends and acquaintances who participated in the latter days of the heyday of the logging era. I gained access to a vast store of
yarns, recollections, and photographs of older residents of the region, as well
as to more formal state reports and histories.

Someday I'll develop a book with the material I've collected. I want the
book to present a man-in-the-street approach to the area's logging history by
de-emphasizing statistical data and concentrating on folklore. The book will
contain a background of historical data along with a succession of picturesque
incidents, stories and legends of seriousness, humor, and adventure that

affected the lives of those who lived in the lumber camps and worked in the Adirondack forest.

I began my informal research just in time, for there were not many old-timers left who could tell what was going on before the days of the Linn tractors when there was still the flavor of the pioneer woodchopper in isolated camps distant from the settlements.

Yes, the lumberjacks and river men, heroes of a romantic saga, whose skill and might provided an income a century ago, are gone today, but for future generations, as well as the present ones, a great amount of material can be gathered to present stories of life in those early days.

The staid facts of logging history are clothed with vivid descriptions of the people who successively lived and worked in the region, and with accounts, often humorous, of events that transpired in early days in Adirondack country.

Those of us who prefer our history informal will be grateful to the old men and women and their relatives for sharing the best of their recollections. Through their memories, the best tradition of historical writing, in my opinion, is a story of the boisterous goings-on of the people who once lived and worked robustly in the lumber woods.

"My great grandfather was a logger," went one man's memory, "so it was that I came to try chewing tobacco. I still remember how he would shift the

A "whitewaterman" maneuvers easily across floating logs.
AUTHOR'S COLLECTION

cud of chew in his mouth to the other cheek, clear his throat, roll his eyes to the ceiling and give his best rendition of any number of log camp songs."

The term "spring break-up" brought these memories to the surface from another gentleman, whose recollections made it seem as if he had just seen spring at his door yesterday. "They came afoot, these men, each with a turkey slung over his shoulder, and each with his own and peculiar kind of headgear. There were caps of coonskin and bearskin, caps of wool, and old hats of weather-stained felt. Mackinaws were of various colors and patterns, and pants—well, just pants which, below the knees, disappeared in the tops of high, laced leather shoes, thick-soled to hold the heavy sharp calks (pronounced 'corks' in lumber-woods parlance) driven into thick sole and heel.

"Some of the men carried their own, time-tested peaveys; others depended upon the supply they would find at their respective camps. Along the rutty road they came . . . ," and so the old fellow continued on, filling several cassette tapes. Conceivably he lived a long life because he never made a habit of chewing Jolly Tar tobacco regularly.

It is just one of hundreds of recollections of the hard-bitten men of the timber woods whose culture is gone today.

🌲 BRUSH AND THE ROAD MONKEY
Douglas and Helen Hays

Rush, the Indian, checked the fire in his kitchen stove. Taking his red plaid mackinaw and knitted cap from the peg by the door, he stepped out into the sharp cold of Adirondack winter. He glanced at the overcast sky, fastened his snowshoes and thought, as he broke trail through the woods, "Only two o'clock. Dark will come early. I better see that young Frenchie now."

Like his friend Andre, the road monkey, Brush had drifted down from Canada. He had cooked in many lumber camps, big ones, some of them. He remembered the one on Dug Mountain Pond. When the men needed a dock for a little evening fishing, they had felled a virgin pine into the lake. The butt end was more than four feet in diameter. It has lasted well, that dock. In fact it still lies with the top sprawled far out in the clear water.

As his snowshoes sifted easily through the light snow, Brush, wrapped in the silence this soft cover gives, remembered the ring of axes, the drone of saws and the sound of men's voices from the busy summer. Many feet of logs had been cut and piled on the skidways and were now waiting to be drawn to the mill.

Life in a lumber camp fifty years ago [1915] was strenuous, but men and horses were well fed and adequately housed. The log cabins were closely chinked, and the chore boy kept plenty of wood for the bunkhouse and cook shack stoves.

Work in the camp went on all year, but summer was the time for cutting. In those days little thought was given to conservation or reforesting. The slash was left as the men moved on to the next stand of timber.

First, the trees to be cut were blazed. Then an ax man chopped a deep cleft on the side of the trunk towards which the tree was to fall. Some choppers used the double-bitted ax, familiarly known as a "widow maker." Next, two sawyers drew the crosscut rhythmically back and forth through the great bole until the tree fell precisely as planned. The trunks were cut into fourteen-foot lengths and the mass of branches left to be cover for small animals and birds as well as a fire hazard for many years to come.

Sometimes, on very steep slopes oxen were used, but in the Canada Lake region of Fulton County, horses snaked the logs out. They were piled parallel to the road on skidways to wait for winter, when they could be drawn to the mill and then sawed into lumber the following summer.

Winter, with snow smoothing the way, made drawing the logs possible. Every lake was used as a road. What a relief it must have been to level off over snow-covered ice after the dangerous descent!

The logs were taken from the skidways and piled lengthwise on lumber sleds, piled so high they towered ten feet above the driver, who sat in front, just back of his team. Driving those huge loads over the mountains was perilous work.

On cold nights the road monkey iced the roads with a horse-drawn sprinkler. He spread sand and straw as needed to keep horses and runners from slipping.

Brush loved the work of the camps, especially this little camp on Eastman Lake, where a colony of gulls nested in summer.

As he walked Brush felt thirsty. Knowing the woods like the back of his hand, he detoured nearer the log road. In summer a spring bubbled here beside a big fern-covered rock. What a time the men had laying the corduroy near that spring! It was all easy now. The snow evened everything. Oh! Yes, here was the spring, black and round at the bottom of an iced funnel that tapered deep through three feet of snow. Brush took the birch-bark dipper that the men kept hanging on a convenient bough. Kneeling, he reached down to scoop up the icy water.

When he reached the road monkey's hut, Andre had just come in from spreading sand and straw on the hill. He stood warming his hands by the small chunk stove as Brush entered.

Andre spoke at once. "Come in. Come in, Brush. Sit by fire. Last night cold. We sprinkle the road. Water wagon like new! She not leak any more. Ice never more heavy, more hard. Oui, plenty sand and straw. All placed before teams go out ce matin. She melt this noon. Now is freeze again. I put more sand, more straw on big hill so horse never slip Oui, brake is good on sled. Horse, too, knows to brake but she need straw and sand. They give grip for horse's foot."

The two friends talked a bit of their work and the prowess of the other men. Competition was fierce within each camp. Ax men, sawyers, experts with the cant hook or peavey vied with one another for skill and endurance.

Presently Brush rose.

"You go now, Brush? Too bad. Dark will come early tonight. This is the day of Sainte Luce. December thirteen. In France we say 'Pour Sainte Luce, les jours augmente dun saut de puce et pour Noel de saut d'um coq.' That be for you, Brush: 'On Saint Lucy's Day, days grow big by jump of flea; on Christmas, by jump of rooster.' Well, so long, Brush, glad you come. I be up for sup."

Reassured that all was well with Andre and the roads, Brush started back, thinking of the longer days to come and the hot supper for the men which he had left preparing in the oven of his good wood stove.

Loggers at the Mill Creek Logging Camp with parts of a logging sled in the foreground.
COURTESY EDWARD BLANKMAN (THE LLOYD BLANKMAN COLLECTION)

🌲 TRAPPERS CIRCA 1900
William J. O'Hern

In the fall 1964 issue of *York State Tradition,* Maitland C. DeSormo led his article, "Heyday of the Hops" with this:

"Older members of the present generation have seen several once-flourishing industries eventually show unmistakable signs of dying on the vine. Some of these have already passed out of existence, and others show symptoms of sliding down the skidways toward economic oblivion. Among these casualties can be listed iron mining, lumbering, the summer hotel trade and the extremely speculative hop-growing gamble."

Pencil to his list the decline in trapping.

Trapping fur-bearing animals is not as commonplace as it once was. The profession has evolved into a part-time sport. "Trappers are a dying breed," a friend told me when I came across him in the woods near my camp. "Some people will tell you we shouldn't even do this—trap animals."

Modern-day trappers would argue. Truth be told, though, the number of men and women interested in this once-common activity has waned, but it is far from fading out.

E. J. Dailey and Richard Wood were two legendary trappers I came across when researching my book *Life With Noah*, which recounts the adventures of Richard "Red" Smith and his life-long friendship with Noah John Rondeau, the Adirondacks' last and most famous hermit. Thanks to the generosity of Dick Woods' daughter, who gave me all of her father's "old trapping photos," the partners' Cold River country trapline adventures can be enjoyed through stories and vivid still scenes. The two young trappers' lives, prior to World War I in a remote section of the Adirondacks, have passed into history, but their activities along the Cold River Trail, the abandoned Santa Clara Lumber Company's winter haul road, live on in the following story.

Trappers in the Cold River Country

Elric J. "E. J." Dailey and Richard K. "Dick" Wood were examples of rugged individualism: they were self-reliant, with strong wills and strong backs. Seasoned native-to-the-territory trappers called the two freshmen "young whippersnappers" and "outsiders" when they first arrived to trap in the High Peaks, a rugged region of the Adirondack Mountains in northern New York State in 1919. In bitter valleys and on strenuous slopes, they endured their share of "baptizing" experiences—lessons learned from the harsh, demanding environment where temperatures often plunged to 40 or more below zero and snow piled up higher than a man's head.

No trap-stealing or other encroachment ever occurred, but the senior Long Lake trappers found amiable ways to christen the newcomers to the Cold River basin. The upstarts were gaining recognition, but it was not because they were skilled at survival, or because they laid down traplines in a fur pocket extending for miles from Headquarters, an abandoned lumber company's camp near Duck Hole in a wild spot deep in the forest, or because one invented a "lure that revolutionized trapping" (his words) or because the other was a professional outdoor photographer.

E. J. Dailey: "Catch all the prime skins you can, but play square with the animals." Photograph by Richard Wood about 1921.
AUTHOR'S COLLECTION

Both men, in their mid-twenties, proved they could substantially support themselves with a good fur check; however, both were better known for their outdoor writing. Several years before they arrived in the Adirondack Mountains, they had built a base of significant readership among outdoor types, both male and female, because of their writings in popular sporting magazines of the day. Both published books that explained trapping techniques. In those books, they also shared their philosophies about the outdoors and told of the trapper's way of life.

In the peace of an Adirondack winter, the writers found much of that cure-all elixir which winter sports devotees look to the mountains to find. At "No. 1" or "Headquarters," their well-stocked Duck Hole shanty, the men found utter solitude in the frozen hush that steals from the forest in winter. A peek out the front door revealed mantles of snow on bush and limb, a frozen river and avenues of pure white set sparkling by dancing sunbeams. The writer-trappers saw the Cold River Country, an isolated pocket of fur, as a sweet spot in the wilderness. Through their eyes, trappers and non-trappers knew the special experience of winter wilderness "that heals and invigorates."

Dailey and Wood conveyed their love for the outdoor experience through words so well chosen that readers could experience the silence that enveloped and rested their tired bodies and gave them new strength for the strenuous tasks of the day ahead. The natural-born storytellers told of the mountains' benefits in their authentic and authoritative voices. The men had partnered not only to trap, but for those Adirondack moments as well.

In addition, Dick Wood's bread-and-butter trade was professional photography. E. J., who would eventually come to be regarded as the dean of old-time trappers, sold trapping supplies, and he also bought fur from other trappers. But Dailey's enduring legacy remains the masterful trapline and out-of-doors tales he wrote, for *Fur-Fish-Game*. For over 40 years, he served as the magazine's "Trapline and Question Box" editor.

Trapping and exploration motivated them. The writers' tales communicated the stirring trials they faced as they traveled along traplines that passed over mountains and through scenic valleys—on trails sometimes obliterated by four to six feet of snow. The trapping partners' travels put them in contact with an assortment of colorful characters whose personalities, dialogue and behaviors they jotted in notebooks. These characters would be woven into magazine articles, sometimes years later. The men also wrote about the animals they encountered. A wily fox became "Keen Nose," and a runaway otter set the stage of "The Otter's Trail."

Dressed to withstand frigid temperatures and steel-headed enough to endure isolation, the partners found their most onerous task was to exhibit patience and restraint toward one another's idiosyncrasies during periods of "rotting snow" (snow foundation softened by rain and/or warming temperatures). During this time, it was impossible to move about easily and the men holed up in their trapline shelter. (The main pathway where Dailey and Wood trapped from is now part of the Northville-Lake Placid Trail, New York's oldest and second-longest trail system.)

All-day card games, checkers and reading were the rule, as well as cooking and eating whenever the spirit dictated. Every now and then time dragged, which led to boredom and cabin fever. Pent-up feelings brought about from living in close quarters would burst into a temporary rift between the partners. Mundane day-to-day habits turned into annoying behaviors. Then, one man, unable to stand the other's habits any longer, would crack and vent his frustration by emptying the entire magazine of his Colt pistol into the log wall directly over the head of his nettlesome buddy—just to break the tension.

Richard Wood's self-portrait along the Cold River Trail.
AUTHOR'S COLLECTION

Wood described the stress in his account of how he spent his first trapping excursion in the Adirondacks in his January 1921 article in *Fur News and Outdoor World*, "Cabin Life." On this excursion, they were accompanied by another man. For an unexplained reason, the three men took nicknames. Dailey was the Professor. The Chef was a buddy who did the cooking. Wood was the Sun Worshipper.

While the wind "intermittently howled outside," and it "either snowed or rained," Wood related, "with considerable regret, the Chef made a ukulele out of a dishpan and fish line." As the "more or less monotonous" days passed, the Professor and the Sun Worshipper began to "appreciate the Chef's art in slinging the dough." Along with eating and smoking, the men played cards. "Pitch led in popularity, but draw and stud poker were very interesting as long as the 'chicken feed' lasted."

Wood was amused by one of E. J.'s habits. "Among the Professor's many sins, I hasten to mention, was a weakness for shaving. Even the Chef was immune from this exigency of civilization. Every day the Professor ran a miniature lawnmower over his mug, claiming a great deal of satisfaction in so doing, but he refused to allow me to shave him with the Marble's Ideal for which purpose I carefully whetted it several hours."

E.J. didn't cotton to Wood's razor-sharp long knife any more than he cared for his choice of reading matter. "I confess to a weakness for French literature—not the Parisian potboiler. Many times as I approached the climax of one of Balzac's delightful intrigues, the Professor snuffed the candle out with his six-shooter in a sort of genuine bravado fashion. One evening this got on my nerves—I was reading De Maupassant's 'Moonlight on the Water,' or something like that, and didn't like to be disturbed, so I emptied the Colt's auto into the wall over Professor's head and that stopped the candle business. The Chef hastily opened the cabin door, whether to let himself or the smoke out, I don't know."

Wood said he originally caught the "Cold River fever" from a "breed guide" he had been trout fishing with. The guide told him he had been in there twenty years previously. He had lived at the Dam Camp while he was a log driver. The ex-log driver-turned-guide described the wildland as a "trapper's paradise, a veritable wilderness in the backyard of a civilized country."

Taking into consideration that considerable change might ensue in a period of twenty years, Wood planned a fall deer hunting exploration trip. His reconnaissance was two-fold. First, it was an opportunity to explore new fur and game country far from his native Tennessee. Second, he wanted see first-hand if the old guide's boast had merit. Wood was not disappointed. His expedition took him into the far back Adirondacks. He turned up abandoned camps, skeletons from the lumbering days and a country that had gone back to its original wild state. "A land of more or less mystery, far back from human habitation," Wood reported to Dailey. The old cut-over country

A view of Oluska Pass from Donaldson Mountain—Cold River Country. Photograph by Robert Bates. COURTESY ROBERT BATES

seemed like an ideal trapping ground to catch fur and to garner plenty of trail experiences to relate later in articles. The deserted lumber shanties would become their headquarters.

So it was that as they trapped along the Cold River mountain country, they came in short-spoken contact with a man who decades later would be hailed as "the Hermit of Cold River Flow."

Noah the Hermit

Six miles downriver from the trappers' Duck Hole headquarters camp resided a cranky woodsman named Noah John Rondeau. He occupied a deserted river driver's lumber shanty known as Dam Camp during the non-winter months. During the winter he relocated to Jungle Camp, a trapline shanty, well hidden near an unnamed peak south of Ampersand Lake which Rondeau called Peek-a-Boo Mountain.

Wood's trapline left Duck Hole in a generally westward direction downriver. "From Camp One I ran a two-day circle line down the river to the big dam and back the next day across the mountains," he explained. "The line followed the Cold River trail, with one big loop around Mountain Pond and another around a mountain peak for marten." The lumber shanty Rondeau used seasonally was his terminus.

In Rondeau's later years, he grumbled that tyros Dailey and Wood weren't the slick trappers they made out to be in print. Instead, he claimed the duo's greatest success at fur harvesting was their ability to catch the numerous field mice that scampered willy-nilly in the Dam Camp, which he most often occupied before pulling stakes and moving to his "Jungle."

Wood hit back that he held never held any admiration for Rondeau. Wood could not endure the frigid Dam Camp without his "sleeping pocket," or air mattress. He found Rondeau had spread over one corner of the floor a thick layer of balsam boughs to be used for a bed, and there was a stack of wood behind the stove. "These things were appreciated," he wrote, "but I didn't have any compliments for the fellow who had carried the stove pipe away. I tried to manufacture one out of tar paper and liked to have burned the camp down. So I opened wide the door, and as the window was out in the opposite end of the camp, the smoke blew out. Also the zero weather froze the cooking about as fast as it thawed on the stove. I ate off the stove top, bacon, skillet bread, raisins and sugar with plenty of strong tea, and immediately crawled into the sleeping bag."

Wood wrote, "I had no time to repair a camp and build a bunk, but by blowing my 'Comfort Sleeping Pocket' up I could crawl into a bag as comfortable as home, and sleep as warm as toast in a place as open as a barn. . . . From under the pillow I extracted two trail friends, a candle and a volume of the classics too dry to read in civilization, and read myself to sleep. When in camp alone far from civilization [and from his partner] I can read with relish such works as the Bible, *Pilgrim's Progress* and *Dante's Inferno*."

Colorful Characters

The Cold River territory was home to picturesque, one-of-kind characters. Among them were transplanted French-Canadian lumberjacks, who worked in nearby lumber camps.

Camp Four, a rough woodsy settlement of several log camps between the Sawtooth and Seward ranges, was of particular interest to E. J. and Dick for two reasons. For one, the complex had a camp store where they bought supplies—but more fascinating were the woodchoppers' stories. One in particular was a curious account of a matronly woman who had been hired as a camp cook. The men claimed that one day she left Camp Four on a trip to an older camp nestled in a peaceful little valley clearing high in the mountains closer to Cold River.

The boys took particular interest when they realized the camp was near Seymour Mountain. They knew the area well. It was a base of several camps with roofs broken in by years of heavy snow. It was also the site of one of their trapline shelters.

What happened to the cook remains a mystery. She never returned to camp. The prevailing theory was that she had been murdered in one of those abandoned cabins. E. J. declared that if he had any predisposition toward spookiness, he might have considered making some shades for the windows when he slept there at night!

Wood and Dailey were amused by a renegade Lake Placid guide's boast that proved to be true. The grizzly woodsman prided himself on being able to put away large quantities of whiskey and, while under the liquor's influence, to shoot his rifle with dead-eye accuracy. A demonstration proved his boast to be God's honest truth. They watched a bullet shatter a brier pipe clenched between a trusting fellow's teeth.

Another guide, a yarn-spinning storyteller, could quote lengthy Robert Service poems about life in the Yukon. There was also a mentally-deranged trapper who never talked to anyone except the postmaster, who sent his furs out for sale, and a thieving guide named Wood (no relation to Richard K.) and his two sons. The guide boasted to city sportsmen that if he wanted to catch fish, "I can catch 'em just as well where they ain't as where they be." He meant he wouldn't hesitate to poach on private preserves.

And then there was the famed controversy regarding the Tupper Lake game protector who arrested hermit Noah John Rondeau for assault. He claimed Rondeau had tried to murder him. As evidence, the game protector submitted his Army campaign-type hat. It clearly showed that a bullet had passed through the top portion that rose above the wearer's skull.

Wise to dishonesty, Rondeau pointed out how he had cleverly marked the ears on muskrats the warden claimed he was trapping illegally. This development turned the table on the game protector. The judge deemed Rondeau was not the wrong-doer, but that the warden was.

If one believed half the witnesses who testified to Rondeau's accuracy with either rifle or longbow, then his shot at the hat was probably nothing more than a well-placed warning. If he had wanted to, he could have killed the game warden.

Late in E. J.'s life, when one could allow an aging trapper's memory some latitude, he recounted to his friend Donald "Jack" Anderson his fondest recollections of the vanished era of trapping in what he affectionately dubbed "the 'Dacks."

In Anderson's book, *Goodbye Mountain Man*, Dailey says of the senior trapper, Rondeau, "He scraped like a madman on a broken fiddle. He once killed a bear with a homemade longbow and sometimes fired any weapon that was handy at folks who approached the place."

Dailey's and Wood's readers were not only treated to the roamings of the partners in a mountainous land, where silent killers stalked at night. They also enjoyed the drama of the natural world that was all around the partners' trapline through the illustrative pictures that accompanied their stories. Wood's early-twentieth century photographic images display the men's battles against snow and cold in a wilderness. There were scenes of the trappers returning to camp from explorations across the Seward, Santanoni and Sawtooth mountain ranges, where hardship, hunger and danger were commonplace.

Such was the life Dailey and Wood experienced in the Cold River Country. Two young men, rugged individuals with strong wills and strong backs who chose to live in makeshift line camps, to brave deep snow and frigid temperatures in order to follow their own call of the wild. How good a team did the men make in the fur business? I believe they were successful, but the financial return never seemed to matter as much as their way of life.

Dailey shared this point at the close of his little book, *Traplines and Trails*: "Before bringing the book to a close, I want to ask the readers once more 'To play fair with the wild things, and give them a chance to replenish the earth with their species.'"

Once, railroad and steamboat whistles were common, and guides and trappers ranged like the mountain men in America's Old West. The Adirondack Mountains (E. J. called the region the "land of the Christmas trees") gradually lost many of their pockets of virgin forest. The lion's share of the present six-million-acre park is built on a versatile, recreation-driven economy. People the world over come to the Adirondacks to hunt, fish, hike, camp, ski, and snowmobile. They come for the trails that wind through the world's most ancient mountains. Where hermits once lived, tourists now commune with nature.

"A trapper is never known by the length of his trapline, nor the number of traps he uses, but by the pelts that adorn his cabin wall." – EJ Dailey. Photograph by Richard Wood. Unidentified subject, 1923.
AUTHOR'S COLLECTION

🌿 RAY MILKS, UNDER THE ICE
Lloyd Blankman

The following account of his experience on the trapline was told to the writer by Ray Milks at his home on August 16, 1964, on the date of the 36th annual reunion of the Conklin family.

Ray's partner, Burt Conklin, the great trapper was ill, so Burt's grandson, Ben Pardee, was with Ray in the woods with headquarters at Burt's shanty on Shirttail Creek. They were trapping for fisher cats along the West Canada Creek, in the spring when the ice in the creek was breaking up.

The night before the accident happened Ben had a dream in which he saw Ray under the ice and for that reason he warned Ray not to go on the Creek. They were pulling their traps for the season. The incident took place about the year 1925 on the Mitchell or second Stillwater on their way to the Buck Pond Stillwater, on the West Canada Creek.

Ray Milks at 68, in 1968.
COURTESY EDWARD BLANKMAN (THE LLOYD BLANKMAN COLLECTION.)

Under the Ice

Ray was warned not to go on the creek but keep in the woods because the ice on the creek wasn't safe. The ice was hard but the water had dropped and air pockets were under the ice everywhere.

Ray strapped his snowshoes on but the snow was sticky, the balsam shoots were everywhere making it hard going for snowshoes. Four or five deer were ahead on the creek where it was easier for them to travel. The water was high due to thaws, then it froze, the water went down and made air pockets under the ice.

Ray tried to cross the creek just below the Buck Pond Stillwater, broke through the ice with his snowshoes and packbasket. Here he was, under the ice in the water. He drifted down stream fifty yards or more and at the same time got his snowshoes off and packbasket, holding on to them and looking for a place where he could break through the ice and lift himself out of the water on top of the ice.

The weather was zero, the water cold and his clothes were frozen stiff. With his snowshoe he was able to break a hole in the ice overhead and after slipping back into the water was finally able after several tries to get out on top of the ice with his packbasket, axe and snowshoes.

He left the trapline at once, went over the mountain, hit the Indian River, where he found his partner searching for him and together they went back to camp. After a harrowing experience Ray was saved.

⚜ TRUE FISHING STORIES
William J. O'Hern

I never met Mortimer Norton, but I would have enjoyed talking and fishing with him. I would try to hold up my end of the storytelling. As for fishing, my casting methods surely would cause as much mirth as some of the angling yarns he could tell, for I have had my share of mishaps. More than once I have started out with a fine collection of flies, leaders, and so forth but have returned with not even half of my equipment left. The flies had flown heavenward and lit on the boughs of alders so thick that they infested the banks, making a pathway almost impossible along a stream. I've slipped on greased rocks, fallen head first into the water, emerged without a dry stitch on, made another start only to repeat my previous performance, only to break my rod.

Once I was chased. He was not a very funny fellow. It happened one day when I mustered up the courage to go fishing where I had not been invited. I was approached by a man about six feet tall and not less than 200 pounds. When a man that size approaches under the pretense that he would like to see your rod because he desires to purchase one, as you fish a posted section of a river that has signs reminding club members only fly fishing is allowed, there is no waiting to see what will happen. I knew there would be no amusing laughter.

I made good time, actually excellent time, hightailing out of there. But the fellow kept up with me. I assumed he must have been a runner or just in darned good shape. After a time he could go no farther. He sat down on a rock in the river's deep ravine to catch his breath. Seeing an opportunity to ease the burning in my lungs, I also stopped.

"Well there," I hollered, "We sure had quite a run."

"Yes indeed," he shouted back between heaves of his chest. "And let me tell you something," he added. "We are going to have another as soon I get my breath."

I have many Adirondack memories. Many of them have to do with bushwhack companions and best fish catches in May and June, with not knowing we would be lost on the way to a trout stream, with hearing a faint call from my friend Mark in the distance on a long tramp to a stream I had learned about from an old-timer who said it was one of the best trout streams in the North Woods and told us not to "wet your line at once" but to go to the head of the rifts and fish downstream, for which we would be rewarded.

But these were not the reasons I convinced my fly-fishing buddy to accompany me. Something compelled us to make our way to this remote trout stream in the interior headwaters of the West Canada Creek.

The stream was unusually low and the fishing was mostly done in the numerous pools and occasional rifts with more water than average. Mark, younger than I and more interested in catching the Big One, managed to mosey ahead. I felt bound to keep track of him. I won't recount the number of times he fell, or the bruises he got from tumbling over logs, and how his hip boots were nearly smothered in mud, or the loss of his favorite smoking pipe. Two hours of hardship were enough for him. "I give up," he said, exhausted and discouraged. "How long has it been since this guy has been back to the creek?" Mark pressed.

I anticipated his reaction to my answer: "About fifty years."

"Fifty years!" he exclaimed. "You took the word of a guy who hasn't been back here in fifty years? How old is he?"

"Slim's eighty-seven," I answered.

"All right, let's get out of here. I give up. I can only hope you get us out and find the trail back to the car."

The long hike back to civilization limbered Mark's disposition so that he admitted he "somewhat enjoyed the trip."

I've mentioned many other streams, ponds, and lakes throughout the wonderful wilderness where I thought he might enjoy trying his hand on the rod, but he has yet to consent to take his "killing flies" to another desirable fishing spot with me, even though I promise, "It's a Mecca."

*   *   *

April 15th is my red-letter day. Sometimes the lakes and larger streams are still frozen—ice doesn't always leave the waters until the end of April or early May—but by the middle of April I begin looking for lakes that are parting with it.

As the days pass and the water is unlocked from its icy grip and the streams and rivers begin to subside from the mad fury of the first freshets that follow the swift melting of the snow, the throng of visiting anglers increases until scarcely a stream or lakelet, however remote, remains unvisited by at least a few enthusiasts. But Fisherman Mark remains convinced that any future trip I guide him on would be to another sucker brook—he being the sucker.

While Mark knows any stream I could lead him to would not have trout "good for toothpicks," as he has told others, he does know the fish in Adirondack waters bite when they want to. He also knows there is no better time, or better fun, than to be fly fishing in May and early June.

As I sit around an evening campfire, I am often forced to endure the light-hearted jests of friends like Mark. "Yeah, that Jay. Watch out if he wants to take you somewhere deep in the woods," someone will say. "He'll lug around a camera all day long for a few pictures and all you might get for the adventure is to catch minnows and snags, and have pine cones drop down your neck."

That may be true. But packs are still shouldered, and we are soon out on the trail. Behind lie Adirondack memories; in front, the hope of another recommended fishing destination in the mountains.

*   *   *

What follows are two accounts of Adirondack fishing trips by Mortimer Norton, writer, conservationist, guide and angler. I am reminded of a saying of Mortimer's. I paraphrase: "I can't fathom folks traveling out-of-state, looking for some elusive fishing vacation when they can get it right here in the Adirondacks—and darn cheap, too. Any man or woman that doesn't like roaming through woods like these and fishing for trout, has my sympathy." I could never be an object of Mortimer's sympathy, for I am usually one of the first to encourage a friend to come along and wet a line.

Mortimer Norton doing what he loved to do—fish!
COURTESY EDWARD BLANKMAN (THE LLOYD BLANKMAN COLLECTION)

🌲 A MISHAP ON PANTHER MOUNTAIN STREAM

Mortimer Norton

S-P-L-A-S-H! broke the stillness of the thick woods, startling me as it came unexpectedly from around a bend in an Adirondack stream. I was standing knee-deep in water, rod in hand, absorbed in an effort to induce a wily trout to leave its home under a large rock, and take up its abode in my creel.

I knew my brother was ahead of me, but for a moment, so interested had I been, I was speechless. This soon passed, and I called out, "What happened, Morgan? Making a dive for one, or did you lose an old whopper as I did a while back?"

"Naw," came back in an angry tone, "I fell in."

We have been on many eventful fishing trips together, but the one we took that and the following day we seem to remember most clearly. It was a Friday in July on which this story opens. In the morning it was hot and sunny on the outside of the woods, but on the stream, where it ran through the deep forest, it was shady and cooler.

Mortimer Norton, 55 years old in 1963. COURTESY EDWARD BLANKMAN (THE LLOYD BLANKMAN COLLECTION)

The night before, Morgan and I had planned the trip while quietly resting in camp after the evening meal was over. We had an ample supply of bait so decided to try to catch a few brookers in Panther Mountain Stream, about two miles from camp. So bright and early the next morning we were on our way up an old wagon trail, which led to our starting place on the stream. The trail went between two high and thickly wooded mountains, and a fine brook ran beside it for nearly a mile. A beautiful picture was presented. Just ahead, where the water slowly trickled down a long, slanting falls, it glistened in the morning sunlight; and the murmur of the little brook, as it wound its way to the road, fell pleasantly on our ears.

At an exceptionally large pool, for that brook, Morgan thought a few good-sized trout might be lurking in some shady covert. True enough, one did leap from the water at that moment, only to disappear again in the shimmering depths. We did not stop long enough to catch it, for we were impatient to reach Panther Mountain Stream. Farther up the trail more trout were jumping, but still we would not give it a try, but kept on, and soon reached our destined point. We figured it was just as well to leave the trout in a small brook alone and let them grow and multiply, as they would probably enter the larger streams later on. We were looking for bigger game in bigger waters.

We had planned to stay all day, as this particular stream flows into Irondequoit Stream and we agreed to fish that also, so had put up a substantial lunch. We both carried our share, but in spite of that we were not to have the pleasure of partaking of it, as you will see later.

After we had fished downstream a short distance we came upon a big, deep pool, with an enormous boulder in the middle. We considered it worthwhile to stop and spend a little time at this delightful spot. We stayed a good half-hour, and Morgan managed to land several beauties by means of his flies, and I caught a few with worms.

Upon walking down a bit farther we came to a large log reaching from side to side, quite a part of it being under water. I dropped my much washed and now faded angleworm beside it, and immediately there was a terrific jerk, snapping the line taut. I was fast to the largest trout we had occasion to see that day. Must have been fully fourteen inches long; a rare sized trout for Panther Mountain Stream. He darted swiftly under the log, but I checked him just before he would have a chance to become entangled around a branch. At once he swerved and shot for the other side, twisted, turned, gave a magnificent leap from the rushing water, dove, and made wild, erratic dashes in all directions. He tried his best to duck under the log to a safe retreat. Another frantic leap and mighty splashing! What fun I was having with this beauty! What a glorious fight he was giving me! At last the trout showed signs of tiring, and after a last great attempt to reach his nook under that log, I hauled him from his home waters.

"Wow!" shouted Morgan, who was behind me, "Don't lose him! Get him over to the bank, quick!" We were more than excited. I swung him towards the bank, but oh! He never got there. In my excitement I had failed to notice the low branches of a nearby maple tree, hanging over the water to the left. The fish naturally had to strike those fatal bows, be knocked from the already loosened hook, and vanish from our sight in two small seconds. Back under the log he darted, and to stay. What a sight! What a moment of deep feeling that caused!

"Darn!" I muttered in keen disappointment.

Morgan fished on ahead of me and was soon lost from view, for I stopped at a small hole to see if it was possible to tempt one out from under a big stone. I made absolutely certain that no branches or anything else would impede landing this time. Presently I had one safely hooked and flopping on the bank. (I do not dehook a fish in mid-stream, as I have lost too many that way. Neither of us had a hand net, so it was a case of swinging each one to the bank for safety.) I had measured the trout and found it to be exactly five and three quarter inches in length-not mentioning its great width. Aggravatingly close! Back it went and I moved on, hoping luck would change. I finally came to a sharp bend and paused to fish a pool. It was here I heard the loud splash which opened this story.

I rushed around to where the calamity had occurred and began laughing so hard I nearly fell in myself. There he sat—right in the middle of the stream, rod in the water, with a seven-inch trout flopping desperately on the line; the creel, which contained his few precious fish, almost capsized; and his much-worn and dilapidated hat floating gently but swiftly downstream. Brother was not in too pleasant a frame of mind at that moment.

"Laugh, if you want to, I don't care, hope you fall in also."

"How's the water? Warm, isn't it," I said sarcastically. "How did it happen?"

"Oh, some darn rock turned over under my foot while I was waiting for that fish (pointing at the now drowned trout) to get a firm grasp on the fly," he flung back.

Morgan was up of course and trying to recover his upset possessions. I dashed after his hat, succeeded in catching up to it, and was bending over to grab the thing, when I stumbled on a pebble and took a *header*. Splash! Plop! I jumped up quickly and hopped to the bank, wet to the hide. Morgan just remained where he was parked and roared. Imagine! When he approached, I bellowed, "See here, brother, when I chase after this doo-hinky again it will be because I'm in urgent need of the tackle that adorns it. Here, take the fool contraption."

We stuck around that sheltered place for about an hour and partially dried. We spread our fish on a large, flat rock and cleaned them. Eleven speckled beauties! How nice they looked, placed in a row! We were anticipating a fine trout breakfast for the next morning. With the cleaning over and everything shipshape once more, we continued angling.

After a short distance the stream parted and flowed around a rocky island. Morgan took the left hand side, I the other. He did not fare so well as there were no pools, and it was very shallow and sandy. I met with favorable conditions, for in walking by a rock I came upon a little stillwater. I was screened by a boulder in front, so cast my line to the opposite bank near some thick alders. There came a swirl, and I felt a quick tug the minute the line touched the surface. A fairly large trout left its home by the alders and took up its residence in my creel, free of rent.

I threw in a few more times. More swirls and more additions to my small stock of fish.

"Hey, Morgan!" I yelled, "Come over here. The fish are hungry. Angling is prosperous." He came on the run, or I should say "roll," for he misstepped and rolled down an inclined shelf of stone. He had some difficulty, from his position behind a boulder, in maneuvering his fly to a place beside the alders. He is good at "flipping the fly" though, so caught more than I was able to capture with the trusty worm.

Moving on from there, Morgan again took the lead, while I lingered behind to fish leisurely along and try thoroughly every out-of-the-way spot. I presently felt a vigorous pulling at the line and brought to light a fine specimen of a "brookie." Believe it must have been at least three inches long. Pity I did not measure it to be exact about dimensions, for I am none too accurate on estimating the correct length, breadth, and thickness of a trout of that size. However, I surveyed him while he dangled in air for a few seconds before he shook off.

"Ah!" I sighed with relief, "I don't have to de-hook him." When they are small like that, it seems good not to have to bother to remove the hook from each, especially when you catch as many as I do.

I proceeded farther downstream, and it was not long before I heard an urgent call from Morgan.

"What's the trouble? Are you lost?" I shouted.

"Come here, quick!" was the reply.

I could not imagine what he could have had that was worth going so "quick" to see, and what provoked such a yell. I ran forward and what I saw speedily convinced me that his joy was well founded. He was proudly holding a ten and an eleven-inch trout that had just been lured by his faithful flies. As the sun shone on the dripping sides of the fish, they glistened and were really beautiful—the colors were so bright.

"Those are *trout*." I remarked.

"Well I should hope to tell you so!" he exclaimed with great enthusiasm, his face all smiles.

"Your creel will feel heavy soon, " I said, as he carefully laid the newest with the others.

I believe I failed to mention a while back a couple of incidents that proved to be of importance to us. You remember that Morgan sat down in the water when he slipped. Well, it happened that he rested on his lunch and it became water-soaked, so he had to throw it away. And I recall, if you do not, that soon after I was flat on my face in the middle of the stream. When I turned over to get up my sandwiches had voted, "wet," so I discarded them. Morgan had been carrying the hard-boiled eggs. Imagine how they looked after he sat on them! Flat and mush, and who likes their hard eggs in that shape? So we had no lunch and, when he caught his last two, it was nearly noon.

We were fishing down Panther Mountain Stream very slowly, adding a few to our supply, when we noticed it was beginning to get cloudy. However, we did not worry as we were just entering Irondequoit Stream and only had two miles to fish.

Nevertheless, we had gone but half a mile when it began to rain hard, and to thunder. We were fortunate in that at this place there was a clearing and an old log cabin and woodhouse stood near the stream. As it was not raining too hard yet we fished in the still-water close by the cabin, and enticed some nibblers to take a worm, sail in the air, and land in the fish basket. Soon it commenced to pour, so we hurried into the welcome shelter of the camp.

Inside we discovered an old rusty stove and some food that must have been fresh when Noah stored away his two cans of salmon in the *Ark*. Besides that there were several rusty pans, pails, and kettles scattered over the floor. Everything in the "kitchen" had seen its last good day of service about fifty and one years previous. In the only other downstairs room there was a broken-down bench, which probably once served as a bed on which to pass the night—not to sleep on, for it looked impossible to enjoy that comfort on an old hard board such as the bench consisted of.

We mounted the ladder to inspect the attic. Here we found a small pile of hay.

"Looks like we chew hay tonight, if we are forced to remain here," suggested Morgan, and added, "unless we can cook some of our fish."

"Go to it," said I. "But as for fodder, I would rather put that chunk of stale bread we saw on the table to soak and squeeze that down."

It rained steadily for four hours and Morgan and I became restless at being cooped up in the musty cabin. The only other noise, besides the patter of the rain on the leaky roof, was a chipmunk which continually squeaked to himself in the corner. It was now five o'clock and would be going on eight before camp could be reached if the rain stopped, which it did not do. At last it let up (if it had not quit our chipmunk friend would have been in danger of losing his squeak) so we left the ancient cabin to plod our way back, accompanied by our thirty-nine trout. Morgan did not want to cook any of them as he thought we could endure our hunger until we got to camp, but I felt otherwise.

We had a long journey on a muddy road before coming to where there was some food, so set off at a brisk pace. The sky cleared, and by and by twilight came. On rounding a curve we were suddenly startled by a deer jumping across the road. He was gone in an instant and we only caught a glimpse of his white "flag" as he bounded into the forest. As darkness fell the stars commenced to shine, and later a full moon helped to light up the way ahead and cheer us along.

The route seemed endless, but finally camp came in sight and we were mighty pleased to see it. Both of us were dead tired and almost famished. Supper was soon cooking and in short order was being rapidly consumed.

"Want to earn some money?" asked Morgan, after the meal was over, the dishes washed, and we were enjoying a peaceful rest before the fire.

"How come this unusual generosity?" I demanded.

"Keep your money, you may need it some day, and I'll keep my seat."

It ended by us both doing our share, and then "good-night" for a much-needed sleep.

It is a mystery to me yet when I hit the pillow. Morgan told me the next morning that I was snorting loud and fast enough to have jarred the bed to pieces, even before he had a chance to unlace his shoes. I claim he is wrong, for I distinctly heard two loud crashes after he had let those same shoes drop.

🌲 FISHING THE TURBULENT WEST CANADA CREEK

Mortimer Norton

After a good night's sleep we found that we felt like putting in another day with the trout, so at breakfast, real early Saturday morning, we discussed the possibilities of securing a few larger ones somewhere else. At that moment we were enjoying some of the trout caught the day before, and cooked by our united efforts. Where to go? After some debating, Morgan, for once, agreed with me perfectly in that we should take the auto and go to the West Canada Creek.

About twenty minutes later, if you had been there, you would have seen two fishermen climb in a car and go bumping down that same dirt road we had traversed the evening before, on our way to camp from the old log cabin by Irondequoit Stream. Also you would have seen Morgan's grand hat (the identical one I had fallen fore and aft in Panther Stream to get the day before) go bobbing up and down and, when he hit the roof, smash flat to his head. He has that thing to this day.

We reached the creek in less than two hours, and parked the car near a tumbled-down shack. At once we rigged up and set out for the falls and pool. We knew from what others had said that some very large trout were in the pool, but strange to relate neither of us could lure any of those old wise fellows to taste our proffered bait. The trout must have been too educated to the ways of fishermen to be fooled by either Morgan's various kinds and colors of flies, or my adult and infant angleworms After fishing there for half an hour, and losing several crawlers by the nibbles of small trout and chubs, besides our good humor, we moved on to fast waters below. Morgan was a bit reluctant to leave without having at least one fish from that excellent pool.

Below a bridge there was another fine pool, so we dropped our lines in and let them drift slowly. I made sure that no obstructions were in the way, as I remembered what the loss had been the previous day on account of a few branches. The bank here was steep and high, so much line had to be let out in order to allow the hooks to drift.

All at once I felt a bite, so bent over a trifle to get in a position to play whatever "bit." This act nearly proved disastrous to me. Some dirt broke away from under my feet and I began to tilt forward at a dangerous angle. I guess I would have been swimming with the fish in two seconds if Morgan had not grabbed me by the coat-tails and yanked me back, upsetting my equilibrium.

Morgan succeeded in landing a ten-incher from this pool, and three more about eight inches in length.

Wilmurt Falls on West Canada Creek. The pool below was one of
Mortimer Norton's fishing destinations. Photograph by Lloyd Blankman.
COURTESY EDWARD BLANKMAN (THE LLOYD BLANKMAN COLLECTION)

At a wide bend in the stream, a half mile below the bridge, there was deep, fast-moving water along the right bank for quite a distance. "Here is ideal water for a big one to be lurking under the bank," said Morgan. "Take it easy now; keep well back out of sight and spend plenty of time here."

He took the lower end of the bend to fish with his flies; I the upper half to try with the worm. He made a skillful cast; the fly lit on the water close to the bank, and began to glide past rocks and little eddies. A wonderful place for the large, sporty trout. Swish! A real one had smashed into the fly and had hooked himself securely. At once he darted for the bottom and under the bank. Morgan quickly tightened up a bit on the line and easily led him out and away from dangerous obstacles near the bottom. Up the trout came, making a ferocious shake, and a mighty splashing. What a beautiful sight to the eyes of fishermen, and what a trout! In a twinkling he had disappeared and then tussled back and forth, up and down, keeping Morgan busy every second guessing his next antic. That was a game trout, and for five minutes he thrashed around in swift water in the middle of the stream, until Morgan led him to shallower spots where he reached down and lifted the speckled beauty from his mountain abode.

Morgan seemed to be having all the good luck, though I caught one almost as large from my end of the bend. During the day my brother captured three others of practically the same size – fifteen inches of fighting fury. These were old natives of West Canada Creek, trout that are rarer and harder to catch these days from that stream, though some fine ones have been taken lately.

Towards noon we came to where the banks of the stream are rocky for a short distance. Here we sat and fished. At first we caught a small number of shiners or "whitefish," as some call them, locally. Our lunches were dry and in good shape this day, for we had not yet fallen into the creek. We expected to, though, since it would be queer if we did not take a nap on the bottom somewhere. We thought it opportune to do away with the eating problem then, as we had keen appetites. One certainly gets hungry after a few hours' healthful exercise in the open.

It was a beautiful spot where we ate. The stream stretched away for a long distance at our left, and finally disappeared around a bend. Trees lined either bank and at some places grew right to the water's edge. The unruly water, as it tumbled over some stones and swept between others, was very white as it broke, and in the sunlight presented a pretty scene.

While Morgan and I sat there enjoying nature and landing a trout or shiner occasionally, we discussed and argued about the ways and peculiarities of trout.

"The reason we do not get more fish is because we keep too near the stream; they espy us and are scared away," was Morgan's opening comment.

"I believe you are right, for trout depend on their eyes mostly to warn them of danger. When they see a man, at once they dart off for safer retreats."

"But what about their hearing?" Morgan asked. "If you drop your sinker in with a 'plop' they are frightened away." To which I replied, "Trout cannot hear." It is through their feeling or sense of vibrations that they are warned in that way. I once read that trout show no alarms when a train rumbles across a bridge over a stream. If you threw a stone into a pool you would see that a trout, quietly sleeping, would not become alarmed until the waves, which cause a slight commotion in the water, from the stone reached him. Here is a saying I think aptly expresses the hearing question:

"If fish could hear as well as see, never a fisher would there be."

"I often wonder what becomes of small trout when they are released after being caught through the eye, or hurt quite badly," Morgan resumed.

"I heard once that these injured ones are often eaten by the larger trout, if they do not die beforehand."

"Another interesting thing to know," I continued, "is that if the wind is from the west or south the trout usually rise briskly, but if from the north or east they do not move or are very slow at it."

When a trout is caught that is undersized, *always wet your hands* before taking it off the hook, or they will die shortly afterward, it is said. Remove the fish gently, and easily slip it into the water at your feet. *Never throw* the trout fifty feet or so down the stream, as some do, just to get it out of your way so it will not bite again, which it probably would not do anyway.

"This fly fishing exasperates me at times," said Morgan with feeling.

"You must have a lot of patience. Look at me with my worm fishing. I usually get about fifteen minutes of sleep between bites. (Not so when the mosquitoes are out by the thousands.) Patience is the main thing in this kind of angling. As an old Scotchman used to say to a fisherman, who showed signs of giving up in despair: 'The first rule, sir, is, keep your flees in the water. Y'll never ha'e a fish unless they're there."

"Well, let's fish a little farther along, and then quit for the day," said Morgan, and with that we started on.

The stream grew wider and the water a trifle swifter, and at a bend we stopped to try the boiling water at the foot of a rocky wall. The view here was splendid, for we could look far off and see the green hills and white houses bordering a winding state road. At this point we caught three more large trout.

Nothing very exciting occurred during the rest of our angling, so after securing a few more, making twenty-three in all, we left the stream and hiked for the road that led back to the auto.

"Well!" exclaimed Morgan, "we didn't land in the creek today, did we?"

"Don't believe so," said I, feeling of my clothes to make sure.

"We have had a fine two days' fishing trip, though, and I dread to think of having to go back to the city."

"Yes, so do I, but we will come here again next year."

"We still lack about three miles of reaching the auto, so let's walk faster," said Morgan.

The old iron bridge over Twin Lakes Stream in North Wilmurt. Edward Binks, an Adirondack League Club employee is standing on the bridge. Photograph by Lloyd Blankman.
COURTESY EDWARD BLANKMAN (THE LLOYD BLANKMAN COLLECTION)

Collection 5
Sportsmen's Camps and
Backwoods Destinations

AS NEWSPAPER COLUMNIST, author of *West Canada Creek*, hiker and kayaker David Beetle so often put it, "The West Canada is a good river to know." Beetle would know. Over the course of a year he tramped his way up and down the stream, interviewed hundreds of old timers, and braved the upper West Canada Creek's powerful rapids many times in his wooden kayak, all in the name of research to gather the first written history of the river's 75-mile course.

Mud Lake is the source of the watercourse. The river winds southwest toward Prospect, fed by outlets from a maze of Adirondack lakes. The mountainous country was once home to Louis "French Louie" Seymour, who lived on the shore of Big West. The West Canada Lakes are distant and hard to reach, but the remoteness doesn't bother the backpackers who, if they arrive during just the right stretch in June, will find the shorelines abloom with pink azalea.

Nature's palette has daubed the West Canada Creek wildwood trails in year-round witchery, from the budding softwoods and hardwoods of spring to the snow-clad evergreens of winter. The entire region was once under the last glacial ice sheets that blanketed the Adirondacks. The glaciers were responsible for shaping the current landscape. Their receding waters left a vast number of boulders and erratics everywhere.

"This wild, hour-glass-shaped high plateau is higher than any other Adirondack land mass." At an elevation of 2,458 feet, Wilmurt "is the highest settled lake in the Adirondacks." Fort Noble Mountain, the highest surface feature in the region, is in the Town of Wilmurt. A fire tower was once constructed on the summit; observers looked out over Nobleboro, West Canada Creek and the South Branch of the West Canada Creek in Herkimer County. Its slopes are a sweep of scented winds over balsam, spruce and pine, and are costumed in brilliant fall colors for leaf peepers, ranging in hue from red to pale yellow.

Author Barbara McMartin's *Discover the West Central Adirondacks* guidebook tells us about the southwest Canada Lakes Wilderness: "Although many trails penetrate its narrow core, parts of it are trackless, making it the most remote and secret area in the park . . . The creeks conceal spectacular forests as well as a dozen inviting lakes." The guidebook reports that "There is currently no view from . . . [Fort Noble Mountain]. In its last few years, when the tower stood abandoned, you could still climb its rickety stairs for the view. However, even to do this you had to ford the South Branch, no mean feat even in low water, because the great hiker's suspension bridge was removed about 1980." The "160,000 acres [would be] the second largest Wilderness Area (after the High Peaks in Essex Country) in the Adirondacks, a bushwhacker's paradise were it not for the difficulty in fording the South Branch and the large blocks of Adirondack League Club and Wilmurt Tract lands that are posted." McMartin's guide emphasizes that the owners "permit *no one* on their lands."

Once, sportsmen and tourist propaganda depicted exciting experiences. Sports sojourned in hunters' camps—bark or pole lean-tos provided by guides who selected camping grounds, felled trees and peeled bark for the shanties, fitted up enticing balsam bough beds on the floors, built shelves and racks, kept the campfires and smudges going night and day, prepared and cooked the meals, washed dishes, told yarns and, late nights or early mornings, left the sports to sleep while they slipped away to return with venison or fish. Those recreationists who sought a woods experience but had more congenial tastes, wishing to avoid living in the heart of the woods but preferring the charms of hotel life to those of camp life, sought out public houses with unpapered pine board partitions rather than the hotels with covered verandahs, barrooms, bedrooms, bathrooms to wash off the dust of forest travel, and dining rooms that offered a well-arranged menu from which to select dinner.

The stories in this chapter touch on a few of the high spots Blankman and Norton learned of or visited in their days of circling the Adirondacks. Most deal with the forest and lake settings in the West Canada region. Almost every turn they took brought them to a point of interest—Spruce Lake, now wild, once filled with trout—Adirondack Whiskey Springs, a lake bed containing an interesting natural resource, and more.

Reading the old recollections is an excellent way to get that old-time "forest feeling." And it's invigorating.

ADIRONDACK FOOTHILLS HOTELS AND TUG HILL

William J. O'Hern

Life in a primitive fishing or hunting shanty can be raw, lacking in refinement, but it can also be an escape from the telephone, newspapers, the work-a-day-world and city living. Sportsmen probably laugh harder, longer, and louder over things that have happened in camp than over things that have happened anywhere else. And some of the warmest memories they come home with are woven around this nomadic existence they enjoyed for years on end.

Twice a year sporting men and women took to the Adirondacks. In May they would spend two weeks trout fishing and the same length of time in the fall hunting white tail deer or black bear. North Woods headquarters might have been a log structure built by a guide for "sports," such as "Red" Jack Conklin's two camps in Wilmurt. One was back a way from the dirt road (Route 8) near Mad Tom Brook; the other was sited deeper in the woods, north of Haskell's Inn, along a cold spring brook called Gulf Stream and within a good stone's throw of the old trail to Twin Lakes and North Wilmurt.

Before reaching their destination, which was usually miles away from home, travelers would enjoy dinner, a night's rest and breakfast at an Adirondack foothills hotel. The West Leyden Hotel was one such stopping place for travelers heading into the Adirondack Mountains.

The hotel stands today. Well over one hundred years old, its appearance has hardly changed from the time George Scholl took over its operation in 1904. It is typical of many Tug Hill inns that once welcomed travelers on their way to the 'Dacks.

Guests pose in front of "Red" Jack Conklin's camp. Conklin was likely the guide for their hunt.
COURTESY EDWARD BLANKMAN (THE LLOYD BLANKMAN COLLECTION)

Tug Hill is known as the "Lesser Wilderness." However, it is less developed, and has fewer roads and many remote regions with thousands of state-owned acres. It is not controlled by a state agency and boasts of more wildlife than the "Great Adirondack Wilderness." It is known far and wide as the capital for snowmobiling, snowshoeing, and cross-country skiing.

Lloyd Blankman said, "Tug Hill is said to have gotten its name from two early settlers, who made their way up Welsh Hill Road, west of Turin. They probably gave it other names at the same time. It was quite a tug."

Hunting and fishing was excellent in the early days. Two Lowville-bound fishermen went on a trip to Crystal Creek by horse and buggy. They returned home with a hundred pounds of trout for each man.

Tug Hill was first settled, more or less, about 1797. Settlers arrived from Massachusetts and Connecticut following the end of the Revolutionary War. Between 1797 and 1804, logging and road building opened the wilderness for farmers to settle along the Black River watershed.

According to Ben Wright's survey of 1802–1804, the lesser plateau contains 375,000 acres of forest and swamp "nearly level." It was late in the fall when Wright started his survey. He wrote, "We have just arrived at the top of Tug Hill . . . mostly swamp and high water, and to make matters worse, we ran out of whiskey three days ago."

In Blankman's travels he viewed interesting sights and learned facts.

The largest spring on the Tug Hill is at a place called Monteola. It is the size of a small house and water rises from it like a water fountain. The outlet is a stream that empties into Mad River, terminating at Mad River Beaver Dam.

A large part of the plateau is now owned by the state and by two or three paper companies. Many sections are now being reforested with spruce and pine, set out by farmers, the state and paper concerns.

There were many hardwoods here, mostly birch and maple. The large virgin growth birch trees were shipped to Poland and manufactured into veneer. The waste material from the hardwood flooring operation, was made into charcoal and wood alcohol. No part of the tree went to waste.

The birches were beautiful white, silver and yellow. The maples were wonderful growths of curly and birds eye, shipped to Germany for use in making expensive musical instruments like violins.

Lloyd Blankman loved to travel. It was his pleasure to seek out (and photograph) "the large, medium, and small hotels and inns that stand today unoccupied waiting to burn up or crumble to the ground," he reported in an "Adirondack Characters" article that featured Fish Creek Hotel.

As a youngster, Lloyd found the hotels and inns "fascinating." Most of the early places he knew in his youth were gone when he began his early hotel picturing-taking odyssey in the 1960s.

"They were rambling buildings," he recalled, "a remnant of an early day. All the Tug Hill and Adirondack hotels advertised trout and venison dinners, and accommodated from a dozen to hundreds of guests. Most places were close to the road where the stages almost brushed the front porches."

Blankman felt, "Something about the memory of an early hotel in the woods, arouses a strong feeling of nostalgia." This was especially true with him each time he talked to oldsters who recalled, as one old timer did, "the quiet of the hills and the soft, smoothing stillness of the lakes and woods." The man, identified only as Frank, traveled with a horse and buggy and stayed at Paul Smith's Hotel on St. Regis Lake in 1914 and the Fenton House at Number Four near Beaver River.

Frank was typical of every old-time Adirondack "sport" (man and woman) Blankman revived memories of. "Before the opening of the fishing or hunting seasons," he told, "I sent word in advance to my favorite Adirondack hotel of the date of my throwing off the cares of town life for the delights of the forest."

Of the fifteen hotels Blankman remembered from his youth, the West Leyden Hotel (once known as the Scholl House) on the rim of the Tug Hill Plateau is special because its architecture is of an earlier time and it stands today. Note the dinner bell on top of the building.

Each time I round the curve in Route 26 on my way to the Adirondacks I picture the old hotel porch, as it might have looked a century ago. There, along the dirt road to Boonville might be found deer hanging. There would be proud sportsmen, with packbaskets and rifles, standing as someone took a picture with a camera. The next morning, they would catch the stage and start for home, taking with them not only game but also Adirondack memories.

The hotel at West Leyden sometime after 1911. The photo came from Mrs. George Witzigman, daughter of George Scholl, who ran the hotel from 1904 to 1911. AUTHOR'S COLLECTION

The old Haskell Inn had fallen into a state of disrepair similar to the St. Nicholas Hotel when this picture was taken. There is still a tavern called Haskell's near the old Inn which may have been part of the original Inn and also served as a stage coach depot.
COURTESY EDWARD BLANKMAN (THE LLOYD BLANKMAN COLLECTION)

🌲 ST. NICHOLAS HOUSE, AN ANTIQUATED ADIRONDACK HOTEL

Lloyd Blankman

The old St. Nicholas Hotel is being torn down by Glen Stevens, who recently purchased the place. Mr. Stevens owns and operates a gas station and general hardware store nearby.

The hotel was built in 1872 by Richard (Dick) Allen and soon after was sold to Nicholas Bush, from whom it derived its name.

Mr. Bush was a native of France and with his wife, their son, Charles, and daughter, Josephine Bush Overacker, operated the hotel for many years, during the time the tannery was in operation.

Mr. Bush had a clock, which he brought from France, which was a curiosity to all, being in the form of a man. With each tick of the clock, "Blinky" rolled his eyes. One day "Blinky" was silent and never worked again. No one ever understood its mechanism, it being of French design.

Mr. Bush sold the hotel in later years to George Freeman, who died there. It was then sold to George Hatch, who conducted a successful hotel there until 1901, when the place changed hands several times, finally being bought by the late Nelson Jarvis, Sr.

After the death of Mr. Jarvis, it was sold at auction to Claude Colton to settle the estate. Mr. Colton turned the building into an apartment house, but it had fallen into disrepair and was regarded as a menace to nearby buildings.

Another old landmark of the Adirondacks is no more, but many people still hold memories of the old St. Nicholas Hotel.

The Nicholas House was an unusual style of hotel.

🌲 MOTHER JOHNSON'S
Lloyd Blankman

Mother Johnson was an Adirondack character. Her place was situated on the Raquette River about midway between Long Lake and Upper Saranac Lake. It was long called the half-way house. Her hotel was ¼ mile above Raquette Falls on the carry around a two-mile stretch of rapids on the river.

Summer travel was quite heavy here. No one ever went by Mother Johnson's without stopping for a meal or a night's lodging. Her specialties were pancakes and hospitality. No one ever forgot the meals served here, in the log house, at the pine table. None was ever turned away, day or night.

Mother Johnson's fat, pleasant face glowed as she served her customers. Her sides shook with laughter as she passed the smoking, russet-colored cakes from the griddle to the half-emptied plates. Soon she won the race as the guests cried "Hold; enough."

She knew how to get up a good feed, venison that was juicy and had actual taste to it. She served fine trout at the table until September 15, when the season closed, and then they didn't have any name.

The Johnsons moved to Raquette Falls in 1860 and picked up a good many dollars from travelers, serving meals and lodging, and by dragging boats two miles over the rough carry by ox-cart at $1.50 per boat. Mr. Johnson had a kennel of the best deer hounds.

Mother Johnson died January 27, 1875, after a short illness, and, at the desire of her husband, was buried on a little knoll back of the house, where her husband was also buried when done with earthly things. The snow was so deep at the time as to make the way almost impassable, and but three, beside the family, were present at the time; but with their aid the body was laid away, with no ceremony save the sad good-byes of those who loved her.

The Piseco Lake House, a turn-of-the-century rural hotel, 1900.
COURTESY EDWARD BLANKMAN (THE LLOYD BLANKMAN COLLECTION)

ADIRONDACK SPRINGS

Lloyd Blankman

All over the woods are to be found hundreds of springs that are one of the main sources of water supply, feeding lakes, ponds and streams. Here, for over 100 years, hunters and trappers have rested from the trail and at these places, have quenched their thirst with clear, cold and delicious water. Here water bubbles up out of the earth, sometimes in large streams. Many of these springs are well known and bear interesting names, such as Clear, Crystal, Whiskey and Mineral.

The writer, in the summer of 1960, rediscovered an ancient and nearly forgotten mineral spring near the outlet of Brantingham Lake. The water from this spring is strongly impregnated with iron and contains some magnesium with a trace of sulfur. This water is clear, cold and delicious, but if left to stand in a bottle overnight turns brown and tastes strongly of minerals.

There are many whiskey springs. One of the most famous is about a mile beyond the cement bridge on the old Joy Lake road. This is a small permanent spring, and is from a small base.

Why Whiskey?

Why is it called Whiskey Spring? There are two versions as to the origin and you may take your choice. When the old road was in full use (1885–1910) the packers and other travelers always stopped here either to drink water, or whiskey, usually both. Some say this is why it became known as Whiskey Spring.

Others say that one time a person started to pour a whiskey drink here and dropped the bottle, which broke on the gravel, and the whole party dropped down on their hands and knees and drank out of the spring, as the whiskey ran into it.

The permanent springs seeping from large gravel deposits and rock crevices keep the brooks running throughout all seasons of the year and thus the springs are of great importance for all plant and animal life in the forest.

Occasional Flow

Some springs issue from gravel deposits that cover bare rock and flow only in wet seasons.

There are two main kinds of permanent springs, one heading from shallow gravel and a light cover of woods soil. Possibly these have an original source from rock crevices beneath the surface and are small but permanent springs.

Another type seeps in regular channels, from beneath large areas of sand and gravel many feet thick, resting on an impervious base.

Take the path to the spring for rest and refreshment. The water is cold and refreshing. Sip a little at a time, pausing often to admire the beautiful scene before you. Few things in nature are more precious to a woodsman than a pool of clear, sweet water. This is what makes a camping place really good. All such places are welcome landmarks.

 WHITE LEAD LAKE
Lloyd Blankman

Just east of Wright's Hotel in Wilmurt, a road leads north into the woods a half mile to a small pond called White Lead Lake. The bottom of this pond is a soft white mud formed by the residue of living organisms, much like coral is formed in the ocean.

This substance was dug out of the lake, pressed into small cakes, placed in open sheds to dry and then put into a kiln where it was heated by a wood fire to burn out vegetable matter, leaves and other impurities.

It was then bagged, taken to the rail head at Hinckley and shipped away to be made later into a silver polish.

Light in Weight

These cakes were light in weight. A barn sack full would weigh only a few pounds. It was first transported on wagons with hayracks. These loads seemed to be as bulky as small loads of hay.

The outlet of White Lead is a small stream, which flows southward a half mile, crossing the hard road just east of Wright's Hotel. It then joins the West Canada Creek just above the Wilmurt Gorge.

Details

The story is, a sow fell in the lake and when they got her out she was pure white and so the lead was discovered and the place called White Lead Lake. Operations were started here about 1870 and a company established in 1873 by John A. Wright of Keene, New Hampshire.

The main product was Wright's Silver Crème polish.

One may still find, here and there, samples of Wright's silver polish in crème or powder form, made from a product of White Lead Lake.

White Lead Lake. Photograph by Lloyd Blankman.
COURTESY EDWARD BLANKMAN (THE LLOYD BLANKMAN COLLECTION)

🌲 LITTLE DEER LAKE

Lloyd Blankman

Grotus Reising, the photographer, took a picture of Little Deer Lake in 1897 from the steep bank near the paths. He took another picture of the same place with two people in a flat-bottom boat. The boat was kept tied where the water from a large spring ran in quite a stream through a marshy shore.

The outlet of the lake is as large as the Conkling Brook where it crosses the Northwood road. Before it was dammed, Little Deer covered about three acres of land. The lake had a sandy bottom and was from three to five feet deep.

It was a great spawning place for trout from the West Canada Creek. The only inlet was a spring brook three or four hundred feet long. The lake is also fed from several springs along the bottom of a steep bank. One spring is near a trapper's cabin, named Broadwaters.

The outlet of Little Deer Lake enters the nearby West Canada Creek just above where the Conkling Brook does. Burt Conklin caught mink, muskrat and trout here at Little Deer Lake.

This lake gets its name from the fact that a grass-like algae grows profusely all over in it and that deer seem to like it better than anything that grows. Deer fed on algae here more than anywhere else you ever saw. They would put their heads way down in the water to the bottom, gather a mouthful of the luscious food, raise their heads out of the water and chew like a cow would chew a mouthful of clover. Deer do not seem to understand "no trespassing" signs. The writer saw recently deer crossing the Northwood road, on their way to Little Deer Lake.

When Burt Conklin, the trapper, built his house nearby, they carried all their drinking and cooking water from Little Deer Lake for household use. Little Deer Lake is well worth a visit at the present time.

Little Deer Lake. Photograph by Grotus Reising, 1897.
COURTESY EDWARD BLANKMAN (THE LLOYD BLANKMAN COLLECTION)

🌿 SPRUCE LAKE COUNTRY, FAR BACK AND LONG AGO

William J. O'Hern

I suppose anyone who likes the outdoors, consults a guidebook, and enjoys traveling throughout the great Adirondack forest shares a need for a special place: a meadow, a summit, fire tower, lake or pond, a stretch of incomparable water to paddle or fish, a favorite trail or a seldom-climbed rocky knob. The list is as endless as people are diverse. The particular place where we can eye the mountain topography, think of a little history or study the pleasing geography can stick in our mind long after we leave it. The thought will soar a tired spirit, refresh a wearied soul, and perk up a sinking feeling.

Spruce Lake is one of those baptismal landscapes that offers a refreshing sight. Located about ten miles northwest of Piseco Lake Village, it is one-and-a-quarter miles long and one half mile wide and lies 2,378 feet above sea level. Few people ever see it, although it is accessible by foot trail on the way in to the home site of French Louie, the old woodsman who once lived at Big West.

Time is an asset. I make use of it as one should a nonrenewable natural resource. While rowing and later, lakeside, nestled in one of three lean-tos tucked along the tight spruce-balsam bordered lake, by a crackling fire, with the freedom time affords, I have looked at fishing pictures that were taken in this vicinity. On the path from the village of Piseco that in 1880 consisted of only three or four families, I suspect the old Indian hermit "Pezeeko," who once dwelt upon its shores, tramped approximately the same terrain of the Great Forest I cover to reach the backwoods lake. Then, the scenery was wild and beautiful. The lake is no different now. Then, the recent explorations and extensive reports on the Topographical Survey of the Adirondack Wilderness, by Verplanck Colvin, served to attract attention in this direction. The lake was richly supplied with trout. Deer fed in the daytime around the almost impenetrable shoreline. It was also the headquarters of a well-liked spruce gum-picking Adirondack character. From his camp at the lake, Tim Crowley packed pack baskets of gum out to the Daniels factory in Poland, where it was purified and packaged for sale.

In time, a twelve-mile sled road extended Pezeeko's footpath. The access afforded guides an avenue for their horses to pull jumpers, and city sports to traverse northwest overland from Piseco to Spruce and Balsam Lakes and more distant trout waters where the tenderfoot sportsmen could whip the streams.

There, for example, through the dense stands of spruce and balsam, the faint muddy footpath around the south shore of the lake joins with a southerly nondescript track that leads to Spruce Lake Mountain and Indian River stillwater. Farther along Spruce's southern shoreline, another obscure trace meanders westerly in the direction of West Canada Creek's headwaters. Illegal all-terrain vehicles have made their mark. Prefabricated bridges lie hidden in bushes to span tributaries where once the Adirondack guide who worked for three dollars a day carried a guideboat, guns and fishing tackle, his bulky pack basket and cooking utensils. He was a one-man traveling camp outfit.

The guide-of-old took pride in his knowledge of woodcraft. Without a murmur he would have made the rough "carry" for miles with a boat on his shoulder and, on reaching a favored location, would quickly set up a camp, and gather firewood for cooking and balsam boughs for a bed. He would cook, wash the pots and pans and perform whatever else was necessary to make a party of tenderfoot sportsmen comfortable and happy.

Back of the outside world beyond the edges of the North Woods, the guide's mind filled with woods lore, he told of his unsophisticated adventures. The Adirondack guide was a valuable companion in the solitude of the deep woods.

There is something marvelous about traveling throughout Spruce Lake country. Its past and geography bring on creative ideas. The creative ideas, in turn, affect emotions of my heart and allow me to dream of past times.

I think of Speculator's Dan Page and forest ranger Jim "Pants" Lawrence. Jim and the West Canadas are synonymous. At age 63, Jim constructed the log bridge across Mud Lake inlet. His way of life and his eccentricities became symbols of Big West, his interior ranger cabin home.

Both men were oldsters but popular personalities in the territory during the middle of the twentieth century. Their knowledge of the land and firsthand stories of backwoods dwellers Johnny Leaf and Adirondack French Louie (Louie Seymour) became legend. Louie had put in a good evening the night of February 27, 1915, at the bar of the Brooks Hotel in Speculator, drinking with Pants Lawrence. The next day Louie died.

I didn't know French Louie but I knew Winfred "Slim" Murdock. Slim, late in life, shared his time with me looking back on his years as a packer for his uncle Gerald Kenwell. Gerald's parents were Adirondack pioneers. On the bank of the South Branch of the Moose River in the Moose River Plains, his parents lived in the 1890s. Their nearest neighbors resided eighteen miles away!

It was while living in the Plains that Lewie, as Gerald spelled his name, came to know the Kenwells. Louie taught Gerald (who was only a young boy) how to care for himself in the woods under all kinds of circumstances. Slim said his uncle told him the woodscraft learned from Louie became "mighty useful in later years." Once grown, Gerald built a fishing and hunting camp along Otter Brook. Slim began packing for Gerald about 1920.

Gerald and Louie's land connection between their camps was roughly the blazed trail to Brook Trout and West Lakes today. It is a long huff between Spruce Lake and the Plains. I've made the trek several times following today's trail system as well as the trackless avenues French Louie and Gerald footed—routes that invited investigation around Mica, Poor, and Northrup Lakes. On one trek I came onto the rotting remains of Gould Paper Company's logging Camps 5 and 6. The exact locations of both camps had long eluded me.

The lean-tos of today, hidden away on the shores of Spruce Lake, make a simple shelter. They offer rough accommodation for today's fishing and backpacking parties. My favorite time at Spruce Lake is not paddling the water, searching for spring holes and fishing, but later in the day when I lay over at a lean-to. Absorbing the warmth from a cracking campfire, I imagine I entertain similar feelings shared by earlier sportsmen, when they would gather around the great back-log fire that blazed at Tim Crowley's hostelry. Camping duffel has changed a lot. The food eaten shares similarities. Bread, pancakes, cocoa, and potatoes are still standard fare. In place of venison (and any trout I don't catch) I carry little tins of tuna fish.

There is something reassuring each time I return to the lake. The early morning air. The deliciously fragrant bouquet of spruce-balsam. Wild flowers. The mud! I've yet to be greeted by an old patriarch coming up for a fly.

The fire and the environment serve as a tonic from the time I arrive home until I start again for distant Spruce Lake and the unfrequented ponds and lakes and wild trout streams in the West Canada Lakes headwaters. I watch the daytime and evening sky and look for new horizons. Connecting with nature and this marvelous Adirondack world fills me with delightful awe.

Retired Forest Ranger Jim "Pants" Lawrence, and woodsman Dan Page beside an Adirondack guideboat.
COURTESY EDWARD BLANKMAN (THE LLOYD BLANKMAN COLLECTION)

Collection 6
The Rural One-Room School

*The Hoffmeister school closing day picnic about 1900. The building is now
the Hoffmeister post office. The photograph was taken by Grotus Reising.*
COURTESY EDWARD BLANKMAN (THE LLOYD BLANKMAN COLLECTION)

ASK OLDER RESIDENTS about their knowledge of an old district schoolhouse in their part of the North Woods, and a handful of the oldest with good
memories will talk about some hamlet you might never have known about.

Their memories, perhaps the only link with the past, might go like this as
they recall a cluster of homes, hardscrabble farms and a small sawmill: "Go
four miles west past the central school in town, turn right on to the dirt road
just before the iron bridge. That's the old creek road. It's narrow, rough in
places. Be careful, there's washouts. More than likely if'n you aren't mindful
you'll scrape bottom with that low-slung car. Better if you had a truck, but it's
passable. Maybe three more miles on up there you'll come to a cross road.
'Bout the only people that travel the old track now is an occasional farm
vehicle, anglers and hunters."

The narratives I've heard generally continue with a description of the land
the abandoned dirt road passes through. Once covered with virgin forests, it
provided a seemingly unlimited amount of timber. Small and large sawmills
dotted the region. The mills were busy places in former times.

"The best trees are gone," they would continue. "Trees more than three feet at the base, there were." Today the forest is second growth. Blueberry bushes and black and red raspberry canes grow in sunny thickets where once animals grazed in cleared land or buildings stood.

"When the sawmills closed, farms were abandoned and the cheese factories shut down afterward." Folks deserted their homes and moved away. "The man years (time of demanding physical labor), like the panther, moose, and pigeon years, are over."

The settlers were rugged and worked hard at logs, lumber and farming.

The accounts of the whereabouts of the schoolhouse resume: "When you reach the four corners, it'll be a bleak looking scene. Don't expect no road sign pointing in four different directions with destinations and mileage, pointing to even more former communities. Them corners was once a busy place. Now all that remains is that school building where a few boys and girls learned the three R's."

Old Forge *Adirondack Express* newspaper columnist Mart Allen has found he gets similar replies to inquires when he interviews oldsters and travels the backcountry. Mart says of his conversations, "One truth is becoming apparent—there was much more human intrusion and activity at the turn of the twentieth century than there is today. Many of the state's wilderness areas were at one time beehives of activity."

Mart and I both enjoy talking to native Adirondackers to learn about by-gone days. One of my investigative trips into the woods might last a day or several. The advancing forest and the clearing choked with fruited brambles are full of stories of times past. If you know what evidence to look carefully for, the remains of old logging roads, holding dams, lumber camps, and home-stead cellar holes are visible. All it takes is to listen to the old-timers and look carefully enough and their stories can come to life. I can imagine an entire sawmill operation with all the comforts necessary to support several families, or a subsistence farm and the subtle signs of its human habitation just by locating laid-up stone foundations, even though the human scars are quickly being erased by an advancing peaceful-looking woods.

Many years have gone by since the isolated communities' heydays. Yet, the tiny communities' lives roll on. Seen through the eyes of a long-retired teacher or students who attended a little one-room schoolhouse, those idyllic years of growing up and attending school in a rural mountain hamlet have become fond reminiscences of golden autumn days, winter, spring and summer, and can be vividly described by oldsters.

Toward the end of his life, author Thomas C. O'Donnell of Boonville, having published four Adirondack histories, began to develop a fifth book. It was to be his recollections of growing up in a family-owned logging camp. Mr. O'Donnell recorded stories of how the teacher grumbled that the make-shift school in the camp, with its low-sloped roof of black tar paper on a renovated loggers' shanty, had inside temperatures bordering that of a blast furnace. The high temperatures might have had something to do with shortening her patience, for she was overheard venting to Mrs. O'Donnell that many of the students "don't know B from bullfrogs."

Concerned that the logging camp community would lose their teacher, Thomas' father rallied the men of the camp to help cut and shape the logs for a new schoolhouse of hewn logs.

In addition to the raising of the new school building, he wrote with nostalgia about his adventurous young teacher who boarded with his family and of his schoolhouse experiences. O'Donnell had fond memories of the peaceful backwoods community, the isolated people comprising fewer than a dozen families, and how his brother and he mastered the ABCs and the multiplication tables, learned the capitals of the United States, had spelling bees, and labored to do cursive writing. Many years had gone by, but the tug of his boyhood years was strong.

O'Donnell's unfinished manuscript rests in a university archives; it has been untouched for decades. I sit reading a photocopy of it and imagine O'Donnell sitting in his North Country house on the hill and hearing the big yellow Adirondack Central school buses go rolling by with their loads of noisy children.

In his Boonville house he shared with his cat, I imagine Mr. O'Donnell closed his eyes and dreamed of past times and of the long-ago school yard. He heard the laughter of a few girls and boys and though his eyesight was failing, he could visualize the rushing river, full of rolling logs, and the one-room schoolhouse where he learned the three R's over a hundred years ago.

Armed with a pad of writing paper, pencils and a manual typewriter, O'Donnell was anxious to run down the road of memories, as anxious as he was on that first morning of school—eager to see the teacher and keen to learn how to read, write and calculate. I presume he recalled his country school experiences with a sharp mind, for his memoirs are full of details of the days before yesterday in a one-room school house in a backcountry logging camp.

O'Donnell begins his journey back in time by telling how his father solicited applicants for the company's private schoolhouse on fanciful note paper.

"Anyone getting a letter on stationery like that would want to come and teach without pay," O'Donnell remembered. He recalls his mother smiling with approval when she saw a pad of custom-printed stationery her husband had ordered. The printer had placed his name in "glorious big Gothic letters across the top of each sheet and something about School District Number 2," he recorded her saying, "and a line on which the date could be put down. And, as if this were not enough, Father had secured envelopes to match!"

Decades later, he reflected that the quality of the paper and envelopes was probably not that good, "yet one of the responses brought a reply from Sadie Cook, who didn't wait for a reply but drove in, a day or two later, from her home over beyond Mount Pleasant. Sadie gave Father to understand that for the thirty dollars a month and board that was offered he might just as well close the deal then and there. The transaction was quickly consummated."

O'Donnell continued, "This achieved, Sadie asked, 'Where is the school-house?'"

"Huh? his father replied."

"It had never occurred to Father that here was a detail to be settled, and with school to open in two weeks! As though it had been settled long ago, however, Father pointed to the men's shanty across the road.

"'We'll take the bunks out for the summer. The term will be over and the bunks put back before the men come into camp in the fall. After all it is only for three months.

"Sadie was shaken. 'Only three months? In the whole year?'

"Sadie's glance took me in as if to say that a kid like that could stand, at the very least, twelve months. Father, however, informed Sadie that we'd start off with three months and maybe next summer we could work five in.

"The next two weeks were given over to feverish preparations for the opening of school, with carpenters brought in. Bunks were removed from the shanty and the necessary furniture fabricated, seats for the children to be made from long pine boards planed to a smooth, satiny finish.

"The results of so much labor were exciting. Along either side of the shanty ran a bench, and in front of it, supported by upright pieces, was a wide board, on a tilt, to serve as a desk. Underneath was a narrower board on which we could keep our books when not immediately in use, ink, pens, pencils, slates and slate pencils and slate rags. One bench was dedicated to the girls, and across the room, facing them, was a duplicate arrangement for the boys. The wide space between the two benches was a kind of neutral territory.

"No regulations covered the manner of getting to the particular place on the long bench which was yours, be it at or near the end, or in the middle, a half dozen feet from the end. It seemed to be within the rules, if you were a boy, to go up to the spot and step over the bench. The more brazen of the girls used the same technique, and there were occasions when the tinier of them went to their respective places and crawled under."

Thomas O'Donnell's older brother, Fred, and his peer Will Jones ". . . used whatever method would attract most attention at the time. Their favorite way was to come in, just before the bell rang, from the front end, squeezing in between the seat and the desk in front. This compelled everybody to rise and the trick was to see how many sets of toes could be stepped on. Eight out of ten was par for the course."

O'Donnell continued with a description of the schoolhouse as he recalled it. "A blackboard, also made by the carpenters, ran across the end of the room back of the teacher's table, the table something that Father had used as a desk and now was loaning to the District. Along the blackboard ran a projecting strip for holding the sticks of chalk, while at one end, on a nail driven into a log, hung a cloth for making erasures."

Entrance to the school "shanty was by a door at the end opposite the teacher's desk. In either wall, the long way of the shanty, were two small windows of four panes each.

"All this was at Father's expense; even the school bell was supplied from our lumber camp—the hand bell used for bringing the men to the house at meal-time. The only cost to the District was what Sadie, in her lighter moments, referred to as her 'income.'

"Thus were the preparations for the opening of school completed. There remained only the business of spreading word of this startling event. This detail Fred and I took on our own shoulders, and right well we carried on. What Paul Revere was to the approaching hostilities at Lexington, not to mention Concord, we were to the opening of school in District No. 2. Sadie's buggy had scarcely rattled over the loose planking of the creek bridge than Fred and I dashed out of the house to spread the tidings. By supper time, so efficient had been our efforts, the story had been proclaimed to one and all, even to regions as remote as those of the Parsons and Harts, that at nine o'clock, tomorrow morning, school would convene in District No. 2.

"Reception of the tidings was much the same everywhere. The response of Mrs. Hodgins, while pleasing to Fred and me, yet would have been more gratifying had it been more universal:

"'Land sakes, boys, you look hot and tired. Come on in and let me give you something to eat!'

"And Bud's 'Give me a piece too, Ma,' equally indicated the attitude of the victims of the impending tragedy."

I remember my first day in school. It was a very joyful one. I lived what felt like miles from the school, and I had to walk both ways. I was also very proud of my brand new-metal Roy Rogers lunch box. The walk was quite a task for a five-year-old boy but, somehow or other, I made it even though creative avoidance moves (and fast little short legs) were called for on the afternoon return in order to avert being hit by a pair of upper-class mates who enjoyed messing with little kids.

I recalled that experience of my first day in school when I walked around the aged one-room school house that stood near the crossroad the creek track led me to. The one-room building was flanked by a sagging woodshed. I entered by the woodshed through an opening where a door once hung. I could smell the accumulated dust of a century.

Having found my destination, and seeing old items, some now antiques, I carefully made my way over the sagging floor. A recitation bench ran along the wall near the teacher's desk. The old box stove was rusted out, although it looked like the occasional person who sought the dilapidated shelter still had built a fire in it. Maybe fishermen warmed their feet as the children once did in winter before going to their seats in the chilly corners of the room.

I picked up a dirty tin pail and a solitary dipper sitting on the floor. The pail and dipper probably held drinking water that was carried from a nearby well.

Sanitary conditions of the dipper and the back houses were crude compared to the facilities twenty-first century society deems essential. In the 1920s, New York State passed laws requiring rural schools to install indoor sanitary toilets complete with vent pipes and lightning rods.

Progress has camouflaged many schoolhouses as camps and houses. Others weather into decay, but if one listens carefully he will hear echoes of ringing school bells and the strenuous play of children during recess.

O'Donnell's experiences are noteworthy as one views images of the early rural schools. School buildings, teacher training and certification, state and local curricula, and local, state and federal taxes that support schools in the Untied States have changed so much since those early one-room schoolhouse days. In O'Donnell's day, teachers often boarded around and their board was part of their salary. Qualification for teacher certification was also simple. Out of his memories comes an entirely different perspective of schools of a century ago.

The original school building O'Donnell first attended served its purpose until the heat of June. It was then that all the men of the neighborhood responded to the need for a better school. The children watched with wide eyes as horses leaned into their collars as they pulled on ropes that slowly moved logs up diagonally placed pole skids while men with pike poles and peaveys held the hewn logs and others made certain that the skids did not slip. The building operation proceeded until a full wall of logs had been raised above the plates.

"From that point on," O'Donnell continued in his recollection, "the job would be for a mason and a couple of carpenters to be brought in from the outside. These men would chink the logs and over the chinking apply plaster; joists would be sawn and put in place for floor and ceiling, and rafters for the roof. Door and window openings would be cut, and so on until the glorious structure would be finished and ready for the opening of school."

The arrival of a shipment of freight and the unpacking of crates filled with schoolhouse equipment was an especially strong memory:

The ". . . morning the crates were unpacked in front of the schoolhouse twelve double seats, each a crackerjack, just like they had in the city schools, were unveiled. And there were a desk for the teacher and a set of wall maps, the kind of maps you pulled down and moved up on rollers with springs, a potbelly stove and a huge bell to put in the belfry.

"The seats when installed were arranged six in a row on either side of the room, beginning in the back with the larger ones, and ending down front with the smallest for the likes of me. Between the two rows, well back, was placed the tall heating stove, with chrome-colored fittings. At two or three intervals a length of wire, with a turn around the pipe and attached to screws in the ceiling, held the long reach of pipe from crashing down upon any kids who at the moment might be attempting to soak up wisdom from the first or second reader.

"The teacher's desk was set upon a low platform running the width of the room. In front of it was a bench upon which classes sat while going through the throes of a recitation. The only concession to memories of the former school was the wood box, which was brought over from the shanty and put in the corner to the right of the door as one entered the building. A civic calamity was avoided when Fred prevailed upon Father to install a larger blackboard than the one in the shanty, one if possible with fewer knots.

"The term opened late in October, and what with sitting comfortably at the shiny oak desks and staring in wonder at the maps, showing the very places that old John Bugby had us singing about, my mind was made up, as I told Edith Sweeting, our new teacher, never to leave the damn place. My scholastic performance thus far must have convinced her that I had something there."

O'Donnell's schoolhouse memories continue. Like other children of the day, all recited the Lord's Prayer and sang a religious song; they mastered the ABCs and the multiplication tables, had spelling bees, and labored to do cursive Spencerian script. Yet, the construction of the school and the curriculum prepared by the teacher were not all he remembered. His most vivid recollections were of the children and the unholy and gleeful pranks of those playmates that he outlined in a chapter titled "Ants and Lunch Pails."

"Fred and I, when school had opened in the new building, began to discuss dinner pails, Fred reminding me that we were the only kids that had never carried our dinner. While we dashed home for a meal the other children were gathered here and there outdoors, as they ate comparing one another's pickles and cakes, and trading a slice of brown bread for a piece of berry pie. By the time we were back at the schoolhouse everybody would have finished his meal and be off somewhere, the girls hunting flowers and the boys down on Black Creek or the river, throwing stones at crabs and stone-rollers.

"'And all we can do is wait for the bell to ring and see the kids come tearing in from the fun they've been having,' Fred would say. I could see he was bitter about the situation.

"'But *we* can eat with our teacher, Miss Sweeting!' Some word would of course be expected of me.

"Fred admitted that Miss Sweeting was pretty swell all right, young like Sadie [their first teacher]. But bushels prettier, the new teacher having soft, chestnut hair and blue eyes. And always laughing when away from the school. At home she played with us children, yet in school next day would stand Fred or me in the corner as soon as she would John Wilsey.

"Our uneasiness was not relieved by new reports of evil doings by some of our favorite children. Millie Green mopping up the floor with True Hodgins! And Rosy Hart finding in her dinner pail upon opening it a live frog! To be told of such glamorous goings-on while we were having a quiet lunch at home was more than Fred and I could endure, and mother did not seem surprised when one day we asked why couldn't we tote our lunch too.

"Mother, it was clear, had been expecting this. 'I have a better plan,' she replied—'to have Pat [their hired man] take your lunch to you each noon. In that way you could have your things hot, and—'

"'But that isn't stylish,' Fred broke in and Mother, trying to suppress her laughter, dashed from the room.

"This business of taking your lunch to school had advantages that we had never dreamed of. Each pupil had a nail, driven into the wall, for holding his hat and coat, in such months as he wore them, and on it he managed to hang his dinner pail as well. You started in on your lunch at the morning recess. The early class in reading had taken a lot out of you and your waning strength would have to be reinforced by one of the two hard-boiled eggs, and maybe a slice of bread and butter.

"At noon you and Nora would sit at the end of the stoop and compare notes on the viands your respective mothers had fixed up. And maybe you traded half of your pie for a go at her cake.

"In spring, at the right time, should spring ever show up, you would get mother to put a cup in the pail, with sugar in the bottom. You started for school a half hour early and planned a descent upon a patch of wild strawberries you had stumbled into the day before.

"A lunch pail filled so lavishly with sweet things as yours would have the disadvantage of being at great drawer of ants. You would mention the menace of ants to Mother and she would take it up with the folks in town who sold pails. Relief never came from any source, a fact that mattered not at all, the berries, to my taste, being just as nice when you had picked off the ants as they would have been before becoming anted.

"After lunch, and before school was called for the afternoon session, you would have with the others a whirl at pom-pom-pull-away, or hide-and seek, and maybe Miss Sweeting would let you wash the blackboard and slates. And if somebody had beaten you to that you might be permitted to pull the long bell rope that came from the belfry through an augur hole bored through the ceiling, thus bringing the rest of the kids tearing in for the afternoon exercises.

"All this, what with staying nights after school, made me practically a denizen of the schoolroom. Completely overwhelmed by the glamor of the new furnishings, I determined never to leave, and Mother declared that the way I was headed I would make it. Nights after school I flatly refused to go home. I was aided in my determination by the vigilance of Miss Sweeting, who, the first afternoon, caught me in the act of clipping True Hodgins on the ear with my ruler. For this I was penalized by being kept after school for a full half hour. Punishment also included washing the blackboard and sweeping the floor. The time passed so quickly that I asked Miss Sweeting if I might not stay on for another half hour. With a remark that the punishment was hurting her more than it did me, she said yes, but be sure to come home in time for supper.

"'Fred will bring it to me, I betcha!' I declared.

"Immediately I set out upon a series of investigations during which I practically wore out the wall maps, first pulling down the one dealing with North America and locating my home state.

"Roused from my researches by a step on the porch, I looked up to see old Pat coming through the door carrying a small basket. It was my supper.

"'Your ma says, says she, she will sind over fer ye a bed, says she!' said Pat.

"This was more like it and, when I said yes, Pat controlling what must have been an impulse to belt me over the head with his cane, turned and went out.

"I finished the last ginger cookie as night was closing in and, no one having turned up with the bed, I concluded that Fred had started out with it but had fallen off the bridge into the creek. This needed looking into and I set out for the creek. Fred was not in the creek and I determined to find him, no matter where my search might take me. I kept straight on and to my amazement I turned up at the house, where he was at the supper table asking Emory Lewis to pass the butter.

"My devotion to scholarly research continued for a week, my persistence causing the family to wonder how long I could keep it up. The end came mercifully when I found the school agog one morning over a fistic battle between Joe Hart and True Hodgins on the way home from school the night before. It could not have been a battle to compare with the Sullivan-Kilrain bout since Joe could only display a scratch along the left side of his face and a touch of sulk in his manner. It was a battle, however, and that settled it for me. That afternoon I joined the after-school procession homeward.

"Fred, apparently feeling that the occasion called for another battle, went into a huddle with Will Jones when we were just nicely getting under way. Presently Fred declared, in a voice everybody could hear, that Tom could *too* lick the socks off John Wilsey. Will said he betcha John could lick the socks offen Tom, if he had any on."

And so went Tom O'Donnell's school house memories. They aren't a lot different from those of many oldsters. Tom was just able to put it all down on paper. He had many other memories of walking home from school. One small adventure that seemed to delight him was to jump off the bridge into soft sand below. Or, when on days it rained the children would build a dam in the ditch that ran alongside the road. Dropping pieces of dry pine in the reservoir and then tearing out the dam, all would watch to see whose "ship survived the mad, plunging flood and would be the first to reach the creek." And then there were always rock-throwing contests and catching fish bare-handed.

When times had been enjoyed, Tom or Fred would remind each other that it was about supper time, and that they should hurry home. My historical search for old country school houses came to a similar ending. I might have been determined to hang around a lone building longer, but as evening drew closer I was committed to turning back onto the dirt roads that led me into the backcountry.

There is an air of peacefulness about the woods that I have always experienced when searching the backcountry. Each year someone tells me of another old place and I take a trip over an old dirt road that invariably takes me past an old school.

Collection 7
A World of Beauty,
a Land of Recreation

BLANKMAN, DUNHAM, NORTON, AND REV. BYRON-CURTISS had a bottomless fund of stories about the people they hunted, fished, trapped, paddled, and talked with in their pursuit of historical information. And I would guess vice versa, for they themselves were all outdoorsmen and characters in their own way. Blankman was also a thoughtful man. He had observed a tendency among outdoorsmen to overlook a significant physical feature of the North Woods, his buddy Mortimer Norton reported—its mountain meadows and wild flowers. To promote appreciation, the noted lecturer on Adirondack characters and wildlife added to his repertoire of programs a slide show expressly designed to remedy this neglect.

He realized, as do thoughtful sportsmen, according to Norton, "that meadow lands in the forest region help to supply a large portion of the natural food, which goes to sustain the lives of both game and fish, and thus these areas are important from the conservation standpoint." His new, illustrated talk was called *Mountain Meadows of the Adirondacks* and was intended to aid folks, through anecdotes, color slides, and specimens, to identify and become better acquainted with the flowers, plants, and trees of this wilderness domain.

Men and women of the woods are usually serious people and not much given to having fun at the expense of the party who may be in their care, and I have decided that all three men, Blankman, Dunham, and Norton, told straightforward stories. Paul Jamieson held that A. L. Byron-Curtiss' *Life and Adventures of Nat Foster* (1897) "is a piece of myth-making." Perhaps to a degree. My research on The Reverend's life has uncovered the idea that he developed the book based on much first-hand information—people's recollections Jamieson might not have considered. But Rev. Byron-Curtiss also had a flair for embellishing experiences.

Lloyd Blankman's lecture reminds me of Fulton Chain guide E. L. "Jack" Sheppard. Sheppard was as interested in looking out for the well-being of the forest creatures as he was his clients. While he was guiding Fred Mather, a "city sport," in 1897, the men were rowing across Big Moose Lake when Sheppard pointed out a large nest in the top of a dead pine after an osprey bid them a welcome or scolding for intruding. Mather didn't speak their language, and so couldn't tell what the large bird was telling them, but he could read English and said, "It's a sad commentary on human nature that along many of the waterways where these infrequent birds had their picturesque nests there were signs: 'Don't shoot the fish-hawks.' The Adirondack guides put up these notices and were willing that the birds should take their toll of trout, bass and suckers in order to see them lend life to the landscape."

Sheppard commented to Mather: "I don't see what some men want to kill these fish-hawks for unless to brag of their skill with the rifle, if they happen to hit one; there are not enough of them to injure the fishing, and most men like to see them sail in the air when no other living thing is in sight, or to see them hover and dive for a fish."

That was a bit of unmixed sentiment and conservation ethic on the part of Jack Sheppard and a credit to him. Blankman felt the same way toward the thousands of varieties of flowers that change month by month throughout the season, that reveal a predominating color overall during each period.

"All wild flowers are classed as 'weeds'," he declares, "but in the old days Indians found that some part of most of them can be used as medicine or food.

"Many people are apparently unaware that several species of wild flowers are protected by law. Some of the more familiar of these, which should not be picked, are the azalea, bloodroot, gentian, ginseng, Cardinal flower, Indian pipe, Pink Lady's slipper, flowering dogwood, Hart's tongue fern, lotus, orchid, trailing arbutus, painted trillium, and white water lily."

Norton pointed out that in "gathering fresh and authentic material for his lecture, of particular interest to members of sportsmen's and garden clubs, Blankman surveyed numerous Adirondack meadowlands for first-hand information.

"Some of these places are broad expanses of waving grass—small prairies— often miles in extent, he says. Here a brook may be filled with speckled trout, its banks covered with the bloom of the crocus, the anemone, violets, grass pinks, wild roses, or azaleas.

"Others are wild marshes covered with many colored mosses, overhung with shrubs among which blossoms the gentle kalmia, blue gentian, the flaming Cardinal flower, the curious side or pitcher plant, and the rare yellow iris."

"One large and famous mountain meadow," Blankman informed audiences, "is the Sacandaga vlaie[4] in northern Fulton County near where Sir William Johnson built his hunting lodge called the Fish House. This vlaie is 6 miles long and in many places a mile wide.

_____

[4] The term "vlaie" is an old Dutch word meaning a low marshy piece of ground, or a meadow. A more common usage on modern maps is "vly," though the term still appears in some specific place names.

"Another of these natural meadows lies along the west bank of the Black River in Lewis County between Lowville and Castorland. And just beyond Fenton's Hotel at Number Four is the mossy vlaie on Beaver Lake that for sheer beauty has no equal.

"In truth, in my estimation I consider the Number Four and Brantingham Lake region of Lewis County one of the richest lands for field plants and wild flowers existing in the realm of the North Woods."

In the Brantingham Lake area, Blankman re-discovered an ancient, nearly forgotten mineral spring near the outlet, whose waters are strongly impregnated with iron and contain some magnesia and a trace of sulfur. He also studied the pitcher plant, with leaves that often hold a cup of pure and delicious drinking water and said: "If you are in need of water, and no streams are around, the pitcher plant in the beaver meadow will contain sips of water."

*   *   *

The most frequent remark all four writers heard from well-meaning people, who listened to the men talk about outdoor adventures was, "Is it possible to visit the wilderness and still retain some creature comforts?" All knew it was possible to take along some luxuries but as seasoned storytellers the men liked to yank chains—even the quiet, reserved Dunham. Questions about a temporary transition from the comforts enjoyed in a "city life" for the perceived freedom and pleasures one would seemingly exchange for a wilderness experience, were fodder for the men.

I fancy Blankman's answer might go like this, punctuated with a merry twinkle in his eyes: "I could tell you some amusing stories of the comical experience of a city gent who was awakened in the middle of the night to find a skunk under his cot, a bear in the grub box, and a porcupine chewing on his tires, but there isn't a single thing you could say to me to tickle the name of the person out of me."

The runner-up could have been Norton's reply: "Now I won't tell you who, but once I was fishing with a professional deep sea fisherman from Massachusetts, a tenderfoot to the Adirondacks, who boasted he was not worried about North Woods mosquitoes when, in jest, I pointed out a Dragon Fly or Darning Needle, as some folks call them, being the biggest insect in the mountains. 'Be jagers, it's surely a big brute,' he replied in a pleasant voice tinged with a winsome coastal fisherman's brogue, but 'You can't fool me. I'm immune to those stinging pests. In the marshes we have actual mosquitoes.'"

In reply the deep-sea fisherman was challenged that he couldn't lie stripped to his birthday suit for three minutes along the shore of Horn Lake.

He accepted the dare and lay face down on a log, but lost the bet when Norton took off his eyeglasses, using the lenses as a magnifier, and intensified a beam of sunlight onto his buddy's backside. The deep-felt ray began to burn, causing him to hatefully slap at the point it shined on. Like a shot, Norton replaced his glasses as his brave buddy groaned and jumped up. "Nope, guess you lost that bet," he said; "now I'll be taking a bite out of the Hershey's milk chocolate bar as quickly as that Adirondack winged devil took one out of you."

A close third might be one of Harvey Dunham's tenderfoot camp guests who stayed with him at Segoolie, his West Canada Creek camp. It seems inconceivable but the novice wanted to try his hand at fox hunting. Harvey took him to a surefire runway and told him: "You stand right here in this barway, and don't let a fox get through." Harvey went off with his hound. Soon the dog began to drive a fox straight to the barway. Mr. Tenderfoot could hear the dog's barking. He later said he had expected to hear a shot from Harvey's rifle. Harvey, on the other hand, couldn't understand why his camp guest hadn't shot. What he learned tickled his funny bone. As the fox approached his friend, he stepped away from the barway, frantically waved his hands and shouted, "Go back. Go back Mr. Fox, Harv don't want you to pass through here."

Amazing as it sounds, it's a true story. After both had a good laugh, the gentleman asked Harvey, "Are you going to write about what just happened in one of your articles?"

Rev. Byron-Curtiss liked to shake his North Woods camp guests with tales about the locals. One of his closest friends was a district judge in Rome, N.Y., a veteran of more than a dozen years on the bench, who held a strong opinion of the country schools' curriculum as opposed to what was offered in the cities.

Knowing his friend's interest in where the three R's were taught, he brought up the subject on a day when the judge was at Nat Foster Lodge. It was related to him by one of the boys who attended at the time. It went something like this:

"There went to an outlying school house a lad that was slow to learn, and it was agreed upon a certain day that another lad that was a better scholar would sit beside him, and coach him along in reading. In the reader was a story of Job. It read that Job was sore with boils. The lad sitting behind, and by the way a quick-witted one, read it thus: 'And Job was shot with four balls,' and the other lad straightway drawled it out in his singsong manner. 'And that was a hell of a charge,' whispered the other lad. 'And that was a hell of a charge' thundered the slow lad, and you can well believe it there was some uproar in the schoolroom, which the teacher did not try to stop, because she was laughing too hard, too."

The singing of the white-throated sparrow, the whispering of soft breezes through pine, the croaking of frogs in marshes, the call of a loon, the tang of forest balsam. No matter if one comes to the mountains with bag and baggage to stay at a hotel or to play golf rather than catch trout or shoot deer, unquestionably one can enjoy a camp life that is convenient yet *feels* a bit primitive.

There are beautiful trails to walk on, lakes to row and roads to drive that take one to trailheads that lead to the wildest regions.

The writers who contributed to this book knew variety is the spice of life. It certainly is the spice of a vacation. It doesn't matter if one might fish, hunt, backpack, climb a mountain, loaf, stay at a hotel or a bed and breakfast, vacation in a lakeside camp or live in a tent. The Adirondack Mountains offer a rich variety in scenery, in entertainment, and in the romance of history.

🌿 A FIELD OF DAISIES
Anne Marie Madsen

"So much beauty in one place" is the motto used by an exclusive Danish Shoppe in Fifth Avenue, New York. This shoppe is noted for its distinctive superb gifts, including priceless heirloom silver pieces designed and created by the owner; rare and charming porcelains; the finest damask; and crystal from the old countries.

The same motto fits perfectly in the small north country village where I have had the joy of living for several years. I have particularly in mind "A Field of Daisies." This field is located in a picturesque spot near historic Constable Hall and close to the Episcopal Church built by the pioneer Constables for their private sanctuary.

Carefully Kept

It is very old but unlike nearly all old village churches. It has been carefully kept and is just as beautiful now, especially the interior, with its costly wood, reverent simplicity, enhanced by magnificent stained windows, rich in coloring and design. It could well be called a miniature replica of great and beautiful cathedrals. The little church is one of the smallest in our state.

In such a setting the daisy field is truly a thing of breathtaking beauty, which words cannot fully describe—you would have to see it. Just imagine about 15 acres of solid daisies! From a distance they stand out like a great ermine carpet studded by the golden hearts of the daisies.

Annual Visit

Every year when daisies were in the height of their beauty I went to the field to absorb the wonder of it. Way out in the field I walked, completely surrounded by daisies and some tall grasses reaching to my waist. Overhead the clear blue sky completed another masterpiece that only God could design and create in such harmony, wonder and perfection.

I've frequently called pansies the "Children of the Garden" and I call daisies the "Children of the Field." In the rain-washed sun-kissed face of a pansy and a daisy you can see the freshly scrubbed face of a laughing, happy little boy or girl with the imprint (in their laugh) of their mother's kiss.

Nearly Gone

Our lovely daisies are nearly gone now, since haying time makes no exception of their loveliness, but again we see the wonder of God's perfect planning. Just as soon as a flower has lived its time each year, it is replaced by another, giving us continued fragrance and joy all through the season.

When or if we sometimes are tempted to give up trying in this conflicting, restless, disturbing world, it's things like "So much beauty in one place" that take heart again and say "no." God is still (and always) here and everywhere. What have we to fear?

TRIP TO THE MOUNTAINS
Lloyd Blankman

Late in Alice Cooper's life, Lloyd Blankman sat down to chat with her. Lloyd's "Trip to the Mountains" is the outcome of their conversation in Cooper's Clinton home.

We stepped on to the station platform at the end of the railroad (Northville) one hot, dusty day in July, 1908, and eagerly looked for the stage, which was to take us up into the mountains. The air in the city was stifling, beaten back and forth from brick walls and pavement, from pavement to stone walls again, till the life seemed all pounded out and there was nothing left to breathe.

Here, at the end of the road to civilization the air was hot, yes, but full of good life and stirring a bit. It tasted of yellow dust, and pine needles, and smelled as though it had heated all the sap of the trees and honey of the flowers till they steamed it full of their perfume.

No Hurry

There seemed no hurry here, the stage driver was loading on express boxes and packages, stowing them under the seats in all the corners and available spaces. Then he picked up the trunks and swung them on the back, roping them in like young animals who were going to try to kick out.

At last he said, "All aboard folks. I guess we're right about ready to start. Let's see, Miss Putnam's pail o' lard, them shoes fer Matie Colson and that bag o' feed fer ole man Huson. Dunno where I'll put the mail bags but I reckon you can squeeze a little closer together."

We climbed in and draped ourselves around boxes and express bundles; I had one foot under the lee of a huge bundle marked perishable, the other one twined about a pail in an impossible curve, and I wondered whether the perishable foods aforesaid might be liquid or just something which would melt, and I pictured my arrival, one foot covered with sticky substance, the other one shaped like a crescent moon from too close adherence to that pail of Miss Putnam's.

We're Off

My thoughts are brought up with a jerk, right here for Tom swishes the long lash, and with a crack, the four horses are off. We lurch and sway around a corner, trot gaily up the long village street and begin our climb up into the mountains.

The old stage creaks and sways, the leather smells hot in the strong sun, we not only taste but are forced to bite the dust now for the yellow sand flies in clouds, and covers us with a cloth of gold for which we care little. Still, it is preferable to a gold lining so we refrain from much conversation.

We climb up a long hill then plunge down a short one, up another, and down again, but always climbing higher and higher away from broiling streets and huddles of people. At the foot of one hill there is an old log hollowed out, which catches the trickle from a spring up in the hillside and is full of the cold clear water. The brakes screech and grate and Tom jumps off his high seat to water the horses.

A Teamster makes his way along a rocky Adirondack road.
COURTESY EDWARD BLANKMAN (THE LLOYD BLANKMAN COLLECTION)

Chance to Drink

"Ef any of you folks wants a drink, this ere's good cold water. Ye can run up the hill a bit and drink right out of the spring hole," he comments.

My partner, Middy is not enticed by the thought of a run uphill, but I untwine my feet from the baggage and climb out and follow the little thread of water up the bank to the place where it comes from the shining gravel as cold and refreshing as the day is hot and dusty.

Middy passed out a cup to be filled for her as though it could taste the same from a civilized cup as from its own cup of clear glittering sand with its rim of fresh grass.

An Empty Seat

When the horses had all dabbled their noses in the old log trough and we were ready to start again I looked longingly at the empty seat beside Tom and all the space for one's feet to dangle in up there. He saw the way my gaze was taking and said, "There's plenty o' room up here if you want to jump up. Ye'll get more dust but ye can see more o' the road."

By way of the wheel, first the hub, then the top, then up on the step and there you are; all right, and with a "Yes, this is great," we're off again. I heaved a deep, deep breath, and looked ahead. What a queer sensation to be swaying back and forth up here in the air, the horses trotting below your feet, and nothing but the fresh air and space all around you.

The road now follows the riverbank and now the mountain peaks come nearer and nearer, as our way winds on through the trees. The country grows more wild and the woods, which come close to the road, stretch away for miles and miles as far as one can see. Across the river the trees step close to the water's edge, then march away and away in ranks and mosses, over the mountains and down in the valleys, their tops one soft mass of varying fullness, with here and there on a mountainside the flash of a white bush standing on a rock or the shadow of a ragged storm-twisted pine outlined against the sky.

Oh, the Wonder

Oh! The wonder of it! The exhilaration of it, to have these mountains always before you, peak rising beyond peak. Always leading your thoughts on and on to seek the way over the next one and still on to a farther horizon with their strength and repose to guide and their sheer beauty to delight you.

Once in a while there is a clearing beside the road where a log house stands. Tom sings out, "Ho, Jean!" or "Hi there, Arnie," and throws down a paper to the waiting child or digs out a parcel from under the seat and hands it to her with a "Guess this be fer yer ma, Arnie. Don't drop it, it might break. How's your brother, better?" and the child's shy answer comes, "No, sir, not much." "Too bad, had the doctor yet?" "He came last night and went this morning but he says it ain't much use unless'n we kin get him to a hospital."

"Well, hope ye'll have better news fer me when I come down tomorrow, Git-up, you, Sam, and off we go."

"Is the sick boy a younger one?" I ask.

"No, he's a big husky chap, the only one in that family that ever was good for anything. The others are spindly, ailin' kids, sick all the time."

"In this air?" I couldn't refrain from saying.

A Sickly Lot

"This air's all right. Nothin's the matter with the air I knows un. They're just a sickly lot. But this feller, he was different, the oldest of 'm all. He went up on Pine Creek a lumberin' last winter. Wuz up there in Pete Harvey's camp. Wa'll, one day, long to'wds the end of the season, he was choppin' down one of these 'ere big white pines. He didn't run soon enough, stayed to give her one more chip, and the tree fell on him. They carried him out's best they could, but his back was pretty nigh broke in two, and he's been lingerin' long ever since. Dunno if the doctor'll get him patched up or not. Hope so. Good feller. Git up Sam."

The air was heavy with all the woodsy odors. The pines were the dominant fragrance with whiffs of wet moss and ferns growing in cool moist places and herbs and summer flowers carried with it.

Up and Up

The mountain summits rose up and up at our right, and at our left, the bank dropped down sheer to the river. We heard a "Hollo-o" in the distance and Tom answered and whipped the horses. "That's the down stage at the turning out place," he said, "Only spot for two miles where we can pass so we allus stop and holler when we git there, and see if the road is clear ahead.

"We looked with pity at the down stage folks. Poor things going back to cares and the sights that burn, the poverty and trouble that one has to see in the city, and we felt our own joy and freedom to the full, in contrast.

"Jest around that next bend there is Candee's, where you're going," Tom's voice broke in on my thoughts. I jumped from the city to this glorious country at his words, and watched for the view around the bend. As we turned the curve we could see the old white inn up the road, with the three great Scotch pines on the river bank in front of the house, and the mountains peaking, one beyond the other, from the opposite river shore to the far distance.

Tom's "Whoa" brought out Mrs. Candee to the other door to greet us and to get her mail and groceries. We climbed out of the stage and rummaged out our luggage. Tom unstrapped our trunks and in another minute the stage was off up the road again and the trunks tied on the back that disappeared around the curve were the last reminders to us of the petty discomforts and annoyances.

Four weeks of freedom and pure pleasure with Mrs. Candee as chief hostess and general mother to us all was the program which made us jubilant.

BUSHWHACKING
William J. O'Hern

I am addicted to secluded off-trail locations. I bushwhack, a seeker of the best wild experience time allows me. I enjoy all sorts of exciting and enjoyable adventures. Perhaps the best experience for me is found in a compass course over a mountain range, through tight alders and witch hobble, picking a route through a spruce bog or a safe passage across water. This convinces me that there is still excitement, and wild spots of a worthy and enjoyable sort, to be had in the Wilderness, Primitive, and Wild Forest public lands of the Adirondack Forest Preserve.

The result could also be that I reach a destination that is infrequently seen by others, hop unnamed headwater rivulets, fish brilliant backcountry ponds, have a go at an unclimbed rock-faced cliff, and see other geologic features the average woods-goer would not chance upon.

More and more I load a light pack, a set of topographical maps complete with interesting contour lines that hint at the ease or difficulty I can expect, a camera, perhaps fishing tackle and without regard to the marked trails set off before or after the flies are thick, or after the hot weather has passed by.

Easy hiking? Friends who have gone argue that the idea and effort are flawed and fail to satisfy the heart of their outing: to travel outside the blazed and beaten paths yet not forego the gratification from creature comforts and mental pressure. My wife, Bette, having climbed to several remote summits, commented, "Why, the view from one mountain top isn't much different from another! These trips are *work*, not pleasure."

Once I guided a fisherman friend to a distant stream. An old-timer had told me it was known to him to be "trouty"—forty years ago. I failed to mention that part to my buddy. Two hours of hiking, I estimated. After three hours he questioned, "How much longer?"

"I'm not sure. Not much," I replied as I glanced down at the map.

Mark asked, "So show me where we are right now."

Not wanting to toss cold water on an interesting time, I provided a vague answer in a confident voice. The reply didn't satisfy him. "Don't circle the area with that stick. Show me your best estimate. Where are we *right now* on the map."

I'm ninety-nine percent right most of the time but because it had been necessary to circle several boggy low areas I answered, "I have no idea at this moment."

Mark's mind collapsed. "*What!* No idea. You mean we're *lost*!"

Eventually we reached the stream. It was almost devoid of water. Wetting a fish line was out of the question. I made a quick check of the map. An interesting unnamed pond was not too far off. I suggested we check it out.

"You'd better get us there fast and I don't want to see any wild animals either," said Mark.

Surely I had taken my buddy to a remote and lonesome place. I have seen the Adirondacks in all seasons, traveled under difficult conditions, and enjoy the different overland experience bushwhacking offers. Mark didn't. He hung close. He didn't like the loneliness, the thought of black bears or the feel of sweaty wet clothing, the disappointing original destination, the miles that would still need to be traveled by foot to reach the truck before night, and his uncertainty of trusting map, compass, and my judgment.

Before returning safely, Mark had an opportunity to fly fish as he puffed on a favorite cigar, loiter and eat in a sweet spot. In later years he accompanied me on several other bushwhacks but has since chosen not to continue this kind of experience.

If I figure up my trail-less trips throughout the Adirondacks, I understand why companions have questioned the practice of bushwhacking. It deliberately challenges one's judgment, stamina, and interest. Bushwhacking has repaid *me* time and time again.

Yesterday, guides were skilled in the woodcraft knowledge required to bushwhack. Their profession required that they know the nature of the territory and provide perfect service. It was essential that their "sports" felt at ease and hunted ground that would benefit the shots taken.

When I load my gear and start for the most interesting ground in the locality I've chosen to travel, in a small way I am duplicating what a guide would do preceding his taking a party into the mountains.

Cold River Valley. A bushwhacker's paradise! Photograph by Richard Wood, 1921. AUTHOR'S COLLECTION

III
Campfire Yarns

The Tales and Recollections of William J. O'Hern

To one familiar with the characters of the Adirondacks, the old-time native men and women were a source of both truth and fiction. A few were so unique in character that regional Boonville author Thomas C. O'Donnell described them as "colorful as the autumn foliage."

In the late 1940s, O'Donnell began collecting tales of the old communities sited in a wide arc that roughly formed a circle around Forestport and North Lake. Many of those backwoods communities are no longer marked on the map—places like Farrtown and Wheelertown, Pony Bob's, Reed's Mill and Enos. His planned book, an informal history, was to be a true-to-life (color-ful) picture of late eighteenth and nineteenth century life in the area providing the source of the Black River. The story of this southwestern region of the Adirondacks was to be told through the medium of the people who inhabited the mountainous area in *Birth of a River*.

A decade earlier, Harvey L. Dunham, author of *Adirondack French Louie*, had begun to preserve memories of the North Woods at the turn of the century. He took great pains to seek out the few old-timers who were still alive. From their reminiscences Dunham constructed *Adirondack French Louie*, a classic history about life in the North Woods.

O'Donnell's and Dunham's research led them to the source of the Black River, in the heart of Herkimer County and nearby companion to the headwaters of West Canada Creek. There they met with Rev. A. L. Byron-Curtiss, who, for almost fifty years, lived at Nat Foster Lodge.

The headwaters area was a paradise for anglers, hunters and trappers, eccentric hermits, lumberjacks and guides in the days before New York State enforced game laws and lumber-harvesting regulations and before the Adirondack League Club's establishment took a large hunk of wilderness out of public domain.

Rev. Byron-Curtiss served as Forestport's Episcopal minister in 1892–1893. He came just in time, for there were not many old-timers left who could tell what was going on before the days of the automobile when there was still the flavor of the pioneers in isolated communities distant from the railroad.

The Reverend collected stories of the days of the log drives, buckboard rides on rocky and sandy roads, and hermits who set up headquarters in bark and pole lean-tos. He became acquainted with Pony Bob, the best horse trader in those parts, and was invited to join the Liars Club, also called by Forestport residents the Harness Shop Senate, which held its meetings in Sam Utley's harness shop in Forestport.

Byron-Curtiss also rubbed elbows with rascals and poachers who practiced inventive ways to beat the law. And, in addition to his connection with renegade hunters, he was friends with the early judges in and around Forestport who gave the game protectors a bad time, as did the Dirty Dozen, who took vengeance on the game wardens assigned to patrol the Adirondack League Club lands.

In time Rev. Byron-Curtiss' avocation of gathering truth and tales, and his own character-like reputation, grew. It was this colorful holy man and his wellspring of material that Dunham and O'Donnell sought for their facile pens.

I never met Rev. Byron-Curtiss. He passed on before I began writing about him. I have a lot of respect for him. His influence on O'Donnell's and Dunham's histories has been great. It's the kind of folklore he collected and folk tales that he used to tell that I'm going to share because I know them best. Folklore is the traditional customs and tales most often preserved orally among a people. But these stories are my versions about The Reverend, some of his cronies, and the mountains he loved. They are only a few of the delightful and charming tales that have been told about life in the Black River and West Canada Creek headwaters. These tellings represent fact and folklore, and, it seems to me, an authentic flavor of the colorful and lively period in which Rev. Byron-Curtiss lived.

Unquestionably, camp life today is totally different from that of the 19th and early 20th centuries. Then, the tourist came with his fishing and hunting outfit and was met by the same guide who had served him for years. Contrast a season now in the Adirondacks with the good old times to which I refer: TV, videos and electronic games, convenience stores and restaurants, and so much more. As a natural result, recreationists, camp owners and vacationers are spoiled—and, to my way of thinking, miss the kind of memories folklore is made from.

*   *   *

The other night, I wanted to feel like I was talking to some old friends again. I asked myself, "Where would you most like to read some memoirs and listen to some of the tapes you made years ago when you interviewed North Country old-timers?" I could have cozied up in my den, but I needed atmosphere.

Then I thought of camp. That would be the perfect place. I'd surround myself with trees. I wanted to be away from as many twenty-first century trappings as possible. Because camp has no electricity and is half a mile back off a permanently abandoned dirt road, the location would be perfect. As I sat in my favorite outdoor lounge chair and gazed at glowing embers on the outdoor fireplace hearth, I fell to reminiscing on the many old-time yarns, tales, and stories I had heard, and especially on an old North Laker, the late Rev. A. L. Byron-Curtiss. A book I wrote, *Adirondack Stories of the Black River Country* had just been released. It centered around the Reverend's glimpse into a long-ago era in the Adirondacks, and it dawned on me that I should set down for posterity some of the yarns, tales, whoppers, and anecdotes I had learned about the bygone mountain characters' remarkable adventures in the lake-dotted wilderness of the southwestern corner of the six-million acre Adirondack Park.

With delight, I plunked down in front of the fire and said to myself, "I'm sitting in a prism of light!" I felt warm, comfortable and peaceful. There was not a sound to be heard save for the cracking and popping of the fire. Instead

This is the original condition of a little 2" x 2" photograph that was taped inside Lloyd Blankman's dog-eared copy of Adirondack French Louie *written by his friend Harvey Dunham. In the picture from Left to Right: Harvey Dunham, Billy Collyer and Lloyd Blankman.*
COURTESY EDWARD BLANKMAN (THE LLOYD BLANKMAN COLLECTION)

of thumbing pages in diaries or turning on the recorder, I just sat, enjoying this blissful feeling and allowing my mind to wander.

My camp is packed with belongings from former Adirondack camps and things once owned by folks who are silent now. Perhaps I should put little labels on each of them so they are not mistaken for trash. There is a string of muskrat traps biologist Roy Tank was given by guide Gerald Kenwell, who told him they belonged to "French" Louie Seymour and he had found them along the Otter Brook many years ago. Sitting on a shelf are tin plates and cups and crockery from the Miller Camp once positioned deep in the wilds above Bear Pond. There is the hand-split and hewed log table that John Ferris fashioned for his Lone Pine camp on the backside of Mount Tom that he attributed to saving his life when, during the November 1950 Big Blow, he crouched under the sheltering table as trees crashed all night long outside his wilderness cabin. Byron-Curtiss' fifty years of camp journals rest on a stool entirely handcrafted from wood that grew in the forest. Leaning against it is the peeled beaver stick my old friend Richard Smith relied on to help him on the last trail walk he ever took. There are so many other articles. I feel the illumination and worth of pleasing times in each of the belongings, each one holding memories, recalling personalities, voices, and the touch of hardworking hands. I feel the tie of true interconnection. I know in my heart that there will be a time when I will reestablish my ties with their cheery, smiling faces. I look forward to that time.

I thought about the correlation between the artifacts surrounding me and the waiting with anticipation for their stories of yesteryear to awaken my mind to an older time in the Adirondacks. Sometimes, it's difficult to listen as the people's voices I recorded, now long dead, come alive. Modern technology really does rekindle the spirit of those who have passed on, and as I close my eyes, I visualize all the places I was when reminiscing brought cheer to the wrinkled faces of aged folk who worked hard all their lives to make ends meet just so they could hold on to the rustic lifestyle they preferred—the excitement and joy of living on their own in the elegant Adirondack Mountains.

But I have their voices on tape. I have the opportunity to share their spirits—that feeling of delicious old times they shared by allowing themselves to be recorded. Their voices reach out to touch friends, family, and those who never knew them. I can contribute a bit of their hearts and lives, share their warmth, experiences, and appreciation for the forested mountains and river valleys that they cared so much for. Hear stories they told and feel the simple, easy spirit of living in the Adirondacks of the past.

I stayed outside by the fire until I gazed only at the dying embers on the open hearth. As I sat there, eyes half closed from fatigue, it seemed as if I was once more a younger man sitting with my old friends listening as they spun their evening yarns.

I will tell you some of the tales as I remember them.

Rev. A. L. Byron-Curtiss shows off a fine catch of trout.
AUTHOR'S COLLECTION

🌲 TALES FROM NAT FOSTER LODGE

These tales are inspired by my reading of the journals of Rev. A. L. Byron-Curtiss and living at his Nat Foster Lodge.

"Tales From Nat Foster Lodge" is a collection of accounts of Adirondack folklore loosely based on the writings of Rev. A. L. Byron-Curtiss and on odysseys of my own throughout the southern Adirondacks, following in his century-old footsteps when he ambled the Black River backcountry.

In these stories, we see an Adirondacks very different from that of the twenty-first century, and a mountain fastness much less developed, more isolated and wild, but as inspiring as it is today. The totality of isolation possible in the early twentieth century can scarcely be imagined now; wilderness adventures of sporting people involved different woodcraft requirements. These woods roamers were entirely on their own when it came to reading map and compass. There were no GPS instruments to keep them from getting lost. The gear they carried was bulky and heavy, they were without communication with the outside world, and they provided their own entertainment. The narratives that tell of such experiences are rich with tales from the trail and the awe for a natural world no longer known.

I envision with no doubt that versions of these lighthearted stories, straight from the Lake Country, were told by Byron-Curtiss as he and his cronies gathered together to swap tales and recount events and adventures of their times, capturing the spirit of the Adirondack backwoods.

Inspiration for my tales originated with entries I gleaned from Byron-Curtiss' camp journals. The Reverend's Nat Foster Lodge logbooks are an Adirondack treasure, a primary document penned by a man who was to many the real and true voice of the wilds of the southwestern Adirondacks' headwaters. To several generations, Byron-Curtiss was the Mark Twain of North Lake's backcountry, a wanderer transfixed by the richness and greatness that he found in practically every corner of the wilds. For almost sixty years he lived in the mountains at Nat Foster Lodge, as the "Bishop of North Lake." His voice—the voice of the common man—reached out to America's news-papers, church pulpits, and nationwide religious and political conventions.

The North Laker lived out his years in a setting of companionship among guides, neighbors and caring friends. While unqualified solitude could always be found just a few steps from Nat Foster Lodge's door, the Reverend felt that living among the forested mountains and the multitude of feeder streams leading into the Black River valley, the regal softwood and hardwood forests and sweet-tasting bubbling springs, brought guides and locals, outsiders and newcomers closer to the natural world and reminded them unceasingly of the Creator's wondrous universe.

Regardless of a guide's individual faith or persuasion, it would be impos-sible to take a client afield to mountain-climb, fish or hunt and not have him absorb these impressions and be inspired. Perhaps this was one of the tightest knots between a guide and his party.

*   *   *

Rev. Byron-Curtiss wrote to Robert Holzworthin in 1936:

> The eleven Adirondack Woodcraft campers you brought to my lodge this past July were a particular joy to me. How thrilled they were, their penned memoranda forever a permanent part of Nat Foster camp history.
>
> > "North Lake! It's simply grand.
> > It's the best place in the land!
> > So here and now I take my stand
> > With cheers to beat the band."
>
> Your, and coworker Metzger's, efforts to make the disadvantaged boys' outdoor experience rewarding equals the best efforts of official guides. The canoe race had to be one of their most memorable experiences.
>
> The contest reminded me of a similar race between Atwell guides and brothers Ira W. and Henry W. Watkins in 1907.
>
> Ira claimed he could out-pull any guide, brother or not. Henry knew his brother had great endurance in a boat and was strong at the oars, but calculated that since he could out-wind and out-distance his brother on the trail, he had a chance against his wiry brother—in a short pull before fatigue set in.
>
> I heard the brothers talking out loud about their contest when collecting my mail at the State House. Since it was only a few days before North Lake's celebrated Independence Day at Nat Foster camp, I asked the guides if I could add them to the day's program. How about a pull to the head of the lake and back? Would that be too far?
>
> "Head of the lake, or anywhere," they answered.

"All right. Better yet, the race will begin at the island opposite the State House flagpole. Your course will pass to the right of Huckleberry and Cranberry Islands, pass through the first Narrows, go through Split Rock Bay into the second Narrows, round Phoenix Island, and return to Nat Foster camp's dock in Panther Spring Bay. It makes a course of approximately three miles."

"We'll bet that," the boys said airily.

I don't excuse gambling, so devised a reward when Ira voiced, "How much?" to his brother.

"The prize will be a pouch of chewing tobacco."

"Covered," they said, spitting on their hands and shaking mine. I would be both stakeholder and judge.

With that we parted, with each brother claiming, "I can beat him," to the small crowd that had gathered at the post office.

The starting gun sounded and the race began. Henry quickly lunged ahead, but Ira pulled steadily and strongly. We could see by using binoculars and from the flags from the observers in boats that as they neared the island they were almost neck-and-neck. Momentarily both were out of sight as they rounded Fox Island, but as they came into view, both guide boats looked to be bow to bow. Then Ira gradually gained the lead, pulling up at the dock several boat lengths and a few minutes ahead of his brother. Ira claimed he was in good shape and was just "warmed up," and ready for "another turn." Henry was winded but not spent.

"That evening the audience talked of the Fourth of July sport around a blazing bonfire.

Ira claimed the tobacco wager I put up was some of the best he had ever chewed.

The good-natured rivalry was typical between guides. Modest entertainment but memories aplenty.

The stories told around Adirondack campfires could be both factual and amusing. Others wandered farther from the truth with each retelling, and that simply made them more appealing. All fit Byron-Curtiss' description: "Modest entertainment but memories aplenty."

Rev. A. L. Byron-Curtiss'
Nat Foster Lodge on North Lake.
AUTHOR'S COLLECTION

🌿 A CAMPFIRE YARN

For almost sixty years, Byron-Curtiss lived a life away from train whistles, vacationing crowds, and the daily activity of bustling Adirondack tourist villages. Usually at night, when he was often alone, he reviewed his day and recorded in his subdued, truthful, straightforward fashion the events that had framed the previous twenty-four hours. Although he penned no tales, I found that his journal entries contained kernels of stories, and enough information to help me shape accurate tales about the best in him, and about the people who surrounded him. The entries indicate that "B-C" and his cronies did not consider their ways of living particularly admirable. There is little of self-regard in the journal accounts. Only after time had held the historical mirror up to B-C's entries did it become possible to gain the perspective needed to realize and reclaim the richness of a past way of life.

Byron-Curtiss: "My camp was built by some men from Remsen, N.Y. About 1887. It was then bought by Michael Bennett, a contractor from Utica in 1896. George Combs, a telegrapher died of pneumonia in the camp September 1899. From superstition and etc., the camp was abandoned for a year. I bought the building through Charley O'Connor of Forestport in 1900. I repaired and improved the shanty in 1901. The rest of the camp's history is to be contained in the following 'log.' The written record will contain a record of guests and visitors, daily events, & entries of game afforded by woods and etc. Nat Foster Lodge, North Lake, Herkimer County, Adirondack Mountains. 1901."

Enough. I'd say finally only this: I'm glad to have had these log books given to me. Adirondack history and lore needs all the protection it can get.

* * *

"Yep," said Burt, Byron-Curtiss' guide for several seasons in the Adirondacks, aiming a stream of tobacco juice in the direction of a chattering chipmunk, "some of these city dudes that come up here deer hunting and take turns having their pictures taken with a bunch of deer and maybe a bear or two hanging up behind them, never shot a gun in their lives and wouldn't know a skunk from a ten-point buck. They couldn't hit the inside of a barn if you closed the door on them.

"I 'member one fellow to come up here two years ago. He was deafer than a fence post and you had to get right up to his ear an holler to make him hear.

"I was pretty busy that season and I had two New York parties on my hands and I'd promised to get them all a deer to take back with them. Well, there was nothing to do but I had to make a drive for him, so he could get back home Saturday night. I told him if he would get up bright and early next morning I'd make a drive for him around Hamilton Ridge. Next morning, when I got up he was snoring like a steam engine and I shook him a little but he kept right on making steam, so I went down to the spring and filled the frying pan with spring water and let about a quart run down the back of his neck, and say, the yell he let out of him was enough to scare all the deer this side of Portner's camp, and I wish I had woke him up some other way.

"Guess he thought a wildcat was tearing him. He was pretty mad, but I got him started and I took him down and left him on that runway you crossed down there by the big pine; I posted him on the edge of the clearing and told him to keep his eye peeled and not shoot till he was sure he could see hair.

"Well, I made that drive away around Hamilton Ridge and scared up a small doe and a big buck, grayer than a whetstone. Saw they was on the right runway and took it easy till I come to where I had left Mr. Man. He was there all right, but I couldn't see if he had seen anything and he said he had seen three but he was so deft they got out of sight before he knew they were there.

"You know what it means to make a six-mile drive before grub and I was getting pretty lank, so I told him we would eat a snack and try it again.

"After breakfast I took him over to the meadows and left him on the edge of Saddleback Ridge, and told him if he didn't hit nothing this time he could go it alone.

"I went away round Beech Nut Hill and scared up another pair and tracked them right up to where I'd left the darned cuss and expected every minute to hear something doing. I climbed up on a rock and there he was right under me and watching them two deer making tracks over the next hill.

"Then he woke up, and talk about the battle of San Juan, it was nothing to the noise he made. He had an automatic, and he was pumping lead faster than a kid could eat chocolate drops, and missing every shot.

"Well, I had covered about thirteen miles and given him five chances and I was pretty disgusted and tired. I saw he was going to make a miss and just as the buck was going over the hill I let drive right over his hat and dropped Mr. Buck right there.

"When I got down from the rock I found Mr. Man dancing a jig around that there buck and yelling like a banshee.

"He was so deaf he hadn't heard me shoot and thought he had done the whole thing himself, and so I let him think so.

"Say, what do you know about that?"

"Beats hell how business keeps up!" was my sympathetic comment as Walter cut him another plug of "chaw."

🌲 A MUDSLIDE ON WOLF MOUNTAIN

"It is with much trepidation that I set down my experiences as a young and newly ordained Deacon in my first church at Forestport," Byron-Curtiss recorded the day he decided to rough out a biography in 1895. Forty-three years later he was still registering natural phenomena and other observations about the region.

On September 5, 1938, when Rev. Byron-Curtiss was living in the Adirondacks, he had a party of two from New Hartford, N.Y., visiting Nat Foster Lodge, his seasonal camp on North Lake. He had placed a tray of cookies on a table between his guests, who were resting in chairs under the roofed porch overlooking the lake, and had returned inside for a pot of tea.

As Byron-Curtiss walked back to the porch all three felt the earth shake. It was a small earthquake; trees began quivering. Dead branches fell all around them. A huge tree on Wolf Mountain, directly across the lake from the camp, crashed over, pulling its roots from the thick soil, exposing the underlying rock mantle. The waters of the lake were lashed into very respectable white caps, and his power and rowboats and red canvas canoe bobbed up and down like corks. Voices from Johnson's Pulp Corporation who were working the slope of Wolf Mountain cried loud—their voices carrying across the water. Mort Mayhew was attempting to steer his boat with the oars, but looked as if he was the most inexperienced oarsman indeed. Mort was obviously frightened and The Reverend yelled encouragement that must have been sounded imperceptible to old Mayhew out in his flat-bottomed scow.

As fast as it had begun, the trembling stopped. "Land sakes," an excited and surprised Thaddeus Zimowski exclaimed. Adelbert Hoggas, the other guest, agreed with a suppressed titter. Then Byron-Curtiss' ears detected an unusual sound. "Sh-sh," pressed the preacher. For a full two minutes, not moving a muscle or flecking a hair or batting an eye, he stood still. His guests half expected to hear such an exclamation as "do tell" come trailing into their ears. "Now what are you listening for?" they asked.

"Come down to the shoreline," he commanded, "and let's take a clear look at the slope of Wolf Mountain."

When the men reached the water's edge they could see across the surface the oddest sight.

In the few seconds the ground had vibrated, the rocking of the earth had loosened the soil. A narrow mass of earth and trees and shrubs and rock began to move slowly downward at first, then picked up momentum. The ground was moving. Such grinding and crashing they had never heard. It lasted only minutes.

Being on the opposite shore, the men were safe from the trees and rocks as they crashed over the slope. The rush took their breath away. Several trees smashed against each other, tossing an assortment of wild creatures into the air.

When the dust had cleared they saw several animals caught in treetops in the jumble at the foot of the slide. Looking through field glasses, they spied two bobcats with cubs, one big buck and three doe, and a big bear with two cubs scrambling for the safety of firm ground.

Well, Byron-Curtiss called for a game of straws. He was about to suggest they draw to see who would take the first shot at the buck when they were treated to a second rare sight. They learned later that one of Johnson's big draft horses became startled at all the ruckus, stepped on a chain of a log sleigh, spooked even more, and the 1,600-pound horse dashed down the mountainside and leaped into the lake. A trough of waves rocked and rolled Mayhew's dishpan boat as the large horse drew ahead of Mayhew, its tail spread on the surface of the water as it passed the old man in the boat. Driver Cliff Turner on the shore shouted commands and directions but the paddling horse ignored his shouted remarks. Seeing the horse leave the water as it ascended the beach on Cranberry Island, the driver got a boat and pursued his charge, but by the time he had rowed to the island the horse had rested enough to leap back into the water and finish swimming the width of the lake, climbing out onto Mayhew's Red Camp's grassy bank. Cliff Turner continued to the opposite shore, calmed the horse, then drove him back across the narrows, following close by in a boat.

"If that don't beat all," each man independently said in their own way of the odd events as they reached the verandah just as a downpour began in earnest.

"It looks as though the rain will be setting in for a spell," Byron-Curtiss remarked, as he observed the sky from the porch railing.

"Oh well, who cares?" said Thaddeus.

"I should worry," echoed Adelbert.

"Right, men," said Byron-Curtiss in a nutshell.

A rainy day in a snug camp is far from a disaster. Rather, it was welcomed as an agreeable chance to offer incense (smoke), talk, read and putter, all without a guilty feeling of wasting time.

It also afforded columnist Byron-Curtiss the material he needed to set down in his next chronicle. In the September 8, 1938, issue of the Boonville *Herald,* the newspaper led Rev. Byron-Curtiss' North Lake column with the eye-catching banner "Horse Swims Lake, North Lake People Treated to a Rare Sight."

🌲 BROWNIE THE SPANIEL

I was thumbing through Byron-Curtiss' photo album when I came across a 1920 photograph of the Reverend sitting in the sun with his dog, Brownie. The picture reminded me of this story, which is claimed to have actually happened to the "old saints and sinners" who hugged the pot-bellied stove on an October night at Jerry and Nellie's North Lake camp.

The couple, I'm told, made quite a pair—between Jerry's blissful carelessness and self-absorption when he got caught up trying to outdo his rivals with fantastic stories, and Nellie's habitual temper "when her dander got up."

That night, Dell Bellinger, the most prolific storyteller, must have caught wind of Nellie's mounting temper as the meeting moved into the early hours of the next day. He might have shaken his head as he watched her movements, seeing clues indicating that one of the couple's comic tiffs was soon to occur.

Jerry wanted to be a good yarn spinner, but in his self-absorption he rarely had a clue as to what was about to happen.

Nellie was one of the most hot-tempered Irish women Dell had ever known, and I believe that when Dell offered a puppy as a prize for the tallest tall-tale that night, he had only one winner in mind. Dell was a trickster and Jerry was often his comic mark.

In my retelling, I have chosen to exclude Jerry and Nellie's last name and the name of their camp. Reverend Byron-Curtiss held that Nellie would have wanted her privacy protected.

*   *   *

Pranks, practical jokes, and tall talkin' were part of the social fabric of the men who gathered weekly at Sam Utley's Harness Shop in Forestport to swap stories. Theirs was a conventional form of entertainment in the days before radio and television made their way to the North Country.

During one such tall talkin' session at a fellow named Jerry's North Lake camp, Dell Bellinger offered a spaniel puppy to the person who could tell the biggest whopper.

That began an evening of yarn-spinning one-upmanship that made all of the men's previous get-togethers pale in comparison.

One by one, the men took Dell's baited challenge—as Dell knew they would. Stories rolled. Each teller remained straight-faced while any kernel of truth that might have given rise to the story was stretched into pure fiction.

Jerry passed the coffee pot around the table to his cronies, while his wife, Nellie, cleaned up the mess of dishes and pie crumbs. Nellie had been catering all night and they were very close to over-staying their welcome. Nellie was tired and she thought that her husband was going to wind up the weekly bull-session after the last pot of coffee had been drained. She felt relieved when she watched the last drop fall into the bottom of Dell's cup, but then Jerry's mouth opened again. It was his turn in the rotation, and he broke into his finest storytelling routine.

Nellie had a high-spirited Irish side and Dell caught her sharp-eyed glare toward her husband. She was not about to let the gathering wind back up. Jerry, who was often the target of the more skilled humorists, never did know when to shut up.

With a loud thump, Nellie got Jerry's attention, as an empty platter slammed on the table. CRACK went the china, followed by a WHIZ as a butcher knife barely missed the coffee mug as it was thrown into the center of the wooden table with dexterity and spirit. The move could not have been timed more perfectly, as her husband declared, "I've never told a lie the whole night."

Nellie was not interested in hearing one more story bigger and harder to swallow than the one before. She was tired and wanted her house cleared out.

Every man at the table knew Nellie had a temper. They also knew Jerry didn't have a prayer if Nellie got going. Sensing that a family riot might ensue when the knife's point slammed into the table, Dell interrupted Jerry's dialogue. It was time to be smart in a world that looked as if it would turn hostile. He leaped from his chair and declared, "Jerry, you're tonight's winner." With that proclaimed, Dell turned to Nellie and awarded her the prize.

"Nellie, you get the pup. Your cooking is nothing short of angel food, and better than any fancy hotel kitchen." All in attendance agreed. Her dinner would have compared favorably with a Delmonico banquet and their voracious appetites did justice to her effort.

That puppy became Rev. Byron-Curtiss' dog, Brownie, for Nellie had no use for the spaniel pup.

"I could have written a weekly gossip column each week for the rest of my life and never run out of tales," the Reverend proudly proclaimed of the social life of his North Lake neighbors.

After that night, the weekly confabs were dubbed "Parting With the Dog."

The "tall talking" Dell Bellinger.
COURTESY THOMAS A. GATES

🌿 JUT THE ROSSER

In a blast of wittiness that elevated Gus fifty notches on Rev. A. L. Byron-Curtiss' I.Q. list and showed off his dormant comic qualities, Gus, an old cook in Gig Perry's logging operation in the woods west of North Lake, sent Jut on a mission to the camp of newcomer Byron-Curtiss, who had begun to vacation at Atwell only one year before. That one-day mission showcased Gus' wit and gave Jut the immortality of appearing in lumber camp stories for years to come.

Among the hands rounded up for Perry's second camp season was big-hearted Jut. In spite of restrictions in his intellectual gifts, he had great physical strength. Jut never could have dreamed that one day he would be written up in a book. Jut was a rosser. In lumber camps, rossers, and scalers, had jobs that required no brains and were thus at the bottom of the list of jobs based on intelligence. A rosser was a man who, after a tree was felled by the choppers, came up to the fallen tree with an axe and handspike to peel the bark, preparing the fallen tree for the buckers who would then saw it into smaller lengths so horses could drag the shorter sections to skidways. Whether the log was drawn to a nearby skidway or snaked out, the peeled end would considerably ease the labor of the horses. From the rollway to the bank of the river, logs would be piled high on sleighs that creaked under the weight of fifteen, twenty, and even more logs, a volume that aroused no enthusiasm in the team.

Jut, like many of his counterparts, was a tall, burly-chested, red-haired giant, prone to believing tall talk about imaginary tricks, wherefore nobody was surprised when, his first morning on the job, he showed up at Rev. Byron-Curiss' Nat Foster Lodge asking Rev. Byron-Curtiss for a left-handed handspike. Jut had dashed at breakneck speed a good two miles through the woods to retrieve the tool that supposedly could not be found at the lumber camp and the blacksmith did not have time that day to fashion.

"Gus says," began Jut as his eyes crossed, "you would be having one, Reverend."

"Oh, so you are the lumber shanty's go-fer."

Byron-Curtiss' face was a study, mostly betraying that all might not be well with Jut. He also enjoyed the harmless hilarity that was taking place. Instead of replying, Byron-Curtiss waved the big man over to the tool shed and selected not one but three of the largest and heaviest lengths he could find from a stock of assorted pieces cut from the toughest and heaviest of all woods found along the river, the ironwood.

"Here you are," he told Jut. "You will have to take all three—they don't say whether they wanted a ten-degree or a twenty or thirty."

Jut's education was extended later with a quill pig hunt one dark night far up on Grindstone Creek. This was Atwell's version of the ancient and reliable snipe hunt, like it in all essentials, and equally uplifting and educational (for the unsuspecting.)

🌿 GILROY O'REILLY'S FISH STORY OF HISTORIC PROPORTIONS

Did I succeed in telling the kind of stories Rev. Byron-Curtiss would have? If Byron-Curtiss or his cronies were around, and I could ask them about my campfire yarns, I would know if I had succeeded. I do know I have rekindled an old-time form of entertainment. To be sure, what I have recreated are the clothes without the man in them. Byron-Curtiss died before I became involved in his Adirondack world. I would have enjoyed interviewing the Reverend. Having actual voice recordings would have helped me to recreate more closely his style.

The old-timer's writings display his life, even though it was not left neatly on hangers but instead as if Byron-Curtiss had stepped out of the clothes and left them on the floor. But then my storytelling might be, in some small measure, an example of what he might have envisioned when he told his pal, Raymond Shawl, "Perhaps someday some student of North Country history will come across my writings and find some value in the scribblings between the hard covers of my journals."

"Gilroy O'Reilly's Fish Story of Historic Proportions" is my last tale. It is an example of how I have taken real people and events and fictionalized them. They are a measure of my contribution to the kind of storytelling I have learned from Rev. Byron-Curtiss—or a measure of how flimsy my contribution to modern Adirondack folklore is without Byron-Curtiss here to guide and improve my technique.

*   *   *

This tall tale originated in a humorous attempt to cajole Gilroy O'Reilly to memorialize the day he took a party of five men and six cases of beer up to his Whiskey Springs camp, once a shanty for loggers left over from the time when men first cut over the West Canada Lakes country.

Gilroy warmed quickly as he carried his guideboat over his head at a pace that his party could barely match. It was a sweltering July day and a haze hung in the sky. As Gilroy strained under the load, sweating as if he had consumed a bottle of Tabasco sauce, he heard claps of thunder and read the distant sky. A wall of threatening gray and black clouds was rolling up over West Canada Mountain.

"Darned if it could be a twister," he told the men as he quickened his step, "one of those tree-snapping, wind-sucking storms that come by every now and then. The camp isn't far now. We can beat the storm if we hurry."

When the camp came into view, Gilroy began barking orders. "There's the camp. Hurry over and secure anything that's not tied down. I'm going to get this boat down near the Stillwater and into the spruce thicket to protect it from falling branches or trees."

Gilroy was running to beat the storm, but it was too late. A burst of swirling wind struck with all its fury, lifting Gilroy's boat up into the air with him hanging on.

Gilroy later recalled that it seemed as if a giant had picked him up like a little toy. "I held on to the gunwales of that boat like burdock on a wool shirt" said Gilroy about the ride.

"No matter how bad it seems," he recalled telling himself, "if'n you hang on, you're in for a great many more adventures, Gilroy O'Reilly!" and he was swooped into a swirling cloud of leaves, evergreen needles, twigs, ducks, water lilies, and herons.

"All at once I was soaked to my skin. Water was moving up instead of down!"

A water spout had formed over West Canada Creek and for a time followed the river. As it moved downstream it sucked the water up, Gilroy and his boat with it. Every so often his head and his feet took turns facing right side up; all the time he clung to the boat. His arms were stressed but still he managed to hang on.

Abruptly, he came to a violent stop. Down came his fishing pole, tackle, bait, a sandwich, cigars and him with his camera to capture the whole mess.

"I was too dizzy to move for a time. I wouldn't have believed it unless I saw it," he recalled, "but when I opened my eyes I found I was in my boat and it was full of trout. The fish must have been sucked up with the water and pitched into the vessel. If that weren't enough, imagine my surprise when I found I was on the top of the hogsback, almost a mile from my cabin."

Gilroy was soaked to his birthday suit and the weather had turned cold after the big storm blew through. Tired and wet, he peeled some birch bark curls from the trees and snapped off some dead spruce twigs from under the sheltering boughs and soon had a warming fire going. As he roasted some trout and dried the cigars, his thoughts returned to his party—his brother Glenroy, his brother-in-law Angus, and the Todd twins, Louie and Stosh. Had they been missed by the funnel cloud? Did the roof survive the big blow?

After a scavenged meal, Gilroy filled his woven packbasket with fish, and knotted cords to the four corners of a woolen blanket and tied them to the limbs of a tree, rather high from the ground like a hammock, and filled it with fish. Hefting the boat over his pack on his back, he had about all the weight he could manage to carry as he hiked down the hill to the camp. The going was taxing as the ground was littered with fallen trees. At times it was almost impossible to make headway without walking back over ground he had just traversed.

It was after dark when Gilroy reached the Whiskey Springs camp. Everyone was inside. He quietly packed the many pounds of trout next to the ice under sawdust in the ice house behind the cabin. He decided he would return for the balance of the over-catch of fish in the morning.

He burst into the cabin to cheers from his party. "You all right, Gilroy?" they asked. "We were getting pretty worried about you," said Angus. "We tried to look for you but there was just no sign."

"And we were, cold, wet and hungry," added Glenroy, Gilroy's younger brother, "and I figured you could take care of yourself."

"Yes sir, I'm all right," said Gilroy, "and I do have a story for you boys, but it can wait till tomorrow. Tonight we should all get some shut eye because the fish will be up early tomorrow and so should we."

At dawn the next morning, the mist, which had been rising from the warm surface of the river, was rolling back up the valley like a great snowy curtain, revealing the graceful low mountains in their leafy green. The hogsback at the edge of the Whiskey Springs Vly was a grand dome from a distance and could be easily distinguished with its hard and softwoods. The mist seemed to linger around its summit like a halo of glory.

"A breakfast fit for a king," Glenroy exclaimed as he buttered liberally another piece of Johnny cake and downed a last cup of strong coffee with cream. "It's a good thing your wife doesn't know you can cook like that, Gilroy."

"And you won't be telling her anytime soon now will you, my wise brother?" Gilroy answered with a smile.

"Now, I want you boys to go down and catch some trout while I attend to a few chores. I expect a nice trout luncheon at about noon."

As the fishing party prepared to leave, Gilroy grabbed his packbasket and headed into the woods to recover the remaining trout. Gilroy knew freshly caught trout cooked better when it had been dressed and a bit of salt rubbed on it, and allowed to lie on ice to further improve its deliciousness. After all were fetched he would fill tin pails full of the beauties, load them into his springless wagon and head to the nearby hostelries. He knew the routine. They often bought ten-pound tin pails from him. But first he would lunch with his overnight camping party.

Upon returning with his second packbasket full of trout, Gilroy found the crew gloating over their big catch. "Three each," said Angus to Gilroy.

"I didn't know you fellers were such fishermen," Gilroy replied. "That's real fishin'."

"Well, it was pretty easy to tell where the fish were," Angus proudly boasted, "when they're jumping out of the water after anything that floats!"

"Just the same," said Gilroy, "not everyone can catch 'em, even when they know where they are."

Angus was pretty good at reading people, but he couldn't read Gilroy. Gilroy never showed any facial expressions and Angus couldn't tell if he was being complimented, or made fun of.

"Say, Gilroy," Angus interposed, "what ever happened to you in all that wind yesterday?"

"You fellows have had so much fun fishin' I don't aim to take the wind out of your fun, but I suspect I caught enough trout yesterday that it would take an accountant to get the tally."

"Oh, come on," said Glenroy with a scowl."

"See for yourselves," said Gilroy as he gestured toward the ice house.

"Well I'll be," said Angus as he swung open the ice house door.

"And that's not all," said Gilroy as he unshouldered his packbasket and spilled the contents onto the ground.

"Ahhhhh! You sonovafox! I should have known what you were doing!" Stosh shrieked.

The old guide just smiled. "If I told you fellas that those fish just fell out of the sky, would you believe me?"

"No," murmured more than one in the group.

"Well, I would have gladly invented a fish story of historic proportions, but I thought it might be in bad taste."

"What you are going to do with all them trout?" Stosh quizzed.

"Why, I'm aiming to fill them into pails and sell the tin pails."

"But what would you do that for?"

"Why sonny," answered Gilroy, turning a kindly face to the younger man whose city upbringing would excuse his unfamiliarity, "you see the law don't allow anyone to sell no kind of wild game at all, anytime. So in the case of trout like these, I just sell the pail and throw the trout in fer free."

Gilroy O'Reilly's stomping grounds on the West Canada Creek.
Photograph by Roy Reehil. COURTESY ROY REEHIL

Postscript

Sure, the photographs Rascal spilled over the floor of my den are of yesterday. That's part of their charm. The images are a reflection and a reminder of a simpler day and time. My Adirondack Characters photograph album is also a kindred "family." It's an Adirondack home. It's a place to come back to, a place to hang my hat, visit with old-timers, listen to a few stories, have a few laughs, and relax from the pressures of the day. Besides, the photos have a life of their own.

The day after I sent the last chapter to my editor, Rascal cried at the kitchen door. I answered his call and there stood my tiger two-year old. He was bloodied from what I later learned was an animal attack. I gathered him in my arms and drove to the animal clinic in my village.

"It's a bad injury," the veterinarian reported. "He needs specialized medical care that can only be provided in our Rome hospital. Leave now. I'll call ahead to let them know you're coming."

Following Rascal's emergency operation to save his life I was told, "His recovery will require a lot of attention." The gash in his side was large. It was necessary to leave the skin open. Inserting a drain was not an option. I answered the doctor's instructions. I felt comfortable taking care of him at home. It was where Rascal would want to be.

During the following week I made two more emergency return visits to the vet's. "Something else is wrong. I should have recognized it the first time you returned with Rascal," the doctor admitted. "I'll need to run a series of blood tests." Up to that point I hadn't even considered what the charge would be, but the nurse first presented me with an estimate before work could begin. Heroic medicine was what I wanted. Cost was immaterial. The doctor promised only his best.

A week following my initial call to the animal hospital a small card arrived in the mail. I opened it and read:

> "True friends never really leave us . . .
> They live on in our memories and in our hearts.
> With Our Sympathies, . . . "

The heartfelt note was signed by Dr. Agrawal and Staff at the Rome Veterinary Clinic.

Rascal had a strong personality. His leap onto the desk knocked over stacks of photos, spilling the originals to the floor. Picking up the scattered pictures led to the crystallization of this book's blueprint. For Rascal, I dug in my writing heels and promised I would not allow myself to be swayed from completing the project I like to think he began.

Writing is not a talent I was born with. But I have found Adirondack historical research a fascinating pastime. It delights the intellect as well as the senses; and authoring, rather a vigorous mental exercise, gives the mind needed relief from the requirements of my elementary school teaching.

I promised myself that no matter what my editor said of the manuscript I would continue this work-in-progress until it was satisfactorily completed. If my friend Rascal could talk, he might have told his attacker he was not going to be threatened on his own turf. I too was determined to follow through with my idea to create a book that sketched the characters of Adirondack men and women whose pictures Rascal had accidentally spilled from my desk.

How does one measure importance? In words? In deed? By the size of one's bank book? By the company one keeps? If the latter were true the people in *Adirondack Characters and Campfire Yarns* would truly be important people. The subjects in this book were called "Adirondack Characters" by their friends. I focused on a style that I felt would make their identities stand out. Call the book a collection of pen-portrait sketches, the pen being able to embellish each photographic image.

If on any occasion you sit on a river bank with an angler or next to an old-timer at an Adirondack diner, say "Hello." The conversation you strike up might be the beginning of your own character-portrait sketching. Those lives you have read of in this book now lie in the shadows of legends. Yet, new giants of tomorrow still live within the mountains.

West Canada Creek. Photograph by Roy Reehil.
COURTESY ROY REEHIL

Afterword

YOU WHO TODAY love the wilds of the Adirondack Mountains, take the time as you backpack along a winding trail, fish a stream, or sit in the warmth of an open fire, graced by the mournful *oo-AH-ho* yodel of a common loon, to think of the future of the mountains. Ahead of slipping into our comfortable sleeping systems set on self-inflating pads inside a ripstop nylon tent set up under whatever weather conditions Mother Nature happens to bring forth, we should consider how each of us can help provide equivalent experiences for future multitudes who will long for adventures such as Lloyd Blankman, Harvey Dunham, Mortimer Norton, and the men and women they wrote about had. People must strike a balance between abundant lives, the natural world and leaving a heritage for future generations. I can put my pen down knowing that *Adirondack Characters and Campfire Yarns* has played a small part in raising awareness of our priceless Adirondack Mountain heritage.

Profiles of Contributors

🌿 LLOYD BLANKMAN, 1903–1973

Lloyd G. Blankman was born in Canton, New York, on June 3, 1903. His father, Edgar Blankman (1861–1924), was an author and a cartographer who made large county wall maps and sold them mainly for use in one-room schools and in law offices. In 1905 he produced one of the Adirondacks.

Lloyd moved to Constantia, N.Y. with his family in the teens and graduated from Fulton High School in 1921. The family moved back to Canton in 1923 and Lloyd graduated from St. Lawrence University in 1927.

He taught school in St. Lawrence County until 1936, when he opened a five-and-ten-cent store in St. Johnsville.

In early 1937 he married Adaline Bowers (1904–1988) of Canton, and they had three children: Elizabeth, Edward, and Bruce, who died shortly after birth.

Lloyd Blankman, visiting French Louie's stone fireplace at the site of Louie's West Canada Lake camp.
COURTESY EDWARD BLANKMAN
(THE LLOYD BLANKMAN COLLECTION)

In 1947 he was forced to sell the store due to his declining health, and in 1950 the family moved to Clinton. During the 1950s and 1960s he was in poor health and couldn't perform any strenuous labor. It was during this period that he became interested in traveling and in writing about the Adirondacks.

Harvey Dunham provided Lloyd with photos and written material. Lloyd was Harvey Dunham's greatest right-hand man when it came to promoting Dunham's book *Adirondack French Louie*. In fact, after Dunham died, it was Lloyd who almost single-handedly continued to give lectures across New York State about early life in the North Woods, helping to sell the boxes of unsold books—its copyright acquired by Maitland C. DeSormo's *Adirondack Yesteryears*. (In later years, DeSormo sold the copyright to North Country Books, Inc.)

Lloyd Blankman died on June 29, 1973, after suffering a heart attack.

🌲 MORTIMER NORTON, 1908–1963

Mortimer Norton was born in Columbus, Ohio, in 1908. Much of his youth was spent at his family's camp on Piseco Lake where he engaged in all forms of outdoor life. At the age of seven he climbed his first mountain and caught his first trout. At sixteen he had his first article published in an outdoor magazine and he wrote for publication the remainder of his life.

In 1935 Mortimer edited a volume entitled *Angling Success*. In 1947, under the pen name of Old Hi, he wrote three booklets published by the Horrocks-Ibbotson Company, entitled *Fishing for the Millions, Salt Water Sports Fishing* and *Pacific Coastal Fishing.* Some of his best known news columns were in *Trails Afield, Outdoor Rambles, Angling Angles* and *Woods and Waters.*

Mortimer Norton. COURTESY EDWARD BLANKMAN (THE LLOYD BLANKMAN COLLECTION)

Although he traveled in many parts of the world, the Adirondacks of New York State, where he lived for twenty-five years, had the greatest appeal for him.

For fourteen seasons prior to the second World War he was director of the Poplar Point Outdoor Camping Area at Piseco Lake, for the New York State Conservation Department.

Piseco Lake was home base for "Mort," where he spent so many hours practicing the art he knew the best, fishing.

In his role as a reporter and columnist, Old Hi was a familiar figure at hundreds of dinner gatherings of outdoor sportsmen and fish and game clubs in Central New York.

Mortimer was rugged, six feet tall, over 200 lbs., straight as a balsam tree and a striking figure to meet in his forest garb or in his street clothes in the village of Clinton. It wasn't easy to break through his reserve, but beneath this he was unassuming, friendly and warm-hearted.

Wherever this naturalist lived he liked to organize classes of school students and direct them on excursions into the woods and fields. He did this in Clinton. He did so in Poland.

Norton was a bachelor most of his life and a world traveler.

When on a fishing expedition in Chile, South America, fifty-year old Mortimer met and married almost immediately, a Chilean woman half his age. Once back in America, living in Clinton, N.Y., Mortimer's wife gave birth to a son. Unfortunately his wife and young son were left to fend for themselves when Mortimer died of a massive heart attack at the age of fifty-five.

🌿 HARVEY L. DUNHAM, 1887–1956

Author Paul Jamieson described Harvey Dunham as ". . . a woodsman by hobby, a commercial artist in Utica by vocation, and a literary artist by accident."

Dunham penned *Adirondack French Louie* in 1952, following almost thirty years of research. The story of French Louie has become a regional classic which elevated the simple trapper-woodsman into the halls of Adirondack legend.

Dunham was born on October 6, 1887, in Saquoit, N.Y. and had an older brother, Raymond, and a younger sister, Florence. He married Bessie Throp in 1912. Shortly after the birth of their daughter Jean, in 1914, Bessie passed away. Harvey never remarried. His sister and parents helped him raise his daughter.

Harvey Dunham.
COURTESY EDWARD
BLANKMAN (THE LLOYD
BLANKMAN COLLECTION)

In June of 1914, Harvey enlisted in the Merchant Marines. After World War I, he worked as a commercial artist, first in New York City, then in Washington, D.C. He finally settled in Utica, N.Y., a short drive from the Adirondack Mountains.

The first writing about outdoor adventure found in Harvey's hand was in a journal dated August 1919. It contains the record of a camping trip to the wilderness north of the Beaver River Flow—known today as Stillwater Reservoir. Harvey traveled in the company of his brother Raymond, Jess Seitz, and a fellow lover of the woods ten years his senior, Bob Gillespie. The well-illustrated and well-written journal details the trio's jaunts, hunts, and trout fishing excursions. It is also peppered with campfire humor, a trademark that Harvey would refine.

The 1919 excursion bonded Dunham and Gillespie. Not only did they become lifelong friends, but they also became business partners, investing in land along West Canada Creek where they constructed cabins that they rented to city sportsmen and wealthy adventurers.

In 1924, the partners developed a second journal. It documents a two-week adventure into the West Canada Creek headwater country. As in their first journal, the vintage photographs and detailed writing display real enthusiasm for the outdoors and the men's flair for story-telling.

The men and their journals will be the subject of an upcoming book entitled *Adirondack Adventures*, by William J. O'Hern and Roy E. Reehil.

Following the release of Dunham's self-published *Adirondack French Louie*, Lloyd Blankman, sought to meet the author. The men found they shared a common interest in Adirondack history. They also shared a passion for camping, woods life and traditional woodcraft. Dunham and Blankman became true friends and some of their favorite memories were of the times they spent at Harv's beloved "Segoolie" camp on Seabury Stillwater.

Harvey Dunham passed away on July 24, 1956, after a brief illness. He was sixty-nine.

🌿 ARTHUR LESLIE BYRON-CURTISS, 1871-1959

The young Rev. Arthur Leslie Byron-Curtiss.
AUTHOR'S COLLECTION

Arthur Leslie Byron-Curtiss was born on November 29, 1871, in Westmoreland, N.Y. He was ordained as an Episcopal deacon in December 1892. In 1892–93 he was in charge of Christ Church in Forestport, N.Y. He found the friendly backwoods community to be of a character he thoroughly admired and was more than impressed with the wild country—he was in love with it.

In 1896, Byron-Curtiss married Wilhelmina M. Hosfelt in Rome, N.Y., where he was working at the St. Joseph's Mission parish. Their first child, Helen, was born in 1897; their second, Joseph, in 1899. In May of that year, Byron-Curtiss realized a dream when he plunked down fifteen dollars of the money he had saved from royalties on his first book, *The Life and Adventures of Nat Foster*, and bought a decrepit shanty, which he dubbed "Nat Foster Lodge." It was there that he spent the happiest days of his life.

A third child, Catherine, was born in 1906, and the family spent many happy days on North Lake. The Reverend rejoiced in having his children with him at camp for canoeing, hiking, camping, and other activities unique to the woods.

In 1913 Byron-Curtiss retired partially from the ministry and could afford to live at Nat Foster Lodge from Spring to Fall. The demands of living at North Lake were fairly easy, but the chronic physical pain of his rheumatoid arthritis along with the heartache of a bitter divorce and the deaths of Helen and Catherine, his two daughters, plagued him. No wonder the intermittent, paralyzing depression he referred to as his "nervous disorder" created a new kind of wilderness with which he had no experience.

Byron-Curtiss prescribed for himself a daily regimen that included prayers, a walk around the lake, writing, visiting and naps. Sadly, in addition to his plan for improved personal health, he self-prescribed alcohol to deaden the pain in his joints. Rev. Stanley Gasek lamented his friend's use of alcohol. "His training taught him to counsel forgiveness, yet it was difficult for him to come to terms with his own demons," Gasek said.

By 1923, Byron-Curtiss had begun writing newspaper columns about his trips, the people, and the legends of the Great North Woods and for half a century Byron-Curtiss recorded almost daily notes in voluminous logbooks.

In 1938 he took up the cause to try to prevent cutting up the Adirondacks with more roads. He advocated more trail-building instead. He wrote in the *Watertown Daily Times* that he foresaw the day when the Forest Preserve would become a patchwork of forest islands, "small in area and affording no real retreat for man, or the wildlife we boast of conserving."

The writings of "the Bishop of North Lake" are an important part of the recorded knowledge of the region, something he may have thought about when he wrote: "Together with a story or two of my own, with observations of natural phenomena, [my writings] are all I can give you of this part of the Adirondacks . . . . Past times should be a part of our strenuous lives today. May I have contributed something to it."

The journals he kept and his first-hand knowledge of the legends of the Black River headwaters give us more than a mere glimpse of an era long past.

The Rev. Arthur Leslie Byron-Curtiss will be the subject of two upcoming books by William J. O'Hern. The first, entitled *The Renegade Reverend of North Lake*, will be a biography.

🌿 THOMAS C. O'DONNELL, 1881–1962

Thomas C. O'Donnell was born in Midland County, Michigan, in 1881. When he was four, his father founded Vestagbury, a family-owned logging community named for his mother. Tom remembers: "It was a good place for a boy to get started in life."

Through his early years Tom lived close to logging rivers that cut across the Michigan peninsula toward Saginaw and the lumber market. "I loved a woodsman who in notching a tree could cut a clean, true V in the bole," he has said.

Having spent a long, distinguished career in editorial and publishing work in New York City, London, Chicago, and Cincinnati, Thomas C. O'Donnell came to Boonville, N.Y., in 1943.

Hunting, fishing, hiking, canoeing and berry-ing took him off the beaten path along backroads

Thomas O'Donnell.
AUTHOR'S COLLECTION

and byways that are now largely abandoned roads. He remained in the Black River Country for ten years before moving to Winter Park, Florida.

His skill-of-pen was his ability to ferret out a colorful picture of early life in the southwestern Adirondacks. During a decade of rambling the forests of the Black River region, Thomas O'Donnell was busy gathering recollections from older residents. Out of that research emerged four books: *Sapbush Run, Snubbing Posts, Birth of a River* and *Tip of the Hill*. His books not only flash back to the bygone days, but reflect the imprint of his warm individuality on the age-old lands he described. Future generations may read and reread his work, discovering the lower Adirondacks as he knew them: forever various and forever new.

Author
William J. O'Hern

William J. "Jay" O'Hern lives in rural Camden, New York, where he worked as an elementary school teacher for thirty-five years before retiring. He and his wife Bette raised five children and today, in retirement they enjoy their many grandchildren.

Jay is a graduate of the State University of New York (SUNY) at Auburn and SUNY Oswego and did graduate work at SUNY Oswego and the College of St. Rose in Albany.

Jay has also worked in the lumber, paper, chemical and metal fabricating industries. Carpentry, handicrafts, gardening, kayaking, backpacking, snowshoeing, mountain biking, and writing are his hobbies.

Years of backpacking taught Jay the Adirondack Mountains' nooks and crags not only had natural beauty, but could be interesting historically. Jay became a 46er in the 1980s and has been a member of the Adirondack Mountain Club (ADK) since 1969. He lectured for Adirondack Discovery for seventeen years, for Sagamore Lodge in Raquette Lake for seven years and occasionally for the Adirondack Museum in Blue Mt. Lake.

William J. O'Hern.
AUTHOR'S COLLECTION

Adirondack Characters and Campfire Yarns is Jay's third book about the Adirondack Mountains, their rich history, and the people who made them their home.

Jay's previously published books include: *Life With Noah: Stories and Adventures of Richard Smith with Noah J. Rondeau* (North Country Books); *Anyplace Wild in the Adirondacks* (a self-published book of postcards); and *Adirondack Stories of the Black River Country* (North Country Books). Articles written by Jay have appeared in the following magazines: *Adirondack Life, Fur, Fish and Game,* and *Adirondac.*

Acknowledgments

The Lloyd G. Blankman collection held by his son Edward Blankman forms the basis of this book. I would like to thank the following people, who generously provided encouragement, information, and documentation, or otherwise assisted in valuable ways: Edward Blankman for the loan of his father's Adirondack collection and support in the initial stages of the project; Gary Meyer, Courier Newspaper, Inc., publisher of *The Courier*, Clinton, New York; Carolyn Davis, Public Service Librarian, Syracuse University; Jean Dunham Keck; Karen Maccraken, general manager of *Fur-Fish-Game;* Ellen McHale, Ph.D., executive director of the New York Folklore Society; Walt Hastings; Thomas A. O'Donnell (grandson of Thomas C. O'Donnell); guidebook author Barbara McMartin for permission to quote from *Discover the West Central Adirondacks;* Francis Seaman, Long Lake Historian; Bruce Cole; Kevin Kaderli; Patricia Cerro-Reehil; Julie Simpson; Lauri Richards; Robert Bates; Thomas Gates; Bette O'Hern for her company on many investigative trips; my frisky cat Rascal, whose action led me to action; Roy Reehil, for his counsel, his organizational suggestions, and his belief that this work could be better than "just good"; and Mary L. Thomas for her editing when called upon. I would also like to acknowledge, posthumously, Glyndon Cole, editor and publisher of *North Country Life* and *York State Tradition* magazines; Winfred Murdock; Thomas C. O'Donnell; Mortimer Norton; Harvey L. Dunham; Rev. Arthur Leslie Byron-Curtiss and Lloyd Blankman.

Neal Burdick took on the knotty job of editing the first and final drafts—a service that, thanks to his efforts, focused my workmanship into an important history of the southwestern Adirondacks.

For permission to reprint material by Lloyd Blankman and Anne Marie Madsen grateful acknowledgment is made to *The Courier*, Clinton, New York. For permission to reprint material by Lloyd Blankman and Harvey Dunham grateful acknowledgment is made to *New York Folklore Quarterly*. For permission to reprint material by Mortimer Norton grateful acknowledgment is made to *Fur, Fish, Game*. For permission to reprint material by Douglas and Helen Hays, and Lloyd Blankman grateful acknowledgment is made to *York State TRADITION*. For permission to reprint a photograph by Fred Hodges, grateful acknowledgment is made to George Cataldo. For permission to reprint a photograph of Alvah Dunning by Seneca Ray Stoddard, grateful acknowledgment is made to the Adirondack Museum, Blue Mountain Lake, NY and Angela Donnelly, Assistant Curator, for her assistance in finding the photograph.

I have made every effort to acknowledge the assistance of everyone who helped. Any omission is an unintentional oversight.

Bibliography

BOOKS

Anderson, Donald. *Goodbye Mountain Man!*. Lenhartsville, PA: Summit House Publishers, 1976. Fourth Printing, September 1989, Commerical Printing Company, New Castle, PA.

Beetle, David H. *Up Old Forge Way/West Canada Creek*. Lakemont, NY & Old Forge, NY: North Country Books, 1972.

Bird, Barbara Kephart. *Calked Shoes: Life in Adirondack Lumber Camps*. Prospect, NY: Prospect Books, 1952.

Brumley, Charles. *Guides of the Adirondacks*. Utica, NY: North Country Books, 1994.

Byron-Curtiss, A. L. *Life and Adventures of Nat Foster, Trapper and Hunter of the Adirondacks*. 1897.

Conklin, Henry. *Through 'Poverty's Vale', A Hardscrabble Boyhood in Upstate New York 1832-1862*. Syracuse, NY: Syracuse University Press, 1974.

Donaldson, Alfred L. *A History of the Adirondacks*. (2 vols.) New York, NY: The Century Co., 1921.

Dunham, Harvey L. *Adirondack French Louie, Early Life in the North Woods*. Boonville, NY: Willard Press, Inc., 1953, Reprinted May, 1970.

Gerster, Arpad Geyza Charles. *Recollections of a New York Surgeon*. Hoeber, NY: 1917.

Hochschild, Harold K. *Township 34*. 1952.

Keesler, Paul M. *Kuyahoora, Discovering West Canada Valley*. Newport, NY: Mid-York Sportsman, Inc., 1999.

Mather, Fred. *Men I Have Fished With*. New York: Forest & Stream Stream Publishing Company, 1897.

———. *My Angling Friends, Being a Second Series of Sketches of Men I Have Fished With*. New York: Forest and Stream Publishing Company, 1901

McMartin, Barbara, et. al. *Discover the West Central Adirondacks*. Woodstock, Vermont: Backcountry Publications, 1988.

———. *Discover the Southwestern Adirondacks*. Woodstock, Vermont: Backcountry Publications, 1987.

O'Donnell, Thomas C. *Birth of a River, An Informal History of the Headwaters of the Black River*. Boonville, NY: Back River Books, 1952.

Raymond, Edward R. *Adventures of Uncle Hatchet*. Forestport, NY: Boonville Graphics, 1989.

Reed, Frank A. *Lumberjack Sky Pilot*. Boonville, NY: The Willard Press. Reprinted by North Country Books, Old Forge, NY, 1965.

Simms, Jeptha R. *Trappers of New York*. Albany, NY: J. Munsell, 1850.

MAGAZINES

Anderson, Robert V. "Fishing Piseco." *North Country Life*. Summer 1960.

Andrews, Geo. W. "Deer in the Adirondacks." *Forest & Stream*, August 7, 1890, Vol. 17.

Beardslee, Lester A. "The Adirondack Guide System." *Forest & Stream*, May 3, 1883, Vol. 20.

Blankman, Lloyd. "North Woods Profile--Bill Potter." *York State Tradition*, Fall 1964.

———. "North Woods Profile—Johnny McCullen." *York State Tradition*, Summer 1965, Vol. 19, No. 3.

———. "Jack Conklin's Moonshine." *York State Tradition*, Fall 1970, Vol. 24, No. 4.

———. "Little Deer lake." *York State Tradition*, Winter 1967, Vol. 21, No. 1.

———. "Grotus Reising." *York State Tradition*, Spring 1965, Vol. 19, No. 2.

———. "Burt Conklin." *New York Folklore Quarterly*. December 1966, Vol. 22, No. 4.

———. "North Woods Profile: George Wendover." *York State Tradition*, Spring 1966, Vol. 20, No. 2.

———. "North Woods Profile-Henry Conklin." *York State Tradition,* Fall 1965, Vol. 19 No. 4.

Burdick, Neal S. "Who Killed Orrando P. Dexter?." *Adirondack Life*, May/June 1982.

DeSormo, Maitland. "Hermits, Guides and Other Adirondack Characters." *Sixth Conference on the Adirondack Park*, St. Lawrence University Conference, June 11, 1976.

Dunham, Harvey L. "French Louie." *New York Folklore Quarterly*, August 1946, Vol. 2.

Douglas and Helen Hays. "Brush and the Road Monkey." *York State Tradition,* 1965, Vol. 19, No. 1.

Fosburgh, Peter W. "Guides and Guiding." *NYS Conservationist*, Oct./Nov. 1949, Vol. 4, No. 2.

Goldthwaite, Kenntth W. "A Winter Vacation That Paid for Itself." *Country Life*, February 1906.

Gerster, Arpad Geyza Charles. "Etching as a Diversion." *The Medical Pickwick*, October 1916.

Kenwell, Gerald. "French Louie." *NYS Conservationist*, Aug./Sept. 1952, Vol. 7, No. 1.

King, Thomas G. "Adirondack Guides." *Recreation,* Sept. 1902, Vol. 17.

H. "Adirondack Hospitality of the Olden Time." *Forest & Stream,* Aug. 27, 1891, Vol. 37, p 106.

Jamieson, Paul F. "Guide and Party." *NY Folklore Quarterly*, June 1966, Vol. 22, p 83-95.

Mather, Fred. "Alvah Dunning." *Forest and Stream,* March 22, 1902, Vol. 58, p 239-41.

———. "Men I Have Fished With. XXXVIII: Alvah Dunning." *Forest & Stream,* April 10, 1897, Vol. 48, p 288-89.

———. "Men I Have Fished With. XLVI." *Forest & Stream,* June 26, 1897, Vol. 48, p 506-507.

———. "Sheppard, E. L. (Jack)—Men I Have Fished With." *Forest & Stream,* June 26, 1897, Vol. 58.

———. "State Registration of Guides." *NYS Conservationist,* June 1919, Vol. 2.

Northrup, M. S. "Wolves in the Adirondacks." *Forest & Stream,* March 6, 1890, Vol. 34.

Norris, Isaac T. Norris. "Uncle Alvah." *Forest and Stream,* March 22, 1902.

North, Mary Remsen. "French Louie, Hermit Trapper." *High Spots.*

Norton, Mortimer. "Summer Time is Bass Time." *Trail Marker,* Utica, NY, July-August 1962, Vol. 1, No. 2.

———. "The Mircle of Mars . . . ." *Trail Marker*, Utica, NY, May-June 1962, Vol. 1, No. 2.

———. "An Autumn Blend of Outdoor Sport." *Trail Marker*, Utica, NY, October-November 1962, Vol. 1, No 3.

———. "Fun Under the Adirondck Sun." *Trail Marker*, Utica, NY, Summer 1963, Vol. 2, No. 1.

———. "A Mishap on Panther Mountian Stream."and "Fishing the Turblent West Canada Creek," *Fur, Fish, Game,* Aug.-Sept., 1929, Vol. 50, No. 3 and 4.

———. "Old Lobb of Piseco Lake." *Fur-Fish-Game*, July-August 1958.

O'Hern, William J. "Trappers in the Cold River Country." *The Trapper & Predator Caller.* 1999 Yearbook.

R., J. Jr. "The Adirondack Guides." *Forest & Stream*, Vol. 20, July 19, 1883.

Radford, Harry V. "Adirondack Department." *Forest & Stream,* Oct. 1901, Vol. 6, No. 8.

———. "Other Adirondack Matters." *Woods & Waters,* Winter 1901-1902, Vol. 4, No. 4, p 12-14.

———. "Adirondack Department," *Field & Stream,* October 1901, Vol. 6, No. 8.

S. "An Adirondack Capture." *Forest & Stream,* Feb. 23, 1895, Vol. 44.

———. "Incidents of Adirondack History." *Forest & Stream,* April 24, 1897, No. 48, p 323-324.

Shepard, Henry P. "I Once Knew an Adirondack Guide." *North Country Life,* Fall 1951.

Smith, Donald V. "'Pants' Lawrence of the Adirondacks." *North Country Life,* (abridged from *New York Folklore Quarterly*, Fall 1953, p 16-19.

Spears, Raymond S. "The Little Known of the Adirondacks." *Field & Stream,* July 1907, Vol. 12.

———. "'Guiding' Not What It Used To Be." *Journal of Outdoor Life,* August 1906, Vol. 3.

———. "Guides and Tourists." *Forest & Stream,* May 3, 1883, Vol. 20.

———. "Adirondack Guides." *The American Angler,* December 18, 1885, Vol. 4, No. 12.

Unsigned. "Brief Tribute to Mortimer Norton." *Trail Marker,* Utica, NY, Summer 1963, Vol. 2, No. 1.

Wires, Emily Mitchell. "Early Days in the Adirondacks." *NY Folklore Quarterly*, September, 1966, Vol. 22.

NEWSPAPERS

Bennett, Edward. "Reminiscences of the Adirondacks." *The Post-Star*, Glens Falls, NY, October 8–24, 1929, Installments No. 1 -10.

Blankman, Lloyd. "Adirondack Characters—Old Lobb, Hermit." *The Courier*, Clinton, NY.

———. "Adirondack Characters—Lobb's Trolling Spoons." *The Courier*, Clinton, NY, April 2, 1970.

———. "Adirondack Characters—Merry Go Round Letters." *The Courier*, Clinton, NY, September 22, 1971.

———. "Adirondack Characters—Milo D. Conklin's Merry Go Round Letter to his Parents (1901)." *The Courier*, Clinton, NY, March 28, 1973.

———. "Adirondack Characters—Mortimer Norton: 1908-1963." *The Courier*, Clinton, NY.

———. "Adirondack Characters—Harvey Dunham: 1887-1973." *The Courier*, Clinton, NY, March 21, 1973.

———. "Adirondack Characters—George Pardee, Sharp Shooter." *The Courier*, Clinton, NY.

———. "Adirondack Characters—Link with the Past." *The Courier*, Clinton, NY, July 17, 1969.

———. "Adirondack Characters—Maynard Phelps, the Old Ranger." *The Courier*, Clinton, NY, July 25, 1966.

———. "Adirondack Characters—Will Lewis and a Fine Catch." *The Courier*, Clinton, NY.

———. "Adirondack Characters—Amaziah D. (Dut) Barber." *The Courier*, Clinton, NY, July 30, 1970.

———. "Adirondack Characters—Enjoyment–Giles Becraft (1850-1893)." *The Courier*, Clinton, NY, March 19, 1970.

————. "Adirondack Characters—Jim 'Brockie' Dalton, Guide." *The Courier*, Clinton, NY.
————. "Adirondack Characters—Nat Shepard: 1865-1922." *The Courier*, Clinton, NY.
————. "Adirondack Characters—Ray Milks, Under the Ice." *The Courier*, Clinton, NY.
————. "Adirondack Characters—Sam Dunakin, Guide." *The Courier*, Clinton, NY.
————. "Adirondack Characters—Forest Runes." *The Courier*, Clinton, NY, February 2, 1967.
————. "Adirondack Characters—The Finch-Conklin Feud." *The Courier*, Clinton, NY.
————. "Adirondack Characters—Old Timers." *The Courier*, Clinton, NY.
————. "Adirondack Characters—The Conklin Sisters." *The Courier*, Clinton, NY, Oct. 23, 1969.
————. "Adirondack Characters—Hunting- or No Horns." *The Courier*, Clinton, NY.
————. "Adirondack Characters—Roscoe and The Bears." *The Courier*, Clinton, NY.
————. "Adirondack Characters—Burt Conklin's Christmas Present." *The Courier*, Clinton, NY
————. "Adirondack Characters—Greatest Trapper of Recent Times." *The Courier*, Clinton, NY.
————. "Adirondack Characters—Woodland Home." *The Courier*, Clinton, NY, Dec. 15, 1966.
————. "Adirondack Characters—Roy Conklin's Trout." *The Courier*, Clinton, NY.
————. "Adirondack Characters—Jack Conklin's Camps." *The Courier*, Clinton, NY, Feb. 27, 1969.
————. "Adirondack Characters—Hotel at Fine." *The Courier*, Clinton, NY, Nov. 13, 1969.
————. "Adirondack Characters—West Leyden Hotel." *The Courier*, Clinton, NY.
————. "Adirondack Characters—Tug Hill Roads." *The Courier*, Clinton, NY, October 26, 1967.
————. "Adirondack Characters—Tug Hill Highmarket." *The Courier*, Clinton, NY, January 26, 1968.
————. "Adirondack Characters—Tug Hill Stories." *The Courier*, Clinton, NY, Feb. 22, 1968.
————. "Adirondack Characters—Hotels (Fish Creek, Tug Hill)." *The Courier*, Clinton, NY.
————. "Adirondack Characters—Lewis County High Point." *The Courier*, Clinton, NY.
————. "Adirondack Characters—Adirondack Springs." *The Courier*, Clinton, NY.
————. "Adirondack Characters—Little Deer Lake." *The Courier*, Clinton, NY.
————. "Adirondack Characters—Spruce Lake." *The Courier*, Clinton, NY, Sept. 15, 1971.
————. "Adirondack Characters—Tim Crowley, Gum Picker." *The Courier*, Clinton, NY.
————. "Adirondack Characters—Grotus Reising." *The Courier*, Clinton, NY, 1965.
————. "Adirondack Characters—Fred Hodges, Photographer." *The Courier*, Clinton, NY.
————. "Adirondack Characters—The Blueberry Girls." *The Courier*, Clinton, NY,
    September 17, 1970.
————. "Adirondack Characters—French Louie." *The Courier*, Clinton, NY, Aug. 29, 1968.
————. "Adirondack Characters—French Louie." *The Courier*, Clinton, NY, Nov. 9 & 26, 1968.
————. "Adirondack Characters—Alvah Dunning, Hermit." *The Courier*, Clinton, NY.
————. "Adirondack Characters—Picnic Time." *The Courier*, Clinton, NY, Feb. 19, 1970.
————. "Adirondack Characters—Trip to the Mountains." *The Courier*, Clinton, NY.
Byron-Curtiss, A. L. "Alvah Dunning Was Famous Adirondack Guide And Hermit." *Lumber Camp News,* July 1942.
Madsen, Anne Marie. "A Field of Daisies." *The Courier*, Clinton, NY.
Northrup, M. S. "Wolves in the Adirondacks." *Forest and Stream,* 1890.
Spears, Eldrige A. "In the Lore of the North Country, French Lewey Was a Pioneer of the Adirondacks." Utica *Observer-Dispatch*, 1938.
————. "Alvah Dunning, The Famous Adirondack Guide." Utica Saturday *Globe*, March 15, 1902.
————. "Dudley House." Utica Saturday *Globe,* Feb., 11, 1905 and April 15, 1908
————. "A Wilderness Guide, Uncle Alva Dunning of the Fulton Chain of Lakes." Boonville *Herald,* June 12, 1895. (Reprinted from "A Wilderness Guide," the New York *Sun*, June 6, 1895.)

OTHER SOURCES
Blankman, Lloyd. Personal papers, photographs and slides of Lloyd Blankman owned by Edward Blankman, Adams, NY.
Glass, Joseph J. Jr. Correspondence and papers from Joseph J. Glass Jr., Attorney at Law, Syracuse, NY, 1986.
Kilbourn, Doris and Thomas. Personal papers, letters, photographs, and camp log books owned by Doris and Thomas Kilbourn, Rome, NY.
Letters to the Editor. *New York State Conservationist,* June/July Vol. 3, No. 6 1949.
Letters to the Editor. *New York State Conservationist,* Dec./Jan. Vol. 7, No. 3, 1952-53.
Letters to the Editor. *New York State Conservationist,* Dec. 1952 - Jan. 1953, Letters by Rebecca L. Conklin.
O'Donnell, Thomas C. Personal papers of Thomas C. O'Donnell housed in the George Arents Research Library at Syracuse University, Syracuse, NY.
Oneida County Historical Society. Scrapbook "Obituarites 1897-1902." UTI. 1.

Index